For
Joyce Portnoy
1949–1998

CONTENTS

SECTION I   The Assessment

This is the first of three chapters in the assessment section of the book. In this chapter, you will answer questions that demonstrate skills you've used to deal with challenges, overcome obstacles, solve problems, and achieve objectives.

In this second chapter, you will be placed in the role of someone who has just been named president of the trustee group for a neighborhood subdivision. The group's usual leader recently died, and the trustees are depending on your leadership to help solve the problems that are plaguing this once beautiful but now dilapidated development. Your task will be to enable the residents to solve their problems and help them regain the peace of mind they once enjoyed in a secure and stable neighborhood.

In this chapter, you will be in the role of a leadership consultant. You have an upscale office where clients come by appointment to describe the difficulties they face in their businesses, and in some cases, their personal lives. Your job is to listen to their concerns, identify the issues, analyze the problems, and then offer recommendations to help them resolve their dilemmas.

To help you identify your proficiency in each of the four competencies, this chapter will show you how to score and interpret your responses to the entire assessment. By tabulating your scores, you'll learn which of the competencies you used most frequently and which you might want to focus on for further development.

> *Those who say that it cannot be done should get out of the way of those who are already doing it.*
> —*Joel Barker, Futurist*

SECTION II   The Competencies

This is the first of four chapters that describe the competencies. In this chapter, you will learn how leaders use directional thinking to set a course for the changes they will persuade others to implement.

Having the presence of mind and taking the time to anticipate the consequences of a decision are important contributors to a leader's success. Consequential thinking considers both the benefits and the potential harm of the leader's intended objectives and the actions required to achieve them. This chapter will help you decide whether to proceed after careful regard for the potential consequences of your decisions.

At the very core of leadership is the ability to persuade people. Persuasion is based on any one or a combination of influence strategies. In this chapter, we'll examine several strategies for influencing people to do what you want them to do. You'll also have opportunities to apply these strategies to your own personal and business situations.

By the time you reach this point in the book, you will have learned how to establish a direction for leadership, anticipate consequences, and use influence strategies to persuade people to follow your lead. The final step is to communicate your thinking in ways that will motivate and inspire people. The communication skills that you'll learn in this chapter will help you effectively deliver your message to countless people using the media or to one person through a provocative conversation.

> *Competency . . . An integrated set of skills that collectively enable a person to accomplish an intended objective.*

SECTION III   Applications

We have no magic here. What we do have is the technology to help you solve your problems.

PREFACE

Are you a leader? Do you want to be a leader? How much do you know about leadership? Could you teach someone else to be a leader? The fact that you've picked up this book and have read this far probably indicates you are at least somewhat interested in the answers to these questions.

Consider some related questions. If you were a CEO, how would you go about identifying the future leaders of your organization? As the head of the training department in a large corporation, what methods would you use to assess and develop prospective leaders and at what levels of management would you concentrate your greatest efforts? In your role as a professor of business, what leadership theories would you present to your students and to what course objectives would you hold them accountable? Your subdivision's board of trustees just elected you president and they are depending on you to rid the neighborhood of vandalism and to help restore property values up from an all time low. What are you going to do? You suspect that the car dealer is trying to take financial advantage of your young son who is trying to buy his first new car. What can you do to help him protect his financial interests?

As these questions point out, from the perspective of day-to-day challenges, leadership can take many forms. Businesses need leaders, but so do communities and most certainly so do families. How can you prepare yourself for the countless circumstances in which you might need to take charge as a leader? Where would you begin? What would you try to achieve? How will you know if you've been effective?

Leadership: 4 Competencies for Success can help you answer these questions and develop the skills that will enable you to take charge as a leader. The development of leadership skills in organizations is largely limited to commercialized, nonacademic methods. While practical and often useful, the validity of these approaches is largely a matter of perception and without academic foundation. By contrast, books written for classroom use often survey research findings and offer little of practical value to a professor who wants to prepare students for the rigors of leading people in organizations.

As a developmental manual, *Leadership: 4 Competencies for Success* is inherently practical for business use, and as a textbook it is based on a solid academic foundation. It was written to fill the gap between the field of business in which there is an immediate need for skill development and the world of academics in which the primary objective is to foster and enhance critical thinking. In short, the book prepares students to think like leaders and it trains business leaders to think before they act.

The book is anchored by 4 Competencies: (1) Directional Thinking, (2) Consequential Thinking, (3) Influence Strategies, and (4) Communication Skills. These 4 competencies form the basis for recognizing the elements of leadership, diagnosing the potential for leadership, and developing programs for building new leaders. They can be used for self-development, for mentoring, and for specific instructional design and course delivery. The book presents an entire curriculum ranging from assessment through implementation.

The Assessment provides the student with a diagnostic foundation to determine strengths and developmental needs in each of the 4 Competencies. By responding to questions from the Assessment, students provide information about how they would use the 4 Competencies to address specific situations, challenges, and dilemmas. In the first chapter, they respond to behaviorally framed questions with answers that reflect how they dealt with such situations in their actual experiences. In the second chapter, they write responses to letters framed as an in-basket exercise. In the third chapter, students develop written reports to simulate work as a consultant who is responding to clients with business-related problems. Chapter 4 then explains how to score and analyze the responses using the 4 Competencies as a guide for understanding their current level of leadership skills and for developing a plan to systematically improve problematic areas.

Armed with a personalized developmental plan, students apply the 4 Competencies to strengthen their leadership skills in the remaining chapters. The competencies focus on how to establish a vision for leadership, identify and manage the risks associated with their plans for change, influence strategies for persuading followers and for overcoming resistance to change, and communication skills for presenting their ideas in ways that capture and maintain attention and interest. In addition, a variety of useful tools are presented and illustrated so students can apply the competencies quickly and effectively. Two such tools are *The Relationship Life Cycle* and *The Speaker Effectiveness Index*.

The Relationship Life Cycle is a flowchart that depicts how relationships begin and evolve and how they either deal effectively with conflict and survive or how they ignore conflict and as a result allow it to escalate and destroy the relationship. The model is illustrated by a case study linked to each step in the flowchart. The interpersonal communication skills that follow are then explained and illustrated to help prevent and resolve interpersonal conflict in both business and personal settings.

The Speaker Effectiveness Index serves as both an assessment and development tool for better understanding and improving presentation skills. Whether using the tool to assess other speakers or as an anchor to baseline one's own skills for later comparison, it provides keen insights into the visual, verbal, and vocal elements of presentations. The model includes checklists for strengths and developmental needs and it offers feedback for improving skills.

To aid the instructor in presenting the material and the students in applying the methods to their own personal and professional situations, *Leadership: 4 Competencies for Success* includes a wide array of instructional tools. These include:

1. The Assessment—the protocols and the scoring instructions.

2. Detailed case studies and examples that illustrate the 4 Competencies.

3. T-Charts that explain and illustrate how to make balanced decisions in light of risks.

4. Flowcharts linked to case studies to illustrate how theory can be put into practice.

5. Q & As that address frequently asked questions about leadership and in particular about how to develop and implement a mentoring program in an organization by using the 4 Competencies.

An Instructor's Guide also accompanies the text. The Guide includes:

1. Teaching tips.

2. Detailed instructions for how to administer and score the assessment, along with examples of completed assessments from actual students.

3. A Test Bank that provides objective-type questions with corresponding answers as well as discussion questions from the text along with suggested answers.

4. A cumulative bibliography.

Field testing began three years ago and approximately three hundred students have used the prepublished version of the book. Feedback has been quite positive, emphasizing:

1. Ease of reading.

2. Real-life examples that enable students to place themselves in the situations that challenge them.

3. A smooth linkage between theory and practice with many examples and illustrations.

4. The practical value of the book (assessment and interview skills in particular) as college seniors prepare for and complete job interviews.

Success stories from students have been frequent and gratifying. One student even mentioned that the skills she learned from the book helped her become a more effective speaker and as a result she raised over $5000.00 for medical research.

Are you a leader? Can you teach others to be a leader? *Leadership: 4 Competencies for Success* will help you answer those questions with a resounding YES!

ACKNOWLEDGMENTS

One of the most pleasant tasks associated with writing a book is to acknowledge and thank those people who have contributed to its development. My deepest appreciation and sincere thanks go to each of these people.

My first thanks go to Elizabeth Sugg, editor in the Career and Technology division of Prentice Hall. Elizabeth's creativity opened my mind to the potential for reaching many more markets than I had anticipated and her patience and flexibility enhanced my own skills as an author.

I was awed by the tremendous contributions of Laura Cleveland and Word-Crafters Editorial Services. To no one's great surprise, we authors take great pride in our work and have significant doubts that our golden words could ever be improved. Enter Laura Cleveland and her professional staff. What a beautiful job they did in suggesting revisions and graciously guiding my rewrites toward a manuscript that became so much better than I imagined it could ever be.

Professors Raymond L. Hilgert and Judy Lamb at Washington University in St. Louis, Missouri, critically reviewed the manuscript. A hearty thanks to both for their honesty, insights, and valued suggestions.

Thanks to my teaching assistants: Rebecca Apperson, Lee Carson, David Cosloy, and Meghan Holland. The developments of the assessments into a sensitive diagnostic tool is a direct result of their contributions. I deeply appreciate all the time they spent scoring, analyzing, and reporting data.

Thanks to all my students who made their assessments available for use in the Instructor's Guide. And a special thanks to Elizabeth Rodriguez for reflecting how a book such as this can make a difference when using leadership skills to help other people.

Thank you to those people who shaped many of the ideas, case studies, and examples in this book. Thanks to Sister Marie Damien Adams, Arnold Aronson, Larry Bradford, Sandra Cotlar, Denny Gendreau, David Gerchen, Michael Higgins, Rick Hendin, Van Kirk, Brenda Konersmann, Gary Kral, Rich Meyers, Beverly Portnoy, and Kevin Tucker. You have each inspired me in your own way and I have learned much from your leadership during the times we have shared.

Many years ago as I wrote the Introduction to my first book, I acknowledged the smiles and hugs from my two children Annie and Benjy as I tucked them in at night before I went off to write another chapter. Today, I again thank each of them whose opinions I now value and respect from their critical perspective as students in college and whose smiles and hugs I still and will always cherish.

To my wife, Lisa—thank you for pointing the way!

Keys to the Competencies

Key	Competencies	Chapter
	Directional Thinking	5
	Consequential Thinking	6
	Influence Strategies	7
	Communication Skills	8

INTRODUCTION

4 Competencies for Success

Are you a leader? Interesting question, isn't it? The way you answer the question will depend on how you define leadership. It will also depend on who you already consider to be leaders.

Leaders imagine the future and then inspire others to create it. Leaders help bring order to chaos and help people find meaning and purpose in their lives.

Leaders come from all walks of life. There are no absolute traits or qualities that universally distinguish one person as a leader and another as a follower.

Often leaders are thought of as those people "at the top" of some organization. Executives, for example, provide a sense of direction to corporations. We also look to government officials to make laws that determine the way we live our lives. However, leadership does not need to be restricted to the highest levels. There are leaders among school children, leaders in community groups, leaders in competitive sports, leaders among friends, and leaders in families.

Do you want to be a leader? That's a different question. People often look to leaders to help solve problems. Leaders point us in a meaningful direction, help us believe in ourselves, inspire our self-confidence, and make us feel that the world is somehow better because of what we've done. Do these things interest you? If so, perhaps you'd like to be a leader.

This book is a guide to help you develop your leadership skills. What you'll find in this book are four "competencies" that will help you do an effective job leading people in just about any situation, not just in organizations.

For our purposes, a competency is "an integrated set of skills that collectively enable a person to accomplish an intended objective." The competencies in this book are (1) directional thinking, (2) consequential thinking, (3) influence strategies, and (4) communication skills.

Why these particular competencies? Most definitions of leadership include some aspect of each one. For example, consider the way John Kotter describes leadership.

> . . . a process that establishes direction, creates alignment, inspires and motivates people to produce change.

By developing proficiency in these four competencies, you will likely be able to do just what Professor Kotter's definition describes. In other words, you will be able to lead people to produce change.

Maybe you already can. Shall we find out? Before we spend much time defining and describing the competencies themselves, we'll try to measure your current proficiency level for each of the four competencies. To accomplish this, you'll complete a leadership assessment such as some companies use to determine candidates for positions of leadership.

Section I is called The Assessment and includes four chapters. The first three chapters will help you measure your ability to use leadership skills to create opportunities and solve problems. The fourth chapter will help you interpret your responses.

Chapter 1 is called The Behavior Interview. In this chapter, you'll be asked to provide information about how you handled situations in the past. Rather than looking for your opinions about what should have been done, the ten questions attempt to probe what you actually did. In other words, they focus on your behavior. The chapter is based on the idea that a person's past behavior is a good predictor of what he will do in the future. For example, if a person had perfect attendance in his last four jobs which spanned fifteen years, there's a good chance his attendance will also be reliable in his next job. If a person's subordinates rated her highly as a manager in her previous jobs, chances are good that her future subordinates will also rate her well. It won't always be obvious what we're looking for in your answers to the questions in Chapter 1. To help measure yourself accurately, simply answer the questions by describing what you actually did.

Chapter 2 is The In-Basket. An in-basket, of course, is a tray used in an office setting to collect mail and other items that require attention and action. For assessment purposes, the in-basket exercise evaluates the ability to respond to the items by making decisions on how to manage them. Our "in-basket" belongs to Mr. Peter Franks who was the head of the trustees for a subdivision called Twin Lakes. Unfortunately, Mr. Franks met his destiny in a fatal car accident. The rest of the trustees unanimously voted YOU their new leader. It is now up to you to respond to the items that have accumulated in the in-basket. What's more, the quality of Twin Lakes has visibly deteriorated, and the subdivision is beset with problems. You must help solve them in order to restore Twin Lakes to its former elegance and stability. Your responses to the in-basket items will reflect your ability to exercise leadership.

Chapter 3 is Ask the Consultant. In this chapter, you will find yourself in the role of a leadership consultant. Your clients seek your advice for help with their business, and in some cases personal, problems. Within the time frame of one-hour appointments with your clients, your job will be to "listen" to their situations, analyze the issues, and then make recommendations that they can use to solve their problems. Through your responses you will be demonstrating your leadership skills.

Chapter 4 is Scoring Your Results. To help you score your responses from each of the assessment measures, you will learn how to link your responses with each of the four leadership competencies. Then, by learning how to interpret and evaluate the scores, you'll find out which of the competencies represent your current strengths and which represent your opportunities for further development.

Section II is called The Competencies. Each of the four chapters in Section II corresponds to one of the four leadership competencies. In each chapter, the competency is defined and illustrated. There are also exercises to help you apply the competency to situations from the assessment and to your own situations as well.

Chapter 5 is Directional Thinking. It sets the stage for the rest of the book, but more important, for the first step in the process of leadership. The chapter explores the concepts of direction-setting opportunities (DSOs) and directional-setting decisions (DSDs). DSOs and DSDs are then linked to the process of establishing direction at both personal and organizational levels of leadership.

Chapter 6 is Consequential Thinking. Having the presence of mind and taking the time to anticipate the consequences of a decision are important contributions to a leader's success. Consequential thinking considers both the benefits and the potential harm of the leader's intended objectives and the actions required to achieve them. This chapter will help you decide whether to implement your decision after careful regard for the potential consequences.

Chapter 7 is Influence Strategies. At the very core of leadership is the ability to persuade people. Persuasion is based on any one or a combination of influence strategies. In this chapter, we'll examine several strategies for influencing. You'll also have several opportunities to apply these strategies to the situations from the assessment as well as to your own personal and professional circumstances.

Chapter 8 is Communication Skills. By the time you reach this point in the book, you'll have learned how to establish a direction for leadership, anticipate consequences, and use influence strategies to persuade people to follow your lead. The final step is to communicate your thinking in ways that others will quickly understand and find meaningful in their own lives. The communication skills that you'll learn in this chapter will help you effectively deliver your message to any number of people ranging from many down to one and across a wide variety of situations, including in the media, on a public platform, in a meeting room or office and even in the privacy of your own home.

Section III is called Applications. Chapter 9 is Frequently Asked Questions about Leadership. Chapter 10 is called Assessment Guidelines and Some Final Thoughts and provides guidance for how you can use the four competencies to respond to some of the items from the assessment.

Leadership: 4 Competencies for Success is intended to be a practical tool to help you decide whether you want to be a leader and, if so, how you can enhance your ability to lead people. In these times when the world is changing so rapidly, we need leaders more than ever to help us find order in the chaos, and worthwhile purposes to help guide our lives.

SECTION I

The Assessment

Chapter 1: The Behavior Interview
Chapter 2: The In-Basket
Chapter 3: Ask the Consultant
Chapter 4: Scoring Your Responses

CHAPTER 1

The Behavior Interview

In this section of the assessment, you will answer several questions as though you were writing a type of essay for each one. The questions are designed to help you recall certain events in your recent past that required you to think and act decisively. As you answer each question, write your responses so that they focus on your ACTIONS rather than on *good intentions,* what you *wish* you had done or what *you think others might have done.*

For example, consider the following question:

Think back to a time when you had to get a lot of things done in a relatively short time. How did you organize and structure your activities in order to succeed?

A "Good Intention" answer might be:

I always organize. Good organization is so important. Without it, you just can't get anything done. I've always done a good job organizing. All my friends tell me how good I am at it.

An "ACTION" answer might be:

I remember a time when our whole team was facing a deadline that was a week away. Then, without warning, our boss told us we had two business days to complete the project. After we whined and moaned for a few minutes, I suggested that we pull out our master planning chart. On the left side of the chart we listed each step of the project. Across the top we had the completion times and names of responsible parties. With all the people standing in front of the chart, we collectively decided what we could compress, what we could eliminate totally, and what would have to remain intact. I took on the role of recorder by standing up at the chart and leading the discussion. We accomplished a great deal by cutting out what amounted to dozens of "nice to do's" that in the end were nonessentials. By pulling together, we extensively revised our timelines, achieved our objectives, and completed the project nearly four hours before the revised deadline.

There are ten questions in this section. One page is devoted to each question. To make it easier for you to later interpret your responses, be sure to focus your answer on a past event that actually occurred in your life. Then, use your answer to demonstrate what you actually did to solve the problem at hand. The more specific you are in describing your actions, the easier it will be for you to later identify your most effective and least effective leadership skills. If, instead, your answers describe opinions and intentions, it will be more difficult later to interpret how to improve your scores from the assessment.

Question 1

Think of a time when you had to make a tough decision when there was no company policy or external set of rules to guide you. Provide background information about the situation, describe how you made the decision, and explain the outcome.

Question 2

What types of decisions do you make on your own, and what types do you make only after consulting a higher authority? Give examples of each and describe how you handled them.

Question 3

Describe a situation in which almost everyone was at a loss as to how to solve a problem and you stepped in, took charge, and solved the problem. Give background information, describe what you did, and indicate the outcome.

Question 4

Think of an important goal you set in the past and explain how you determined its importance and what you did in a step-by-step manner to achieve it. Finally, describe the outcome.

Question 5

Describe a situation in which a higher authority blocked your progress in achieving your objectives. Give background information, explain how you handled the obstacles, and describe the outcome.

Question 6

How have you handled people who are difficult to get along with? Describe a situation in which you were effective in getting such a person to cooperate and explain what you did that made a difference.

Question 7

Describe a time when you made a mistake that reflects your own need for improvement. Think of a specific situation, provide the background information, explain what you did, and describe the outcome.

Question 8

Think of a situation in which you used your creativity to solve a work-related problem or one with friends or family. Give background information, explain what you did, and describe the outcome.

Question 9

Describe a time when you had to convey some unpleasant news to someone and then helped them deal with the reality of that news. Explain the circumstances, what you said, how the other person reacted, and what you did to help them deal with the situation.

Question 10

Describe a situation in which you held a minority opinion but were successful in changing the opinions of others who held the majority point of view. Give background information, explain what you did, and then describe the outcome.

CHAPTER 2

The In-Basket

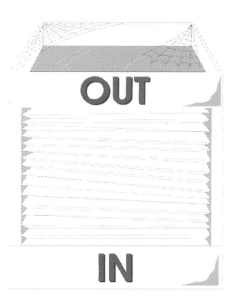

Introduction

An in-basket exercise is frequently used to evaluate leadership skills. An in-basket is a tray or basket that is used to collect items that require some type of attention or response.

In the exercise, the in-basket belongs to an individual who is called on to exercise leadership to solve the problems that the items portray. The items alert the "leader" that he is in the midst of a crisis that requires immediate action and expert skill to handle and resolve.

In this exercise, you will discover that you have been drafted as a leader by your fellow trustees in a neighborhood subdivision. The former leader was recently killed in a car accident. Now everyone is counting on your guidance to help them deal with problems that range anywhere from a barking dog that disturbs the neighbors to possible termination of county-provided services such as trash collection and snow removal. Your neighborhood is depending on you.

Instructions

The in-basket is divided into two sections: background information and correspondence. Before beginning the correspondence, be sure to familiarize yourself with the background information.

Write your response on each of the correspondence items as though you were actually responding as the president of the board. Do not write a description of how you "would" respond. Instead, write an actual response. For example, in response to a memo written to the president by John Jones

DO NOT WRITE,
"I would tell John to call Mr. Smith."

INSTEAD, WRITE ON THE MEMO ITSELF,
"John, this is in response to your above memo. Call Mr. Smith."

Sign the documents with your name or initials as if you actually intended to send them out. When you have completed your responses to the correspondence, proceed to Chapter 3.

Background Information

Peter Franks is dead. You just received word on your answering machine. You and your family have just returned from a two-week vacation. As president of the board of trustees for your subdivision, Twin Lakes, Peter was looked on as the neighborhood's leader. Jill Greenwald, the vice president, left the message and asked that you call her as soon as you return. You phone Jill who tells you that Peter was killed in a car accident shortly after you left for your vacation. He was alone in his car, and no one else was injured. An emergency meeting of the board is called, and you are unanimously voted the next president. Jill and the rest of the board are aware that you will be leaving tomorrow for a ten-day business trip. However, they would appreciate it if you, as the new president, would answer the trustee correspondence that has piled up since Peter's death. You agree. Jill gives you the stack of correspondence. You decide that you will complete it tonight since you will be leaving first thing in the morning for your business trip.

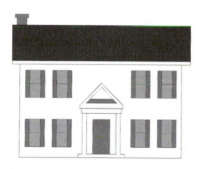

On your way home, you think through the business of the subdivision that you recall as a board member from previous meetings. When the general contractor completed the subdivision twelve years ago, he had an attorney draw up the bylaws and then held an open meeting to elect the board. In general, the objectives of the board are to ensure that the quality of the subdivision is maintained and that future developments are consistent with the wishes of the homeowners and the rules of the community. The bylaws empower the president to make unilateral decisions for the welfare of the subdivision, but to consult with the other members of the board whenever practical.

Twin Lakes is not without its problems. Many residents are bitter and frustrated that the ambitious plans for a pool, tennis courts, a golf course, and development of the two lakes are locked up in some file cabinet in the county offices. Homes are suffering from neglect, lawns go unmowed for weeks, many neighbors refuse to speak to one another, and "For Sale" signs sit for months in front of vacant houses. The subdivision has already lost some of its county-provided services due to decreasing occupancy rates. Further reductions may be on the way.

Now, you have been elected the president. It's your chance to do something about Twin Lakes Development. Before proceeding to the correspondence section, read "A Letter to Our New President" on the next page.

A Letter to Our New President

By the time you read this, I'll have already explained that you've been unanimously elected our next president. You should know that everyone has a lot of confidence in you. The board has not been the most cohesive group of people. Peter tried, but we need your leadership.

On the next page of this letter is a list of the people who wrote to Peter within the last few weeks. By now most but not all of them know what happened. You can assume the people from outside the subdivision, such as the chief of police, do not know. You may choose to say a few words to explain the situation before focusing directly on their concerns.

Please let me know how I can help. If you want to call any meetings or need any special letters written, don't hesitate to ask. I'll see that it gets done.

Peter and I had our differences, but I will miss him. Glad you are the one to take his place in this position. The subdivision needs you.

Warmest regards,

Jill Greenwald, Vice President
Twin Lakes Development

Correspondence List (Additional Members of the Board of Trustees Are Listed Below)

Trustees
Barry Jenkins
Jerry Connors
Tex Silverstone
Kevin Corbin
Jane Reynolds
Allen Lavell

Additional Trustees
Melony Wilson
John Gates
Roberta T. Bringel
Jill Greenwald (Me)

Residents
Willa Meyers
Mohammed Akbar
Perry Shetler
Pauline Frisco

Community Members
Bill Watson
Chief of Police

Walter "Ace" Acme
President
Acme Snow Removal

E. (Doc) Brown
President, Bd. of Trustees
Clocktower Homes

Rona Peters Pakstein, VP
Leadership Dev. Assoc.

Wilford R. Bevel
County Supervisor

C. L. Sheathing, President
Sheathing Real Est. Dev.

The Correspondence

Peter,

Larry Kaplan, VP from Emry-Smith, Inc., moved into Twin Lakes last week. He gave me his plans for the pool he intends to have built in his backyard. They don't comply with the bylaws. Do you think I should tell him the plans will have to be changed? Maybe you should do it. Maybe we should change the bylaws. After all, this guy is important. What do you think? Let me know ASAP.

Barry R. Jenkins
Associate Trustee
Twins Lakes Development

Mr. Franks,

I am sick and tired of the Fitzgeralds' dog barking all hours of the night. It is pathetic that these people are so inconsiderate of their neighbors. I paid good money to move into Twin Lakes, and furthermore, I pay dearly for the subdivision fees. Now I expect you to go over to the Fitzgeralds' and give them "What For." Otherwise, I just might shoot that damn dog!

Willa Meyers
Twins Lakes Resident

To Mr. P. Franks:

Dear Sir:

I have just answered a knock at my door that was most disturbing. The Christian Call To Grace Association informed me that I should place lighted candles along the sidewalk in front of my house on Christmas Eve to light the way for the Holy Family. I was nice to these people, of course. But I think this is an invasion of my privacy and might even be unconstitutional. Whether or not I am a good Christian is my own business, and it is my own business whether or not I want to observe my religion in my neighborhood and in front of my house. This sort of thing should not be permitted. Please put a stop to it.

Your neighbor,

Mohammed Akbar
Twin Lakes Resident

P.S. Also, can you do anything about the Fitzgeralds' dog barking all the time? It's driving me crazy.

Mr. Franks,

My family and I moved into Twin Lakes about six months ago. We've been very happy and enjoy the subdivision very much.

I am writing to express a concern about the bylaws. I feel they should be changed in several significant ways. I would be happy to talk with you about my concerns whenever it is convenient for us to meet.

Thank you for your interest.

Perry Shetler
Twin Lakes Resident

Peter,

We've got some trouble brewing. Burglaries in the subdivision have increased over the summer months. The police have been pretty unresponsive, and the neighbors are getting scared. I don't know what to do about the situation. I know you asked me to look into security and neighborhood watch associations, but I don't know where to begin. Help.

Jerry Connors
Associate Trustee
Twin Lakes Development

Mr. Franks:

We at Acme Snow Removal pride ourselves in the quality of our work. That's why we value our relations with Twin Lakes Development. I must express my concern, however, about the outstanding bills for our services last winter. I have spoken with Allen Lavell, your treasurer, many times. But I keep getting the run around. Can you either straighten out Mr. Lavell or pay this bill yourself? It would be a shame if we had to cancel our agreement with you for this winter. Your home-owners will have major hassles slipping and sliding down those giant hills of yours.

Walter "Ace" Acme, President
Acme Snow Removal

Hi ya Pete,

How the heck are you? Listen, I need to get something off my chest about the last couple of board meetings. You know, being from the old school, I don't mince words. So, I'll tell you straight out. Everybody on that board is so damn polite. No one ever argues with anyone else. Whenever you, as the president, say anything, heck they all shut up and end up agreeing with you. That's not healthy, boy. I happen to know that there's a heap of tension building up in these people. If I were you, I'd get them to speak up. Otherwise, there's no reason to have any meetings at all. You can just make all the decisions by yourself. Hope you don't take offense at this. Glad to talk more if you care to.

Tex Silverstone II
Associate Trustee
Twin Lakes Development

Pete,

Edward Wilson from Racine, Wilson and Endicott Construction Company called me the other day. They want to make an offer on the acreage we own on the other side of the lakes. I've heard rumors that the county might be rezoning for office space. Wilson and his boys would love to get their hands on our land. That would be a disaster for us. What about the golf course we have planned, what about the swimming pool? I don't want to get you upset, but sometimes I think our goals for this development are pretty fuzzy. If we don't decide what we want Twin Lakes to be all about, we may end up worse off than we are now.

Do you want me to meet with Wilson? Do you want to meet with him? What should I tell him? Apart from Wilson, maybe we should try to make some long-range plans that we can stick to. I don't know.

Kevin Corbin
Associate Trustee
Twin Lakes Development

Mr. Peter Franks, President
Twins Lakes Development

Dear Mr. Franks:

I will be brief. As president of the board of trustees representing Bell-tower Homes, I must protest your overtures inviting construction firms to bid on your excess acreage, acreage that is directly adjacent to Bell-tower Homes. We at Belltower are dedicated to preserving the peace and tranquility of our residential development. Informed sources have told us that one of your trustees, a Keven Corbin, is offering your acreage to construction firms. Do you realize this is like playing with fire? Don't you understand that you're inviting initiatives for county rezoning? We'll have no future.

Once these firms get a piece of this land, they and their lobbies can exert powerful influence on the county government to consider rezoning. Placed on the ballot, the rezoning issue will be controlled by the big money in this town. In no time at all, there'll be offices and shopping malls and used car lots and God knows what else ripping away at the beauty and quiet we all love and cherish in Belltower.

We will not tolerate your solicitations to entice construction firms. We will fight you every step of the way. Please advise me of your intentions.

Regards,

Everett Brown
President, Board of Trustees
Belltower Homes

Peter:

Below is a copy of a letter I received from Rona Peters Pakstein reminding me of the speech I agreed to give to the Leadership Development Association. First of all, I never agreed to do this. I don't know where they got my name. Second, I have no idea what to say, much less how to say it. I'm scared to death to get up in front of groups.

How about you doing this? You're much better suited for these types of things. I'd really appreciate it.

Let me know as soon as you can. Peter, I really don't want to do this!

Barry Jenkins
Associate Trustee
Twin Lakes Development

Copy for Peter Franks
To Mr. Barry Jenkins:

Thank you for agreeing to speak to our local chapter of the Leadership Development Association. Just to make sure we're both on track with the times and dates, etc., I wanted to send you this letter.

The meeting will be held the first Wednesday night in November at 8:00. You'll be introduced by our president, Larry Masterson. Larry plans to mention that you'll talk about how a board of trustees works to plan and develop a subdivision. Your talk is scheduled to last from approximately 8:10 until 9:00 with time built in for questions. The meeting will be held at the Downtown Holiday Inn in the Wilshire Room.

We are all excited about your talk and are honored to have such an outstanding member of our community address our group.

Please do not hesitate to call me if you have any questions.

Best wishes,

Rona Peters Pakstein, Vice President
Leadership Development Association

Response to Rona Peters Pakstein:

Mr. Franks,

Isn't it time you did something about all the weeds growing in the cul-de-sacs? I've been humiliated when my friends come to visit me and I overhear them commenting to one another about the condition of our streets. It's terrible.

Please take care of this matter at once.

Pauline Frisco
Twin Lakes Resident

Peter,

You asked me to submit an expense report to our treasurer, Allen Lavell, for the conference I attended on behalf of Twin Lakes. Of all the gall, he rejected over half of my expenses. Come on, now. I made some decisions on behalf of Twin Lakes that I felt would motivate the county to reconsider some of their restrictions in this subdivision. These decisions included buying a few drinks and paying for the meals of two of the county representatives. If our treasurer would have bothered reading my report, he would have realized that they paid for two of my meals to reciprocate. By the way, I'm still working on the county to lift some of its restrictions on us already, thank you very much!

Look, Peter, I made what I thought were reasonable business decisions. I feel our treasurer is being petty and shortsighted. Please reconsider my request.

Jane Reynolds
Associate Trustee
Twin Lakes Development

Peter,

It's time again to collect neighborhood fees. As you know, I have done this for the past two years and I'm getting tired of it. These people out there are a bunch of tightwads, and someone should come down hard on them.

And that brings up another matter. Look, Peter, I'm trying to do the best job I can as treasurer. Every time I make a firm decision that would either save our money or help us raise more, you overturn it. Maybe you should be treasurer. I think I've done one heck of a job for Twin Lakes. It would be awfully nice if you'd stand behind me once in a while.

Allen Lavell, Treasurer and Trustee
Twin Lakes Development

Dear Peter,

I am getting fed up with the board dilly-dallying around as far as the gangs of hippies, hoodlums, and crackheads on their motorcycles using Twin Lakes as a thoroughfare. I wrote a letter to Bill Watson, the chief of police, and told him we'd had just about enough.

Just wanted to let you know I stepped up to this challenge and took care of it. I think my letter should scare the wits out of him. What this board needs is some tough leadership. No reflection on you, of course.

Madelyn Westridge
Associate Trustee
Twin Lakes Development

Memo

To: P. Franks
From: Chief of Police, Bill Watson

1. This is to acknowledge correspondence from one of your trustees, Madelyn Westridge.

2. Ms. Westridge filed a formal complaint on behalf of Twin Lakes.

3. She asked me to respond directly to you regarding the complaint.

4. Regarding the issue of motorcycle gangs using Twin Lakes as a thoroughfare, I will ask one or two of my patrol cars to look into the matter.

5. Please let me know if we can be of further assistance.

Mr. Peter Franks, President
Board of Trustees
Twin Lakes Subdivision

Dear Mr. Franks:

The purpose of this letter is to inform you that certain county services
to Twin Lakes Development will be discontinued in 180 days from
today. Census results just compiled reveal that occupancy in Twin
Lakes Development has dropped below the 75 percent required to
maintain county services.

The county services affected include trash pickup and street repair. As
you know, the board of trustees of Twin Lakes is currently responsible
for street maintenance (snow removal) and street lighting. The provi-
sion of utilities will not be affected by this ruling.

You have 160 days to either appeal this ruling or document that occupancy in Twin Lakes Development has reached 75 percent. If you are
successful, trash pickup and street repair will continue. The additional
services of street maintenance and street lighting will be restored when
Twin Lakes Development can document that occupancy rates reach the
required 90 percent level.

Please do not hesitate to contact me if you have any questions or would
like further information.

Sincerely,

Wilford R. Bevel
County Supervisor

Mr. P. Franks
Twin Lakes Development

Dear Mr. Franks:

Permit me to introduce myself. My name is Cheryl L. Sheathing. I am the broker-owner of Sheathing Real Estate Development Corporation. I have just opened my offices here in town and would like an opportunity to meet with you.

A few days ago, while driving through various suburban developments as I routinely do when I move to a new location, I took the opportunity to familiarize myself with Twin Lakes. I understand from other real estate brokers that Twin Lakes has gone downhill in the last few years. Agents have trouble selling Twin Lakes homes at market value. Residents often overlook their lawns, many homes need maintenance, and in general, Twin Lakes is regarded by many of us as a plague to steer our clients far away from.

Mr. Franks, I see a gold mine in your subdivision. I have specialized in turning around neighborhoods like Twin Lakes. I see what once was a magnificent residential area now suffering needlessly. What the residents need is something to get excited about. We need to energize them and focus them to care about the beauty that is waiting just under the surface of Twin Lakes Development.

Imagine filling up Twin Lakes with vibrant neighbors that care about one another. The plans for the pool and tennis courts and golf course could be just months from ground breaking if we go about it in ways that I know can work. Think of the pride everyone will feel as Twin Lakes competes with other neighborhoods in swimming meets. Can't you just see the kids lining up to take tennis lessons, and even us older type kids driving our carts up and down the golf course? There's no limit to what we can do. Those lakes out in your back section will make for unbelievable sunsets, not to mention expensive homes we'll build right on their shores.

Mr. Franks, making Twin Lakes work is not just a matter of screaming at your residents to mow their lawns. It's not just a matter of plugging up holes in your streets. We need to build a community, a community that's filled with fun and with pride. Within a year, Twin Lakes homes could sell at premium prices. Who knows, we might even think of buying up that neighboring acreage to develop other sections.

Call me, Mr. Franks. Twin Lakes is waiting for us to meet and get down to business.

Warmest regards,

C. L. Sheathing, President
Sheathing Real Estate Development, Inc.

Response to C. L. Sheathing:

CHAPTER 3

Ask The Consultant

To help you learn some important skills for leadership, the first thing we'll do is put you in the role of a leadership consultant. Let's say that you've opened up a consulting practice. People seek you out for advice to help them improve their own leadership skills. You run your office sort of the way a doctor runs a medical practice. An office administrator, who functions as a receptionist and secretary, sits in an outer office that oversees a nicely appointed waiting room. At the time of a client's appointment, your administrator notifies you and then directs the client into your office.

You schedule one hour per appointment. During the hour's time, you allow 40 minutes to visit with the client. The client then leaves, and in the remaining 20 minutes, you review the notes you have taken, gather your thoughts, and then draft a letter for your administrator to type and send to the client. The letter contains your summary of the client's problem, your analysis of the issues, and your recommendations for solving the problem.

Today you have six appointments. They are as follows:

8:00–9:00	Lester Stipple	CEO—Stipple Manufacturing
9:00–10:00	Horton Kramer, MD	Kramer Internists & Associates
10:00–11:00	Beverly Jacoby, RN	Fairchild Medical Group
11:00–12:00	Mike & Kathy Wilson	Personal Consultation
1:00–2:00	Barbara Collins	Collins Video, Inc.
2:00–3:00	Steven Beasly	Marks, Kensington & Beasly, Accountants

Your role as their leadership consultant will be to hear their concerns, analyze their problems based on your knowledge of leadership theory and leadership skills, and draft a letter that summarizes your conclusions and offers your recommendations.

You: Come in, Mr. Stipple. Please sit down and make yourself comfortable. I received your letter and I've been looking forward to meeting you. How can I help you?

LS: Well, my company is running up against some hard times. I've all but given up on salvaging it. I'm about to declare bankruptcy, but a friend of mine from the lodge suggested that I come see you first.

You: I appreciate the good words from your friend. I'll certainly do all I can to help. Mr. Stipple, you say this is your company. Are you the sole owner?

LS: I'm the majority stockholder. We are now publicly traded. I took over the company from my father. He founded Stipple's in 1939 and single-handedly ran the company until he retired in 1978. That's when I took over. We decided to go public in 1982 and are now governed by a board of directors. They pretty much leave us alone, and I've run the company the way I thought best. They've been good to us, and we've been good to them.

You: Please tell me about the business—your product line, customers—anything else that you think I should know.

LS: Are you taking notes there?

You: Yes, is that a problem for you, Mr. Stipple?

LS: Nope. But that pen there that you're writing with . . .

You: Uh huh.

LS: The tank that contains the ink is more than likely one of our products.

You: You mean everything that's inside the plastic housing?

LS: No, no. Just the tank that contains the ink. The ink itself, the ball point, and the plastic housing are all supplied by other contractors. We make the tank.

You: Is that your only product?

LS: No, it's only one of them. Stipple Manufacturing is in the business of supplying hardware piece-parts to the stationery industry. Most people don't think much about our products even though they use them all the time. At least, they have been using them all the time. That's the problem.

You: Why don't they use them anymore?

LS: Because of the computer revolution. The consumption of paper for office supply and communication is decreasing rapidly. We're in the electronic age. In fact, I'm surprised that you're not taking notes on some sort of palm-top computer. It warms my heart to see a good ole pen-to-paper setup here.

You: Okay, I'm getting the picture. So besides ink tanks, you manufacture other types of items that we use with sheets of paper.

LS: Yep. Our list of products includes paper clips, staples, binders to attach erasers to pencils, springs for ball point pens, the ink tanks for the pens, clips for clipboards, and strips for the hard straight edge on rulers. Everything we manufacture is made of metal; each item is a piece that is used to support the stationery industry.

You: Fascinating. You are exactly right. I've used these products all my life and I've always taken them for granted.

LS: The fact that you've taken them for granted never was the problem. What is the problem is that you're not using them very much anymore. That computer on your desk has eliminated your need for many of our products. Let me show you. Can I borrow one of your clipboards?

You: Uh, I don't think I have one. I can check with my administrator outside.

LS: Don't bother. That product is virtually obsolete.

You: Surely you're not saying that staples and paper clips are obsolete as well.

LS: Not yet. But the problem is that the market is shrinking rapidly. There simply isn't room for all of the companies who are now in this business. Stipple's is strong, but how long can we compete with the big guys like Acco and Charles Leonard, Inc.? Sooner or later, those of us smaller companies will drive each other out of business, and eventually the big guys will swallow us up. We employ 2,300 people in several cities. That's a lot of families who depend on us to put food on their tables. It's also a lot of medical bills, clothes, and college educations that come from the fine work we've done at Stipple's.

You: So what we're dealing with is the loss of potential income and your very ability to survive due to the high-tech electronic industry that is reducing the need for your products.

LS: Exactly, and I'm not sure there's anything someone like you can do about it.

You: Well, let's find out. Do you mind if I ask you a few questions?

LS: Go right ahead.

You: I'd like to start with how your organization is structured. Tell me about your levels of management, starting with you as the CEO, and take me all the way down to your operating levels.

LS: We have seven divisions. Each division corresponds to one of our products. At the head of each division is a president and a series of vice presidents that report to him or her.

You: What are the roles of the vice presidents?

LS: It depends on the divisions. Generally, each division has a vice president for product design, manufacturing, and marketing. They have directors who report to each of them. Going down the hierarchy are the general managers, branch managers, group managers, and down at the operational level there are first line supervisors.

You: What's the rationale for having these multiple layers of management within each division?

LS: When I took over the company from my father, Stipples was entirely centralized. Old Man Stip, as they called him, made all the decisions. There was good and bad to that. I remember being in a meeting one morning when I was a vice president. My father arrived that morning about 6:30 instead of his usual 6:00 A.M. He asked his secretary where all his boys were. That's what he called all the presidents and VPs. She told him that they were in a meeting. He was somewhat surprised.

"I didn't know anything about this meeting," he said. "What's the purpose of this meeting?" She said that she wasn't sure, but that he could find them all in the Stipple conference room down the hall.

"I know where the Stipple conference hall is, Gladys," he barked. "What I want to know is why they're having a confounded meeting that I didn't know about." So Dad pranced on down the hall, opened the door, and cast his eyes on Jim Vanders, one of the presidents. He motioned for Jim to come to him.

"What's going on here, Jim?" Stipple asked directly.

"Good morning, sir. As you can see, we're just having a little meeting so we can decide the best option for the Graser project. We thought we needed a little help so we called in a consultant," Vanders explained.

"A what?" my father asked in a menacing tone of voice.

"A consultant . . . He's come highly recommended," Vanders replied unsteadily.

"I see, a consultant, is he?"

"Yes, sir."

"Has he had his coffee yet?"

"I believe he has, sir," Vanders responded.

"Good, good. What about one of those donuts? Has he had a donut?"

"Why yes, sir, indeed, he had one of those chocolate donuts."

"Fine, fine. Now that he's had his coffee and his donut, pay the man what we owe him and send him on his way. The only consulting you boys need is from me. I'll tell you what you need to know. The meeting's over. Tell everyone to get back to work."

You: What a story. So he ruled the place with an iron fist, hey?

LS: And a heavy one at that. But as strong willed as he was, he had a warm heart. All of us from the executive suite to the factory floor felt that he really cared about us. One of our electricians told me a story once that I'll never forget. Way back when he first opened up shop, my father put an ad in the newspaper for workers of all trades. This electrician responded, and my Dad invited him out to personally interview him.

"Son, I like you and I think you'll do a fine job for us. We need electricians to make sure all of our equipment keeps humming right along. How about it, can we shake on it? Would you like to work for Stipple's?"

"I sure might, Mr. Stipple. But before I say yes, how much can you pay me?"

"To start, I'll pay you 75 cents per hour plus overtime at time and one half."

"No offense intended, Mr. Stipple, but down at the union hall I can get jobs at $1.25 an hour. I've got a wife and a young daughter and I need the money."

"Young man, all I can afford right now is the 75 cents. But if you come work for me, I'm going to take care of you and your family. We're going to grow, and you'll grow right along with us. We'll all be one family and I want you to be part of it. My boy, if you want it, you'll always have a job here at Stipple's."

And that's how he made everybody feel. Like he was looking out for us. If you crossed him, he came down hard on you so you'd never forget it. But be loyal and hard working and you were part of that family.

You: Things changed when he retired?

LS: Not right away. I remember when I tried to make my first decision as the new CEO. My father still came in every day. He didn't like the decision I made.

"Lester, that's not a good decision. Here's what I want you to do instead."

"Dad," I said, "you don't understand. I'm the CEO now."

"No, Lester, you don't understand. You may be the CEO, but I'm still the boss!"

Now, to answer your question, why have all these multiple layers of management? I want to drive decision making down through the organization. While he was in charge, my father clearly made the lion's share of the decisions. That's probably okay for a company that's just getting started. But certainly, by the time he retired, my father's company had outgrown my father. At least it needed to outgrow my father. So I tried to move us in a different direction. My intent was to share power and that's why we have multiple layers of management.

You: What is your role, then?

LS: To do just that. In other words, when my managers come to me and ask me for a decision, I tell them that they get paid to make the decisions. I'll certainly help wherever I can. When they disagree with one another, I'll referee. When one gets a bit too uppity, I'll bring him back in line. By and large, though, they run the show. They know their own product lines better than anyone else. So it's up to them to make a go of it.

You: With each president and vice president running their own divisions, what does Stipple's stand for? What do you as the head of Stipple's want the customer to think of when they think about Stipple Manufacturing?

LS: What they always have thought about. Stipple Manufacturing makes quality pieceware to support the stationery industry. Our real customers, those folks that use paper clips and staples, probably don't even know we exist. But they can count on us to make sure they have good quality pieceware when it comes to the work they do with paper in their offices.

You: What are your hopes for Stipple's in the near term?

LS: Son, I want us to survive. I'm no longer sure we can do that for much longer. You already know about the trends in the industry. Fewer and fewer folks are using paper goods in their offices now. And not long from now, offices will use paper supplies less and less. So we need to work on staying afloat. If that means driving out the smaller competitors, so be it. If that means merging with them, I'm open to it. If one of the big boys wants to swallow us up, I won't go down without a fight.

You: How do you feel about change?

LS: What do you mean?

You: If surviving means that Stipple's will have to do business differently than it has before, are you open to it?

LS: Not if it means doing anything that will hurt my employees or my customers.

You: Absolutely not. Research clearly shows that the most profitable companies in any industries are those that do business ethically. What I'm asking is whether you would be open to changing the way Stipple's is structured and organized. Just like you made some significant changes when your father stepped down, would you be open to making some changes now if it could increase Stipple's chance to survive?

LS: If it really meant that, yes, I would be open to change.

You: Very well. I thank you for your candor, Mr. Stipple. I enjoyed talking with you. I never realized how much I myself depended on your company. My next step is to take some time to think about our conversation. Then I'll send you a report with my thoughts and some recommendations for you to consider.

LS: I'll look forward to it, and thank you for your time.

To: Lester Stipple
        President, Stipple Manufacturing

You: Come in, please. Make yourself comfortable. How can I help you?

HK: Thank you. I'm Horton Kramer. I am a general surgeon here in town with Kramer Internists & Associates. I never thought I would come for a consultation like this, and I have to tell you, I'm a bit embarrassed.

You: Dr. Kramer, you're in good company. While I am bound to maintain the confidentiality of my clients, rest assured that many prominent and distinguished professional folks just like you have sat in that very chair. Please feel free to tell me whatever is on your mind.

HK: Maybe the best thing I can do is to simply relate the entire story. I'm painfully aware of every detail. It began when a young woman I'll call Tina scheduled an appointment for a breast exam. She had found a lump and was very anxious about it. We discussed her concerns in my office before the examination. I'll tell you as accurately as I can what she told me.

> "I told myself it was nothing—probably just something that would go away in a day or two. But it still haunted me. I found a hard, round lump in my right breast. I would stand in front of the mirror night after night tracing its shape with my index finger, trying to pretend it wasn't there. But it was.
>
> I'm thirty-two years old. I got divorced six months ago and I decided to return to graduate school to finish a master's degree in architecture. Lately I've been almost incapable of concentrating on schoolwork.
>
> Dr. Kramer, I've never had a breast lump before. My best friend lost her mother to cancer and it started from this kind of thing. I can't help feeling that I'm living with some sort of time bomb that sooner or later is going to explode."

I took detailed notes as Tina answered questions about her medical history. I tried to listen with as much warmth and compassion as I could because she really was anxious. At one point during the session, Tina told me that she appreciated my patience and concern. She said she was reassured that she was in good hands with a doctor who had as much experience as I do.

My nurse then came in and escorted her to the examining room. I described to Tina exactly how I would conduct the examination. I explained that I would stick a needle into the lump to see if any fluid could be drained out. After I finished, I gently patted her on the back and told her to get dressed and then we could talk in my office.

When she knocked softly, I told her to come in and sit down. Just after the examination, my nurse wanted to let me know how Tina was feeling.

> "Dr. Kramer, Tina told me that she feels protected by you. She has been listening to you and finds your voice to be soothing and reassuring. She's beginning to feel much better about hearing whatever you are about to tell her."

I was glad that Tina felt confident about my skills. That kind of attitude is so helpful when a doctor is trying to help patients help themselves. I picked up Tina's file and explained to her what I found.

> "The lump appears to be the size of a small peanut. I extracted a little fluid from it, which is a good sign. I really don't think it's anything to worry about."

I then made a few notes, after which I closed the file. I told Tina that on her way out she should schedule her next appointment about two months from now. At that point, Tina reached for her purse, got up from the chair, and started to walk toward the door. She hesitated for a moment and then asked,

"Isn't two months kind of long to wait? Shouldn't I be coming back sooner than that?"

I walked around my desk, put my arm around her shoulder, and said that I didn't want her to worry.

"Worrying is the very worst thing you could do. Now go on about your life and just forget the lump's there. Come back again in two months and we'll take another look at it, okay?"

She said okay, but I knew she was still upset. It was as though she thought I was giving her more of an order than a question. Later on I found out that she had become extremely angered by this.

"Who does he think he is, telling me to forget it's there? How can any woman be expected to forget that there is a lump in her breast? Get on with my life, he tells me. He's made me so mad that at least I've forgotten how scared I am."

When Tina came back for her next appointment, I reviewed my previous notations in her chart, then I traced the outline of the lump. I then told her that the lump hadn't changed at all and I instructed her to make her next appointment for three weeks from now. I reassured her that all was under control and that she should hang in there. Then she let me know that for her, the appointment was not yet over.

"Dr. Kramer, I don't mean to be rude, but I don't feel as if you've told me anything. I can't just be expected to wait day after day while this thing is growing inside me. I'm not sleeping or eating and I can't concentrate on my studies. Isn't there anything you can do now?"

I wrote her a prescription and told her that I wanted her to take one of the pills I prescribed every four hours and one before bedtime. Tina gratefully took the prescription and then asked me if the pills would dissolve the lump. "Dissolve the lump?" I asked. I told her that of course they wouldn't dissolve the lump; they were tranquilizers.

Once again, I later found that this moment had been particularly troubling for Tina. From her perspective, she had waited two months for this appointment. She would have to wait another three weeks before she would know anything more. It was at this point, feeling helpless, that she decided to contact her gynecologist for his opinion.

The next day I got a call from Terry Mills, a highly respected gynecologist in the area. He wanted to know if I had any idea how upset Tina had been. I asked him to tell me more.

"Tina asked if I could see her right away. I told her she might have to wait in the outer office until we could work her in. She agreed to wait for however long it might take. She explained what had happened during the two appointments she had with you. I conveyed to her your strong reputation in the medical community and said your articles have been published all over the world.

She asked me point blank what I thought of your diagnosis and the way she said you treated her. After examining her, I told her that I didn't feel anything that made me suspicious.

She then wanted to know if I could do some exploratory surgery or maybe even a biopsy. So I suggested that she get a mammogram.

She wasn't sure why a mammogram would be useful since she already knew she had a lump. I explained that it would serve two purposes. First, it might help determine if the lump was malignant based on its specific shape. Second, it would establish a baseline for comparison for future observation. If the results proved negative, I assured her that she would sleep a lot better until she was examined again. If it turned out to be positive, at least she would know now instead of waiting another several weeks until her next surgical visit. Tina asked me to call you and give you this information."

I was enraged. How could Mills undermine me and what I was trying to do for this patient? I felt as if he had gone behind my back and caused this patient to have doubts about how I treated her. In my judgment as a surgeon, there were no alternatives. This gynecologist was way out of line. But—and this took all of my will power and professional demeanor—I didn't say anything, at least to him.

I decided to give Tina a call. I told her that I had talked to Dr. Mills and that I strongly disagreed with his advice to her. I have to admit that I wasn't very nice and my tone of voice was loud and probably harsh. I told her that Dr. Mills was obviously not familiar with the latest research. I explained to her that the radiologic journals made it clear that mammograms should not be used on women under forty unless there is a clear reason to justify the risk of the exposure to the x-rays. I could tell that Tina was now confused.

"But at least I'd know something. I would know one way or the other. I'd know something. At least I could do something."

I told her that if I thought a mammogram had been indicated, I would have ordered it. I went on to remind her that the lump in her breast gave no palpable signs of being malignant. I warned her that she was overreacting to all of this and that is why I ordered her to take the tranquilizers. I asked her when her next appointment was. When she told me it was in three weeks, I told her to make sure she kept it. I also made it clear that I expected her to make a decision who her doctor was. If she decided on Dr. Mills, that would be fine with me and she should simply let me know so I could send her records to him. If she wanted to remain my patient, I expected her to stop this doctor shopping and wasting her insurance company's money.

Of course I knew my behavior would inflame Tina. I felt entirely justified as a physician to give her this information in the way that I had. Later I found out what she did with it shortly after she left my office. She called Dr. Mills. She was totally confused by what seemed to be contradictions between what we independently told her. She felt that I wanted her to believe that Dr. Mills didn't know what he was talking about. So she called him and asked him about it. He let her talk for as long as she needed to and then proceeded to address her concerns.

"You know, I can understand Dr. Kramer's position. The research in the radiologic journals states very clearly that women under the age of forty should not undergo mammograms for the purpose of routine screening. At one point we hoped that mammography studies could be as much a part of a checkup as taking blood pressure. You see, many women don't check themselves for breast lumps. So we all hoped that mammograms, like the Pap smear, would be an almost failsafe mechanism for detection. Unfortunately, because exposure to any x-ray carries a certain amount of cancer-inducing risk, the routine use of mammograms for screening purposes was abandoned. You, on the other hand, have already performed the screening portion of the exam by finding the lump yourself. Your case at this point is clearly beyond the screening stage. The mammogram can now give us a pretty good indication if that lump is cancerous. Now, what about the risk? You have every right to know about it. Out of every million women who at the time of the mammogram did not have breast cancer, one of those women will develop it as a result of exposure to the radiation. Under the circumstances, I would advise you to have the procedure done."

Tina then asked Dr. Mills what he would tell his own wife to do if she were in Tina's predicament. He said, "I would tell her to have the mammogram." Again, what I later found out was how grateful Tina was that Dr. Mills not only told her to have the mammogram, but told her in a way that was comforting and reassuring.

As for me, I take my own comfort in the fact that the results of the mammogram were negative as I had suspected they would be. In my judgment, Tina was exposed to that radiation needlessly. The reason I'm here is because I am angry that I lost this patient. Where did I go wrong? I did everything I could to give her the best medical care. Yet she turned to another doctor. Is there anything you can do to help me understand?

You: She's okay now, isn't she? You diagnosed it correctly, and there was no cancer, right?

HK: There's no doubt in my mind about that. The cancer is not what I'm here about.

You: Go on.

HK: Tina is submitting a complaint to the Medical Ethics Society regarding my demeanor. She told me that she originally considered filing a medical malpractice suit, but changed her mind because the lump turned out to be benign. But she is furious with me for the way she says I treated her. She made it clear to me that she would try to get my license revoked.

You: What do you hope to accomplish?

HK: I contacted my attorney who suggested that he and I make an offer to Tina.

You: An offer? What kind of offer? Was your attorney suggesting you buy her silence?

HK: Absolutely not. On the contrary, in fact, he asked her if she would drop her allegations of ethical misconduct if I would agree to take some lessons in bedside manner.

You: Did she agree?

HK: Conditionally. The agreement is that she will hold off on the charges if I can substantiate I have become more sensitive to the needs of my patients—the, uh, emotional needs.

You: What is she asking in the way of proof or verification that you've turned over a new leaf?

HK: A letter from you.

You: Me? Why me?

HK: Do you know Dr. Mills?

You: Oh, I see. Dr. Mills recommended me as a consultant for you.

HK: That's right. And by now you know how she feels about Dr. Mills. As far as she's concerned, he walks on water. So, that's it. I need this letter from you, and I expect that you're probably going to put me through the ringer in order to get it. Will you help?

You: I'll do everything I can. Give me a few days to outline a plan that will help you develop interpersonal communication skills.

Consultation Report

To: Dr. Horton Kramer
        Kramer and Associates

You: Welcome, Ms. Jacoby. I understand that you are the director of nursing services for the Fairchild Medical Group.

BJ: That's right. And that's why I'm here. I'm having some trouble pleasing both my superiors and subordinates at the same time. Seems like no matter what I do, someone is upset. Of course, my main concern is the welfare of our patients. So far, the quality of our services is still second to none.

You: You say that you're having problems pleasing both your superiors and your subordinates?

BJ: Yes. The problem centers around a weekend seminar I've been planning for the last two months. When I first mentioned the idea back then, my nurses seemed to be in favor of it.

You: Before we get much further, can you give me a bit more information about the Fairchild Medical Group and what your role is?

BJ: I'm in charge of dispensing nurses for home health care. The home health care division is one part of the Fairchild Medical Group, which is a privately owned complex of medical services. Another division within the Fairchild organization is patient relations. The personnel in patient relations are the ones who are contacted by the referring physicians. They make the initial visit to the patient's home or residential treatment facility.

You: Are there problems between your two divisions?

BJ: That's putting it mildly. The PR people make the treatment plan in accordance with the physician's orders, but they make promises that we simply cannot keep. You see, they don't actually treat the patients. We do that. They are supposed to determine what the patient's treatment needs are going to be and then give us a detailed report that we can follow up with. Our job is to assign one of our nurses to the case who will then dispense treatment according to the plan.

You: Sounds reasonable so far.

BJ: So far it is. The problem comes in when the PR people write treatment plans that are beyond our abilities. You see, we feel that they are trying to make Fairchild look good to the physicians so the referrals will keep coming in. So they write up treatment plans for round-the-clock nursing care to be provided by nurses specialized in whatever condition the patient suffers from. I think that if someone were to look into this whole thing from a legal side, Fairchild could get into a great deal of trouble. I've even thought of talking to our company lawyers, but PR is not out and out lying. Some of our nurses actually are specialists. But they create havoc for us because when our less experienced nurses or our nurse-generalists arrive to treat a patient who was expecting a cardiac nurse, the patient has a fit, or the family has a fit and guess who gets the brunt of it?

You: The poor nurse who showed up to do the job.

BJ: Exactly. Our nurses get all the blame for the promises made by others that they had nothing to do with. They are harassed, ridiculed, and a lot of times treated more like housemaids than professional nurses. What complicates matters is that a few of them have yelled back at the patients or their families. Some of them have even walked out. You can imagine how PR feels about us when they get complaints from irate families or, worse yet, from physicians who threaten to cut off referrals.

You: Have you tried going to your superiors? That way, maybe you and PR could work out your differences through a neutral party.

BJ: PR refuses to sit down with us. They see themselves as the sales force for Fairchild and claim that it is up to us to keep the customer happy after the sale has been closed.

You: And what does your boss say?

BJ: That would be Grace Swanset. She's told me to just handle it and make the problem go away.

You: Let me see if I understand so far. Fairchild gets the physician's referral, which is then turned over to PR. PR makes the initial contact with the patient or patient's family and establishes a treatment plan. The treatment plan is in some way glorified to make Fairchild look good in the eyes of the physician. Happy physicians make for more referrals. Am I on target for now?

BJ: Yes.

You: The treatment plan calls for specialized nurses from Fairchild, which PR clearly knows will not be provided. When nursing staff are dispensed from home health care and arrive to deliver care, either the patient or the family feels that they have been lied to because they have not received the type of provider that PR said they would.

BJ: That's right.

You: The patient or the family gets upset, your nurses get upset in response, and PR gets upset because of the complaints they get back from the patients. As a result, PR blames your division and won't talk further with you to try to resolve the problem. And when you tried to get help from your boss, she tells you to handle it and make it go away.

BJ: As you can tell, I'm exasperated by all of this.

You: Of course, it must be terribly frustrating. What I don't yet understand is the issue about the weekend seminar and the trouble you're having with the nurses who report to you.

BJ: I'm probably the cause of the trouble. I think what I'm realizing is that I'm just not cut out to be in a leadership role.

You: It's understandable that you're questioning yourself. Before we come to any conclusions, let's keep talking awhile. With your help, I'm sure I can learn more, and then I'll be happy to share my thoughts with you.

BJ: I haven't told you about Virginia Murphy yet. Virginia was my predecessor as director of home health care. Most people thought of her as a dictator. She was mean, unfair, and just a downright nasty person. Under Virginia, you either put up or shut up. The turnover in the department was like a merry-go-round. People left in droves only to be replaced by unsuspecting, inexperienced nurses fresh out of school who came to us in droves because we paid so well. If any of the more experienced nurses tried to complain, we knew Virginia had the power to get us blackballed from the profession. She made it clear in her own way that we would never work again if we ever crossed her. It was almost like a prison working under Virginia. People were in constant fear of her. Home health was not a fun place to work. It's really amazing what people will put up with for the money—at least for a while anyway, until they just couldn't stand it anymore. Those who were able to find other jobs got out. The rest of us just learned to live with it. Then when Virginia retired and they put me in the director's position, I made a promise to myself that I would treat these nurses with the dignity and respect they deserved. I have probably gone to the other extreme, though, and have become too lenient. I've lost all control. They're late to their assignments, they're rude to the patients, and they've become excessively demanding. In the last few weeks, they've banded together and insisted that the only way they'll continue to put up with the PR situation is if they get more money. They're already the highest paid group of nurses in the community. Last week I went to Grace and asked for more money. She conditionally agreed with the stipulation that I would get control of them and stop asking her to intervene. Now that they have more money, they're still complaining, and Grace won't listen to me any more. So I'm caught in the middle, and I am all out of power.

You: And what about the seminar?

BJ: The seminar was an idea for teaching our nurses how to handle the tirades they face when they walk into the patient's residence. After all, the problems are created by PR, but our nurses are getting the brunt of the anger. So I figured that we could train the nurses to calm the patient down and solve whatever problems they could right then and there. In that way, the nurse could then go about giving the patient the best treatment possible, and as a result, Fairchild's good name could be preserved. We've hired a professional training group who specializes in this sort of thing.

You: Sounds like a good idea to me.

BJ: When I first brought it up, all of our nurses thought so too. We planned to get away over a weekend at a local retreat facility so that we could combine the workshop with a nice relaxing time. Up until the last couple of weeks, the plans were proceeding on schedule. Then some of the nurses started pressuring me for more money. I resisted initially, which I'm sure caused some resentment. By the time I asked Grace to agree to a raise, two or three of the nurses started trying to convince everyone else not to give up their weekend for the workshop. As it stands right now, only three people out of the twenty that we have paid for plan to attend.

You: How have you reacted?

BJ: I have done a complete turnaround in the way I've been treating them. Unless they show up for the retreat by 9:00 A.M. on Friday and stay clear through until Sunday noon, they will not have a job to come back to on Monday morning. When Virginia Murphy treated them like that, she got results!

You: Do you think you'll get results?

BJ: I'm so confused and frustrated, I don't know what I think anymore. I simply don't know what to do. I've got a workshop coming up in less than forty-eight hours that will cost the firm over $3,000 whether or not we go through with it. Only three people said they would attend, and I have threatened everybody else with their jobs. On top of all of that, Grace refuses to help me any further. All I can hope for is that somehow you can advise me how to bring some order to this situation.

You: Well, clearly, we don't have much time. Once you leave, I'll put some thoughts down on paper, fax them to you, and then you can give me a call early this evening. I'll try to lay out what I think you should do in a step-by-step fashion, and then we can talk it through tonight.

To: Beverly Jacoby
        Director of Home Health Care
        Fairchild Medical Group

You: Good Morning, Mr. and Mrs. Wilson. Please come in. What brings you here today?

K: We appreciate your seeing us. We've been married for just over a year now, and we're realizing we've got some problems.

M: No, you think we have some problems. Your mother thinks we have some problems, or at least I have some problems.

K: We're constantly disagreeing and fighting with each other.

M: She's right about that.

You: Okay, what I'm puzzled about is why you're coming to see me. I'm happy to talk with you, but I primarily work with folks who are having problems within business settings. How is it that you've come to see me, and what are you hoping we might accomplish together?

K: When I realized that our marriage might be in jeopardy, I went to our family doctor, Dr. Mills. Do you know him?

You: Ah, yes, Dr. Mills is a fine physician. So, did Dr. Mills suggest that you two come see me?

K: Uh huh. He gave us the names of several referrals, but suggested you particularly because you specialize in working with business people.

You: I'm sorry, I'm still not sure why he would refer you to me for help with a marital problem.

K: Well, both Mike and I are professional people. Mike is in sales, and I've just joined a law firm. Dr. Mills thought you would be the best person to help us.

You: Okay, makes sense to me. How would you like to proceed?

K: Dr. Mills suggested that because you specialize in business, we might want to first write out what's been happening and present it to you so you could get a flavor of what our relationship has been like. May I share that with you?

You: Please do.

K: Okay, well I guess it started shortly after I joined the firm, the day of our first anniversary.

I had recently passed my state law boards and joined a large new practice. I developed my own caseload and won several disputes both in and out of court. Although I really did enjoy my work, I deeply believed that my husband should always come first. On this particular day, Mike and I had been married for one year. Starting three weeks earlier, I began rearranging my schedule so I could devote the entire day to preparing to celebrate our anniversary.

   I spent most of the morning at the market buying food for the feast that Mike and I deserved. Dinner would begin at 6 o'clock with Caesar salad by candlelight. I then planned to serve prime rib with Japanese vegetables. Red wine would complement the dinner, with enough left to toast our happiness for the next seventy-five years.

   After scrubbing the house to a sparkle during most of the afternoon, I began preparing dinner around 4 o'clock. I left word at the office to have Mike call at home since he usually tried to call at least once a day. I set the table with a white linen tablecloth, china, silver and lead crystal stemware. As I finished the table, I admired it and was proud that Mike and I would soon be sharing the evening. For a fleeting moment, I felt a pang of disappointment that Mike's applications to medical school had been rejected and I also regretted that I had been pressuring him so much to give up the field of professional sales.

That started me thinking, and then my thinking quickly turned to worrying. I sometimes wondered in agony if I was really all that different from my mother. I didn't consider myself to be nearly as critical or judgmental. I certainly hoped that I didn't belittle Mike at all—much less the way my mother often belittled my father. No matter what Dad did, it never seemed to be good enough for Mom. She always found something wrong with what he said or how he looked. It was pathetic how he put up with it for all those years. Of course, my mother treated me the same way as I was growing up and, for that matter, she still does. I would all too often hear my mother remind me, "You can't keep a house and home together, and please a husband, and have a career all at the same time." And then there was her constant reminder, "And Kathy, honey, why Mike? He'll never amount to anything. He'll flit from one job to another and, you mark my words, one day you'll catch him playing around on you with another woman."

These thoughts always upset me. I hate my mother for always being so negative. I guess the reality of it, though, is that I also worry that there might be some truth to what she says. Sorry, Mike, but that's what it comes down to.

Anyway, as I continued to prepare for our special night, I cleared my mind of all these horrible thoughts. I love Mike dearly and I reminded myself how wrong my mother was. By 5:30 I had everything ready to be served. I quickly showered and put on the new dress I had bought especially for this evening. At about 5:40 when the phone rang, I remember dreading that it might be Mike calling to say he'd be late. It wasn't Mike. It was my mother.

"I'll bet he hasn't come home yet, has he?"

"No, mother, he hasn't," I told her.

"Did he at least say he'd be late?"

"Mother, I've got to go. Besides I want to keep the line clear in case Mike needs to call. He'll be here."

"If you had gotten call waiting like I told you to, you wouldn't have to worry about other calls and you wouldn't have to keep cutting me off."

"'Bye, mother."

At about 6:20, the phone rang again. This time I felt sure it was Mike. I was already angry that if it were him he would be calling to say he'd be even later. But I was also relieved that at least he was calling.

It turned out that it wasn't Mike. It was my secretary calling to tell me that a judge had changed my court time from 9:30 to 8:30 tomorrow morning. She apologized for calling tonight of all times because she knew how special the evening was going to be. She decided that I would want the information regardless and that's why she made the call. I thanked her for her good judgment and told her how I appreciated her thoughtfulness.

By now I was starting to worry. There was no sign of Mike. The candle had dripped down on the tablecloth and the wine had already lost its chill. The tears welled up in my eyes as I blew out each candle and slowly poured the wine into the sink. I thought about calling Mike at his office, but I didn't want him to think I was checking up on him. I flipped through every magazine on the table, filed my nails, and finished an open bag of peanuts. "Oh, the hell with it. I know he forgot. I might as well admit it to myself. How could he forget?"

I finished clearing the table, wrapped all the food and put it away, and then put on my pajamas and flannel robe. At 9:30 I heard the key turn in the door. Mike opened the door and walked in.

"Hi Honey, what's for dinner?"

I completely ignored him. I tried to cover up my rage. I knew if I said anything, I would be an open book.

"Kath, what's wrong?" Mike continued.

"Do you know what time it is?" I asked in a tone of voice I knew he could barely hear.

"Honey, what's the problem? Why are you giving me the cold treatment?"

"You really don't know do you?" I asked more as a challenge than a question. "Where have you been? Do you have any idea what I've been doing since 8:30 this morning?"

"Kathy, I'm very tired. I don't know what the problem is. I don't know what I'm supposed to know and, to be honest, right now I really don't care. I'm hungry, I want to eat, and then I want to go to bed. I'm sorry, Kathy, but when you clam up on me and give me the silent treatment like your mother, I can't read your mind."

"How dare you compare me to my mother!" I screamed back in rage. "My mother has nothing to do with this. Look on the mantle and see the card my mother remembered to send on a day that obviously means nothing to you."

Mike glanced at the mantle and was noticeably jarred when he realized what the card meant and that he had forgotten our anniversary.

"Kathy, I did forget. I am so sorry, honey. I've been so wrapped up in this Slater account this week that it completely slipped my mind."

"Mike, why is it that everything comes before me?" I asked, raising my voice.

"Come on, Kathy, don't make more out of this than it is. And lower your voice; the whole apartment complex will hear us."

"I don't give a damn about the apartment complex! Right now I give a damn about the fact that our marriage doesn't mean anything to you. Or maybe I should say that I don't mean anything to you."

"Kathy, listen." Mike pleaded.

"No, you listen!" I interrupted. "It's one thing that you forgot about today, but at least you could have called. Do you know what's been going through my mind since 6 o'clock tonight? I didn't know whether you were in an accident or in bed with another woman. In fact, I still don't know for sure whether you were with another woman. I purposely didn't call you at the office because I didn't want to seem like a nagging wife. But damn it, Mike, not even a lousy call to say you were tied up."

Visibly upset Mike said, "You know, you think that because you're the lawyer in the family and that your mother keeps reminding you that you're married to a salesman that I don't do anything important. Well, let me tell you something. Because I worked my tail off tonight, I might end up closing an account that no one else has been able to touch. One way or another, you've got to rub it in that I don't have what it takes to be a doctor. You think doctors' wives complain if their husbands can't get to a phone?"

"I'm not married to a doctor, Mike. Besides, that's not the point. You've got this stupid complex about being a salesman. Don't throw that up in my face. All right, so you didn't pass the medical entrance exams. Forget it, already. I'm sick and tired of you bringing that up every time we fight about something. Regardless of whatever you were doing tonight, you could have broken away for five minutes to call."

"So I didn't call, so I forgot our anniversary, so I failed at that just like I failed the tests. Let's face it, sweetie, you'd better decide if this is what you want, because you ain't going to get much more from me. Nothing I do is good enough for you and I'm getting sick of it. You treat me just like your mother has been stepping over your mealy-mouthed father for the last umpteen years. Well, you may be like your mother, but I sure as hell am not going to let you trample all over me."

"Stop it!" I screamed.

"No, you stop it!" Mike yelled in revenge. "When's the last time you showed me the slightest bit of . . . "

That was all I could take. Mike kept pounding at my weak spots. Each time he mentioned my mother, I felt my heart beating harder and harder as if it would burst. The only way I knew how to fight back was using Mike's sensitivity about his test failures. I had been so excited about what could have been such a beautiful evening, I couldn't understand what was now happening. I just want us to get past all this ancient history and make a happy life with each other.

You: Mike, you've been awfully quiet. Would you care to add anything?

M: No, that's pretty much the way it happened. I'm amazed she remembered it all so clearly. I suppose she's right. I don't want to lose her. Do you think you might be able to help us?

You: Well, let me make sure I understand. You care for each other, and you want to make your marriage work. What seems to be happening is that you have different expectations of each other. That's not uncommon, particularly after the first year of marriage. What I propose is that you give me a few days to think about what you told me today. I'll share my thoughts and my recommendations in the form of a letter that you can expect to receive in three to four days. Once you've each had a chance to read it over, talk about what I've said and the recommendations that I'll be offering. If you want to talk with me further about the recommendations and what we can do to get started, or if you have any questions, give me a call.

To: Mike and Kathy Wilson

You Hi, Mrs. Collins. Please make yourself comfortable. How can I be of service to you?

BC: Please call me Barbara.

You: Great.

BC: I'm having problems with the manager of the video store I own. He's incredibly talented and in so many ways good for the store. But at the same time, he's so strong willed. His temper and his determination can cloud his judgment, and when that happens, he's not so good for the store. So, I'm not sure what to do. Should I fire him? Should I scold him? Should I learn what I can from him?

You: It would help me get more of a handle on the problem if you could go back to the beginning and tell me why you decided to employ him.

BC: My husband Nathan opened the video store about a year before he died. At that time, neighborhood video stores offered warmth and friendliness to a following of local customers. It wasn't like it is today with the large video conglomerates that have all of their operations computerized, and where the service is impersonal. Nathan saw this coming, but his dream was to keep our store focused on our customers. He felt we could grow as a store and even become wealthy some day all from treating people with dignity and care. When he died, I was lost. I just about sold the store. I didn't know how to run a business. Nathan's dream or not, I knew I would be in way over my head. Then someone told me about John Baker.

You: He's the one you're having problems with now?

BC: Yes, and I should have seen it back then. The clues were there. I just didn't pay attention.

You: Clues?

BC: At the suggestion of one of Nathan's best friends, I called John. I explained that I was about to sell the store, but I would reconsider if we could come to some agreement for him to manage the whole operation.

You: So you wanted to be like an absentee owner?

BC: Well, that's what I thought I wanted. The problem was that I didn't know enough about the business to understand what a mistake I would be making by giving him nearly unlimited power and authority.

You: In what way?

BC: John let me know that he had successfully managed several stores owned by the big conglomerates. He talked the business, he knew the industry, and he oozed self-confidence.

> **John:** Mrs. Collins, you've seen my references, you now know that I've significantly increased the profits of all the stores I've managed, and you have my commitment that I will not only guarantee your business will survive, but you will have financial security and peace of mind for as long as I'm in charge. All I want in return is a fair wage, an opportunity to earn a partnership, and your assurance that I will have unlimited authority to make the decisions I need to make in order to honor my commitments to you.

I was totally sold. What more could I have asked for? In Nathan's honor, the business would survive, and the store that he left behind would be taking care of my financial needs. Already I was experiencing peace of mind.

You: It was too good to be true?

BC: It certainly was. John paid lip service to the condition I placed on the agreement that he treat people with dignity and respect and that the customer would always come first. That's the way Nathan wanted it. I also let him know that I expected the video rentals to be high quality and under no circumstances were we ever to carry any movie that had been X-rated. He agreed.

You: And?

BC: Needless to say, he didn't live up to the agreement. Oh, we're making money for sure. The problem is, we're doing it in all the wrong ways. At first, things were great. John had a grand reopening sale offering rentals at special incentives like half price, extended rental periods for no extra charge, free popcorn, and even coupons for restaurant take-out services. We made money hand over fist.

You: Then what happened?

> BC: I first became aware that there were problems when I got a call from one of our high school "co-op" employees.
>
> BC: What's wrong, Scott?
>
> S: Mr. Baker fired me.
>
> BC: Why on earth would he do a thing like that?
>
> S: I was watching one of the movies when he came back to the store after his lunch break.
>
> BC: What's wrong with that? You weren't ignoring any customers, were you?
>
> S: Oh no, Mrs. Collins. There weren't any customers in the store at the time. I wouldn't neglect the customers. Nathan taught me better than that last year when I first started. I tried to explain that to Mr. Baker, but he said I was insubordinate and lazy. He told me I was fired and that I wouldn't be getting my check for the last two days because he said I was ripping off the company by not working and by watching movies without paying for them.
>
> BC: My word. Scott, don't you worry. I'll speak to Mr. Baker. Rest assured, you are not fired, and you will get paid.

Later that week, I got a call from Mattie McCoy. Mattie was our very first customer the day Nathan opened the store. Mattie called me and was just beside herself. When she got her mail that day, there was a letter from our store addressed to her. It was a bill for fifty cents. Fifty cents, can you believe it? John was invoicing her for fifty cents because she didn't rewind her last movie. And to add insult to injury, he wrote out a warning that if she neglected to rewind her next movies, he would personally revoke her membership.

You: Did you say anything to him?

BC: Not as yet. It was the next thing that happened that really got me upset, and that's what caused me to talk to him. Yesterday, I went into the store to pay some bills. I kept my office in the back, and the kids who work for us know to bring the mail back to the office that John and I share.

You: From what you've told me, I'm surprised that John didn't demand his own office.

BC: Since I'm there so infrequently, the arrangement was fine with John. Anyway, as I was going through the mail, I noticed an envelope with a suspicious return address. The label read "The Xtasee Collection." I opened the invoice, traced the video codes to our inventory and discovered to my utter shock that we now owned and rented over 400 X- through XXX-rated movies. That was the last straw. I had no choice but to confront John. After all, he had broken his agreement with me at least three times that I now knew of. He was out on the sales floor at the time. I caught his attention and motioned for him to come back to the office. I told him what I had heard from the co-op student and from the customer. I also showed him the pornographic movies that he had been concealing from me.

> **John:** Mrs. Collins, don't come in here all of a sudden after five months and start playing boss with me. You have absolutely no reason to complain. You have record profits, and your time is yours to enjoy. If I'm going to continue making this store work for you, you need to back off. Don't breathe down my neck because if you choke me you'll end up choking yourself.
>
> **BC:** John, I am extremely upset. I feel like you've betrayed my trust, dishonored my husband's good name, and humiliated our employee and our customer.
>
> **John:** Mrs. Collins, I suggest you think very carefully before you make any rash decisions. I have just about had it with these wimpy employees and these prima donna customers. We need to get a few things straight if I'm going to continue to make this work. I'm still convinced that we can make this store the most profitable and financially secure store in the entire region. In fact, I've been meaning to talk to you about setting our sights on buying out one of the local conglomerates. From there, the sky's the limit. Work with me, Mrs. Collins. Don't ruin it for both of us.

That's when I said I'd think it over and we could talk again in a few days. In the meantime, I told him to take a few days off until I could sort things out. Now I'm here and I'd like your advice. If I lose John, I'll lose the store. If I keep John, I'll lose my self-respect and I'll forever feel like I've somehow cheated on Nathan. What do you think?

You: I think I can help you. I'll need a few days to get my own thoughts together about options for you to consider.

BC: When and how will I hear from you?

You: I'll be sending you a letter that you'll receive by the day after tomorrow. Once you look over my recommendations, give me a call and we'll talk about some possible next steps.

To: Barbara Collins
        Collins Video, Inc.

| | 2:00–3:00 | Steven Beasly | Marks, Kensington & Beasly, Accountants |

You: Mr. Beasly, come in. Tell me why you wanted to see me.

SB: I'm one of the senior partners in a large accounting firm here in town.

You: Of course, I've heard great things about the firm, and I'm honored to meet you.

SB: Thanks, I appreciate the kind words. I'm afraid I was a bit too eager to recommend a promotion for one of our junior accountants. His name is Jerry Williams. May I tell you what happened?

You: Absolutely, please do.

SB: Jerry joined our firm about five years ago and has been a rising star ever since. He turns accounts around in record time, helped us weather IRS audits without a scratch, and as you can imagine, the customers are crazy about him. So, I pushed for his promotion. Needless to say, it's been stormy seas ever since.

One of our firm's partners, John Kensington, had staunchly opposed Jerry's promotion. The other two partners, myself and Roger Marks, had assured Jerry that they would get Kensington to support him, but we weren't successful. There was no way that Kensington could actually block Jerry's promotion. The corporate bylaws stipulated that advancement within the company required affirmative votes from only two of the three partners. Surely the promotion was deserved. After all, a great deal of the firm's financial stability during the last several quarters stemmed from Jerry's close scrutiny of the corporate books. Even so, Kensington was making his life miserable. I know Jerry wonders if Kensington perceives some weakness in him that Roger and I have somehow overlooked.

The problem surfaced just recently one morning at 8:40, when Jerry approached the conference room. He took out a handkerchief and patted his forehead. His hair fell down across his eyebrows and he threw his head back, trying to force it into place. He smiled politely at Kensington. Kensington nodded his head. Then Kensington picked up his glasses from the table, put them on so they rested somewhat forward on the bridge of his nose, and said, "Now, perhaps we can begin."

The meeting did not go well. Kensington questioned several conclusions that Jerry had reached in his report. The division that he had taken over recently had lost several prominent accounts.

"Williams, I don't understand where your head is, man!" Kensington barked. "You can't go giving away the firm's services like this. People expect to pay for quality. Hell, why don't you just take out an ad in the newspaper with 50-percent-off coupons?"

"John, this proposal came from our marketing division," Jerry said in his own behalf.

"Don't hand me that," Kensington retorted. "You signed the damn thing. At least you could have proofread it."

He flipped through the document, showing Jerry several pages that he had marked in red. Then he shoved the proposal across the table.

"Looks like you've got your work cut out for you as a manager, doesn't it, son?"

Looking down at his agenda, Kensington went on with the meeting.

"All right, what other bright ideas do we have to talk about today? Let's get on with it."

Jerry was mortified and humiliated. He was sweating profusely and his skin had lost all color. As soon as the meeting was over, he stormed into the secretarial pool and threw the proposal on Theresa Sanchez's desk.

"You told me you proofread this damn thing!" he yelled.

"I did," Theresa said meekly.

"Well, these aren't gold stars," Jerry said as he flipped through the pages. "Kensington caught all these and chewed me out in front of everyone at the staff meeting."

"Oh my God, I'm sorry, Mr. Williams," Theresa said, obviously ashamed for her oversights.

"I'm sorry," Jerry said mimicking her. "You made me look like a complete idiot to the head of this company. What the hell were you doing when you were supposed to be proofreading this, huh? Dreaming about doing the hat dance with one of those illegals you run around with? Maybe if you'd stay the hell away from those morons you could concentrate on your work. It's going to take me months to shake this off."

He ripped the proposal in half, threw it down at her computer and abruptly left the room. Janet, Theresa's coworker, brought her a box of tissues.

"You know, Theresa, you could get him on discrimination for that. The EEOC wants to know about people like him. He had no right to talk to you like that."

Theresa reached for the tissues and tried in vain to hide her remorse. She looked down the hall toward her supervisor's office, hesitated momentarily, then slowly walked toward it. About an hour later, Jerry's secretary notified him that Mr. Kensington was calling.

"Should I put him through, Mr. Williams?"

"Yes, of course."

Jerry took a deep breath in hopes that he could cover up the quivering that would undoubtedly be in his voice. Jerry's internal phone line rang once and he immediately picked it up.

"Yes, John, this is Jerry."

"Get in my office right now," Kensington ordered, then abruptly hung up.

You: Did Kensington fire Jerry?

SB: Close, he suspended him. Then he called me into the office. Kensington's a powerful man, but we're equal partners so he can't hurt me. But he's livid—and rightfully so. What Jerry said to Theresa could put our firm in a great deal of jeopardy.

You: Did Theresa file charges with the Equal Employment Opportunity Commission?

SB: She said she plans to file charges. As far as I know, she hasn't done it yet.

You: What are you hoping we can accomplish by working together?

SB: I'd like to make things right with Theresa, of course. I'd also like to salvage Jerry. He's a fine accountant. With the right direction and guidance, I'm convinced he could develop into one of the company's top executives. I know he's far from it now, but in time I think that could change. I'm interested in what you think.

You: I need to know more of what you see as Jerry's strengths, not so much in the accounting area but more in the area of leadership.

SB: Jerry is able to look far ahead when it comes to solving technical problems. Oh sure, he made a dumb mistake on his report a few days ago, but we all do occasionally. Kensington doesn't know him like I do. He's great at finding ways that seemingly unrelated problems fit together. Then he comes up with one solution that fixes all of them at the same time. Once he gets this concept in his mind, he convinces his coworkers of how his approach makes sense and then shows them that they can solve their individual problems by collaborating with one another. If we don't find a way to salvage him, not only will he lose a great career opportunity, but our company will lose the potential for developing a great leader. In the meantime, I need to figure out what to say to Kensington and how to make things right for Theresa.

You: Thank you for the explanation. My next step is to reflect on what you've told me and then send you a letter that summarizes my thoughts and outlines my recommendations. You'll receive it in a few days. See what you think after you've read it and then give me a call.

SB: Thanks, I'll talk with you soon.

To: Steven Beasly
        Marks, Kensington and Beasly

CHAPTER 4

Scoring Your Responses

Now that you've reached this chapter, you've hopefully completed each segment of the leadership assessment. You've answered the behavior interview questions, addressed the correspondence items in the in-basket, and given your recommendations to each of the clients that came to you for guidance and advice.

The process of assessing leadership skills is practiced throughout the field of leadership development. Experts have developed many approaches to assessing and developing leadership skills, and many questions have been investigated. Some of these include:

How can we identify and measure the skills that make leaders effective?
Can leadership be learned, and if so, how can it be taught?
What are the differences between leadership and management?
Is leadership related more to intelligence or to personality?

Academicians as well as business organizations have tried to identify and measure the skills that make leaders effective. Some of these approaches include personality tests, intelligence tests, measures of learning new behaviors, and ratings by associates of performance and competence. The assessment method that we've used in the first three chapters focuses on behavior. The reason we have focused on behavior rather than on measures of intelligence, personality, or even opinion is because a behavior can be observed. It is either there or it isn't. Its existence is not a matter of opinion. So, for our purposes, certain behaviors must be present. If they are, then we can describe them in terms of their effectiveness as leadership skills. If they are already effective, we want to identify them as such and support their continued use. If they are ineffective, then we want to eliminate them or replace them with behaviors that are effective.

Let's consider the case of Dr. Kramer. When his patient Tina wanted some reassurance that her breast lump was not cancerous, he responded by saying, "Now go on about your little life and forget it's there." His response can be considered a behavior. As a behavior, it was observable. If played back to him on a tape recorder, he would agree that he did say those words. Tina would agree that she heard those words. Having established that Dr. Kramer spoke the words, we are now in a position to evaluate their effectiveness. Were they helpful to Tina? From Tina's perspective, they were anything but effective. Is there another behavior that Dr. Kramer might have used that Tina would have found effective? Probably so. Then, as a developmental objective, Dr. Kramer could be presented with an alternative behavior that he could try out. If that behavior achieves his objectives as Tina's physician and it achieves Tina's objective for reassurance, then we could conclude that the new behavior is effective.

The three assessments in this section gave you opportunities to discover how you might respond in certain situations that require leadership. The behavior interview questions asked you to respond to a given situation by describing something you actually did to solve a problem. That something were behaviors. The in-basket exercise asked you to write out an actual response to each of the situations. Once again, the responses we were trying to pull from you were behaviors. And finally, the consultant situations simulated what you would actually say or do to help your clients solve their problems. As before, the objective was to focus on your behaviors. So just as with the example of Dr. Kramer, now we're in a good position to examine your behaviors to find out if they would likely be effective if used as leadership skills.

Before we begin the process of interpreting your responses, we need to establish a frame of reference for leadership. We'll start with a definition, and then we'll list a set of leadership skills against which you can evaluate your responses from the assessment.

One of the most widely accepted definitions of leadership is by John Kotter, professor of organizational behavior at the Harvard Business School. According to Kotter,

Leadership is the process of establishing direction, aligning others to that direction, and inspiring and motivating them in order to produce change.

Compare this definition to the literally hundreds of others in the literature and you'll note that Kotter's definition captures the essential elements of leadership, namely, vision, communication, influence, and change. With this definition in mind, let's consider a framework for assessing the effectiveness of your responses.

A Framework for Assessing Leadership Behaviors (the 4 Competencies)

1. Directional Thinking (DT)
2. Consequential Thinking (CT)
3. Influence Strategies (IS)
4. Communication Skills (CS)

Directional Thinking

Kotter's definition begins with the process of establishing a direction. Some writers in the leadership literature refer to this process as "vision." A vision is where the leader wants to end up. Often fueled by the imagination, it is a place or a part of reality that doesn't yet exist. It is what the leader wants to create. President John F. Kennedy led us toward a new direction when in 1960 he proclaimed that we would put a man on the moon by the end of the decade. For those of us who heard those words as he actually spoke them, we could "see" that picture in our mind's eye. To use Kotter's terms, that picture was the direction that President Kennedy established. By contrast, when President Jimmy Carter tried to establish a direction, his messages were not as clear as those of President Kennedy. One author described President Carter's vision as the back side of a tapestry—the colors formed an image, but the picture was fuzzy and indistinct.

A direction communicates where the leader wants us to end up. In order to do that, leaders use directional thinking. They know where they want us to go. The captain of the team imagines the trophy, the CEO of a business visualizes the smiling board members, the mother sees her newborn as a twenty-one-year-old receiving her diploma at an Ivy League college, and a young scientist "hears" the surgeon general proclaim that AIDS has been cured. A vision is what the world will be after the leader has caused it to change.

Directional thinking is the behavior needed to develop and shape a vision. It is the process of thinking ahead instead of waiting passively for things to happen. One way to determine how much directional thinking you typically use is to look back over your responses in the three assessment measures. To what extent were your responses proactive rather than passive? To what extent did they establish a direction for change?

For an example, go back to the in-basket and reread the letter from Cheryl Sheathing. Do you notice anything interesting about her letter? It is visionary. Unlike the other letters, which focused on a detail level, Cheryl's focused on a "higher-level" solution. She described a community that almost everyone would want to be part of. As you read her words, you can imagine a neighborhood that is truly beautiful, fresh, spirited, and fun. This was a direction that she was establishing. Certainly, it was futuristic, but it was within reach. It made you feel good. It made you want to get involved.

That's the beginning of leadership. It starts with directional thinking. What evidence of directional thinking do you see in your responses? Go back and look for it. Using the letters "DT," mark any of your responses that reflect your use of directional thinking. Chapter 5 will concentrate on how you can further develop your skills in directional thinking.

Consequential Thinking

Leaders dream big dreams, but so do a lot of people who aren't leaders. What are the differences between them? Certainly one difference is how effectively leaders can persuade others to do what they want them to do. Many people have good ideas that just die on the vine because they can't get others to listen to them. Leaders get people not only to listen to them, but more important, to believe in them. Suppose, however, the leader is persuasive and the followers are convinced, but the idea itself is not a very good one. Suppose that once the idea gets implemented, it is harmful. If the leader anticipated the potential harm and in fact intended it, does that say anything about the quality of leadership? Depending on your point of view, it might. You might believe that any leader who knows that an idea could be harmful and goes ahead with it anyway could not be a very good leader. Others would disagree and say that it is not the leader's intent that determines the leader's effectiveness. Instead it is the leader's ability to establish the direction, anticipate the consequences (whether good or bad), decide based on the anticipated consequences whether to proceed, and if so then go on to convince others to implement the action required to produce change.

The presence of mind to anticipate the consequences is called consequential thinking. If not done, it is as though a car is set in motion without a driver. There is no one in control of what happens. By being aware of potential consequences, the leader is in effect steering the forces that produce change. In fact, the prospect of the consequences may cause the leader to stop any further action. Or by envisioning what might happen as a result of a particular course of action, the leader may decide to modify what is said or done along the way.

Once again, an example might help. Consider Dr. Kramer's behavior toward Tina. From his perspective, his intentions were to help Tina. He gave her the instructions she needed as a way of providing the best medical care he could. All she needed to do was to follow those instructions to the letter. His vision was that she would be cancer free and entirely able to continue with her life's activities. Viewing this perspective as a direction for leadership, it is entirely appropriate and certainly potentially effective. Proceeding from this vision, Dr. Kramer attempted to convey his directions to Tina. In Kotter's terms, this stage would be described as "alignment." That is, it was important for Dr. Kramer to help Tina understand what he was trying to accomplish through his treatment. The problem was that Dr. Kramer's attempt to align Tina didn't work. She misunderstood his intentions. While he was trying to diagnose and calm her fears by prescribing a pill, she perceived that he was trying to treat her condition ("Will this dissolve the lump?"). As the confusion continued, Dr. Kramer became more and more directive and confrontive with her ("Are you the doctor or am I?"). Clearly, at this point Dr. Kramer was out of control as a leader. He didn't anticipate the consequences of his actions. Instead of easing Tina's mind and moving her back to her daily routine without worry, his behavior made her more anxious and caused her to seek advice from another physician. In short, he didn't use consequential thinking. He didn't take the time to think through the step by step consequences that might result from a particular pattern of behaviors.

Looking back at your responses to the assessment, can you find any indications that you used consequential thinking? If so, make a notation of where it occurred by writing "CT" for consequential thinking. Chapter 6 will focus on how you can further develop your skills in consequential thinking.

Influence Strategies

The most dynamic part of leadership is the process of transforming a vision into reality. To do that requires the ability to persuade people to do what you want them to do. How did President Kennedy convince us that putting a man on the moon was such a good idea? What made the tens of thousands of people travel to Washington to hear Dr. Martin Luther King tell us about his dream? What made you decide to buy the car you drive, the house you live in, the clothes you wear, or the hair products you apply? Many patterns and routines in your life are actually the results of the influence strategies that someone else carefully planned. These strategies are designed to work based on your needs and desires. And whether spoken or not, visible or invisible, your needs and desires are apparent to those who intend to influence you.

Leaders persuade us through their influence strategies. We've already seen how Dr. Kramer's influence strategies were not effective in persuading Tina. By contrast, John Baker was very effective in persuading Mrs. Collins to hire him as the manager of her video store. What was it that he did and said that proved so convincing to her? To understand John's strategies requires that we first understand Mrs. Collins's needs. As the owner of the video store, she was totally inexperienced. The store was her husband's idea. After he died, she continued to need the financial security that the store provided, but she lacked the ability to run it. So, her primary need was financial security. The store was a means of providing it. Her secondary need was someone to run the store for her. John fit the bill. Not only was he experienced, but he was also self-confident. His behaviors convinced her that he would not only make the store work, but that her husband would be proud of the way he ran it. He acknowledged her husband's objectives and her desire to fulfill them. Then he outlined a plan that would achieve them. By so doing, he honored her husband's memory, and he demonstrated how her need for financial security could be met through his plans for the success of the store. His influence strategies could be observed through his promises to meet her needs. In that regard, he was quite convincing. Through these strategies, he was successful in getting the position.

Chapter 7 will focus on influence strategies and will help you develop your own. For now, look back over your responses to the assessment. Wherever you find an example of where you tried to persuade someone, note it with "IS" for influence strategy.

Communication Skills

Once a leader "sees" the world in a new way, that leader must communicate that picture if the vision is ever to become reality. Others must "experience" that vision for themselves in order to picture themselves as a part of it. The process of enabling followers to experience the leader's vision as though it were their own is what Kotter describes as alignment.

In order for alignment to occur, the leader must enable the followers to experience the vision as if it were already real. These types of behaviors are all part of effective communication skills.

Sometimes leaders get up on a platform such as a stage or stand in front of a camera in order to address large groups of people and give formal presentations. Other times leaders simply meet with another person and communicate on an interpersonal level. Whatever the setting, effective presentation skills include a message that is clearly organized, a method of delivery that is provocative and dynamic, an openness to participate conversationally with an audience through questions that are either rhetorical or interactive, and of course, good listening skills.

Consider the example of Dr. Mills whom Tina consulted for a second opinion after her experience with Dr. Kramer. He listened to her concerns and then summarized them in his own words to reflect his understanding and compassion. Then he explained a complex procedure in terms that Tina was able to grasp despite her high state of anxiety. Even though he wasn't speaking to a group and his audience was made up of only one member, Dr. Mills used communication skills to achieve his purposes. He calmed Tina down, helped her understand, and enabled her to make an informed decision.

Can you find examples from your assessment responses that demonstrate how you used communication skills (either on the platform or interpersonally) in order to help align others to your vision? Next to each one, write "CS" for communication skills. Chapter 8 will focus on how you can further develop these skills.

Analyzing Your Results

Step 1—Raw Scores. Go back through each of the three assessments and locate wherever you marked responses with "DT," "CT," "IS," and "CS." Count only those responses that reflect a behavior or action. Do not count any responses that reflect an opinion or intention. Enter the total for each of the competencies in the designated quadrants at the end of the chapter. Compare the total number of responses in each category. The comparison will give you a rough idea of how often you used competencies from each of the four categories. The example below illustrates the raw score comparisons.

RAW SCORES

DT 15	CT 7
IS 21	CS 42

Step 2—Competency Ratio. Divide the raw score for each competency by the total number of responses. For example:

DT = 15
CT = 7
IS = 21
CS = 42
Total: 85

Calculate the Competency Ratios:

DT: 15/85 = 18%
CT: 7/85 = 8%
IS: 21/85 = 25%
CS: 42/85 = 49%

COMPETENCY RATIOS

DT 18%	**CT** 8%
IS 25%	**CS** 49%

Interpretation

The most frequently used competency in this example is "CS," that is, communication skills. The competency that is used least often is "CT," or consequential thinking. With these results in mind, it is interesting to consider the leadership profile.

There is some indication that this person establishes direction. However, there is relatively little evidence that she considers the potential consequences of that future course or of the activities that will take place in order to develop it. Most of this person's leadership is reflected in communication skills. She is probably very highly social and finds it easy to talk to people. Is she persuasive? Somewhat—as reflected by an IS ratio of 25%. In summary, here's a person who lets others know what she wants and is at least somewhat aware of the need to use communication skills to influence people. Is she focused? To some extent, as reflected by a DT ratio of 18%. But with a CT ratio of only 8%, this person may be a loose cannon, seldom considering the consequences of her decisions.

Recommendation (For Previous Example)

Pay primary attention to the chapter on consequential thinking with secondary focus on directional thinking. After completing the chapters, return to the assessment and look for opportunities to improve the scores by revising responses that include CTs and DTs.

Summary

The example illustrates how you can interpret your own responses and identify the pattern that should guide your development. For now, you can consider the higher ratios as your stronger competencies and the lower ratios as those in primary need of development.

Keep in mind that the raw scores and ratios are based entirely on the frequency of your responses. They do not likely reflect the knowledge that you will soon be developing in each of the four competencies. Once you finish each of the chapters and apply the competencies through the various exercises and study guides, retake the assessment. By doing so you will accomplish two important objectives. First, you will very likely improve your scores in each of the four competencies. Second, you will respond with a broader knowledge of the four leadership competencies. Your answers will more likely reflect your ability to chart a course for the future through directional thinking, demonstrate that you are on a solid path through consequential thinking, provide evidence of how you inspire and motivate others through influence strategies, and illustrate how you deliver clear and well-organized messages to virtually any size audience through communication skills.

RAW SCORES:

DT	CT
IS	CS

COMPETENCY RATIOS:

DT	CT
IS	CS

SECTION II

The Competencies

Chapter 5: Directional Thinking
Chapter 6: Consequential Thinking
Chapter 7: Influence Strategies
Chapter 8: Communication Skills

CHAPTER 5

Directional Thinking

Directional thinking is the thought process that a person goes through, whether individually or within an organization, that ultimately produces a vision or establishes a direction. The process consists of two major steps: (1) a direction-setting opportunity (DSO) and (2) a direction-setting decision (DSD).

Direction-Setting Opportunities

A DSO is an event that occurs in a person's life. The event may be something that is ordinary and routine, or it may be remarkable and extraordinary. Whatever its degree or magnitude, the DSO presents an opportunity to change a particular course of action, that is, to redirect the activity from one direction to a different direction. To illustrate, let's first consider some fairly ordinary kinds of DSOs.

Imagine that you're driving your car one day and all of a sudden, the transmission locks up in second gear. You can still drive the car, but only up to about fifteen miles per hour. Today marks the fourth time the transmission has broken down. Your dealer had assured you that the problem had been completely repaired, but now you have serious doubts as to whether it can ever be fixed. Your doubts are fueled by the negative press about the make and model of your car. Your DSO? Should you keep the car and continue trying to get it repaired, or should you get rid of it and buy a new car? The direction-setting opportunity is represented by the events that have just taken place—namely, the car broke down today and this breakdown has been preceded by three others. You now have an opportunity to set a new direction, that is, to buy a new car. If you choose to buy the car, that decision will move you along a new path in your life in which you'll undoubtedly meet new people and have new experiences. Of course, you can continue along the same directional path and repair the vehicle, which you've already done three times. If you choose this path, your relationships and your experiences will remain pretty much as they are.

Another example is the opening of a new grocery store in your neighborhood. Since moving into this neighborhood, you've shopped at one particular store. You know where all the food items are located, and you've become friendly with the store manager and employees. Shopping at this store is part of your routine. You go to this store at just about the same time each week and are greeted mostly by the same people. Now you are presented with an opportunity to change the routine pattern in your life by choosing to shop at the new store.

Now consider an example with the potential of even more significant change to your life. Imagine that you have received a gift of free admission to the local riverboat casino. You decide to try your luck at one of the high-stakes card tables, and within a few minutes you win a great deal of money. On the next round, you bet it all on what looks like a sure thing. The player next to you sees your bet and doubles the amount. You're convinced he's bluffing because your hand is so strong. You clearly don't have the money to put down, but you do have that very expensive, though sentimental, piece of jewelry your partner gave you. Once again, here's a DSO. The opportunity presents itself to win big, fold and lose only your previous winnings, or ask for a marker at the risk of losing the jewelry and perhaps your partner's respect and affection. What will you do? In this case , the DSO is a bit different from those in the earlier examples. In the first case, your car broke down. You couldn't help that. In the second case, a new store is opening up. That's beyond your control as well. Your choice is presented by the opportunities that sprinkled themselves along your path. But in this case, you made a conscious choice to go on the boat and a conscious choice to play the game and make your bets. The DSO is not accidental, but rather one that you created and to a large extent one that you control.

The next example is the most significant type of DSO, one that occurs at a time that represents a transition in your life from one stage to the next. Consider when you were contemplating where to go for college. This decision usually occurs at the end of your junior or the beginning of your senior year in high school. Your choice of college will likely shape the rest of your life. It could very well determine an intertwined chain of events beginning with your choice of courses, who you will meet in those courses, your choice of careers, who will hire you, how you will be promoted, and so on. Given a different choice of colleges, you might never have met the person you married, and your children from that marriage would never have been born. Clearly, this type of DSO sets the direction for the rest of your life. The first three DSOs could certainly have life-shaping influences, but not to the extent of this type of choice.

In general, there are two types of DSOs—those that occur arbitrarily through forces outside your control and those that are intentional. The car breakdown and the grocery store examples are arbitrary DSOs. The gambling and college selection DSOs are those that you create.

Leadership involves both types of DSOs. When a crisis challenges a leader, it represents an arbitrary DSO. When a leader chooses to establish a direction or to develop a vision, that leader is creating a DSO.

An interesting example of an arbitrary DSO is illustrated in the movie *Independence Day*. When the president is safely aboard Air Force One and learns that the invading aliens have destroyed the White House, he comes to a painful realization. His DSO first occurred when the alien ships moved into position and hovered over all major cities in the United States. Had he given the order to evacuate the major cities at that time, his decision could have saved millions of lives. Instead he waited, and the result was massive loss of lives. Because this circumstance was beyond his control, it can be considered an arbitrary DSO.

Another example of an arbitrary DSO that actually occurred was the movement of missiles into Cuba in what we now know as the Cuban Missile Crisis. President Kennedy had nothing directly to do with positioning those missiles. Their existence in Cuba presented him with a DSO.

A third example of an arbitrary DSO is when Tylenol capsules were laced with poison, causing the deaths of several innocent people. The DSO was placed in the hands of Johnson & Johnson, the manufacturer of Tylenol. They had nothing to do with the contamination, but because it occurred in their product, they were faced with the decision about what to do.

When someone decides to move into a leadership role, it is usually the result of an intentional DSO. For example, John F. Kennedy contemplated whether or not he wanted to run for president. Martin Luther King Jr. reflected on how to communicate his dream about equality among all people. Rosa Parks looked up and down that bus and thought about where she wanted to sit. Steven Jobs imagined that he could put computers in every school and maybe even every home. The Wright Brothers wondered about heavier-than-air flight. Benjamin Franklin questioned if gas could be ignited to produce room light in place of candles. And sometime shortly before 1886 in Germany, Karl Benz wondered if horseless travel could be accomplished by a carriage with a motor. These people, each in his or her own way, changed the world. They didn't wait for an apple to fall from a tree and hit them on the head. They intentionally created opportunities that would cause them to make decisions. The decisions that follow a DSO are called direction-setting decisions (DSDs).

A direction-setting decision occurs when you choose between the existing pattern and a new direction. Once you make a DSD, it will change your course and put you on a road that leads in a different direction. JFK became president, Martin Luther King, Jr. held his freedom march, the Wright Brothers flew at Kitty Hawk, Benjamin Franklin invented the lightbulb, Steven Jobs founded Apple Computer and invented the Macintosh, Rosa Parks refused to sit in the back of the bus, and Karl Benz invented the first automobile. As a result, their decisions not only changed each of their lives, but would subsequently shape the course of our lives as well.

Direction-Setting Decisions

Leaders make decisions as a result of DSOs. Some of the DSOs are the results of events that surround them and are therefore arbitrary. Other DSOs are the ones they themselves create and are therefore intentional. The decisions that leaders make establish new directions. How do they know how to make these decisions? When should they wait for opportunities, and when should they create them? How can they be prepared for opportunities that could cause harm? How can they take advantage of opportunities that could prove useful? What's the best way to make a decision to ensure that it's a good one? Should they make decisions alone or should they involve other people? How much should they allow other people to influence their decisions? These and other related questions are what we'll be dealing with throughout the rest of the book and in particular throughout this chapter.

Let's begin by considering what happened when a woman, her husband, and another couple were denied admission to a movie in a local theater. We'll call the woman Jill; her husband, Max; her friend, Leslie; and the friend's husband, Ed. Here's what happened.

Directional Thinking in Personal Leadership

Jill, Max, Leslie, and Ed wanted to see a particular movie. To avoid a sell-out crowd, they decided to buy their tickets in advance. So they went to the theater box office at 4:30 and bought their tickets for a 7:00 show. They then went to a nice restaurant to enjoy a leisurely dinner. They returned to the theater at 6:45 only to see a "Sold Out" sign under the listing for their movie. When they tried to get in, the ticket taker told them that their performance was sold out.

Jill: Sir, you don't understand. We already have tickets for this performance.

Ticket taker: I'm terribly sorry, Ma'am, but we sold out by 6:30.

Jill: I understand. There are no more tickets to be sold. But look, we have four tickets, so please let us in.

Ticket taker: I can't.

Jill: What do you mean, you can't? Here are the tickets.

Ticket taker: The performance is sold out.

Jill: I want to speak with your manager.

Ticket taker: Certainly. Mr. Jenkins, this patron would like to talk to you. I explained to her and her party that we're sold out for the performance they want to see. They already have tickets.

Manager: I'm Pete Jenkins, the theater manager. How can I help you?

Jill: This is ridiculous. Look, we have four tickets for this movie. We got them at 4:30 to make sure we could avoid a sell out. Now you're telling us that the movie's sold out. This doesn't make sense.

Max: Maybe they could give us free tickets to another show.

Jill: Be quiet, Max. Sir, I don't understand the problem if we already have our tickets.

Manager: The problem is that our doors for this movie opened at 6:30. By then, everyone had tickets, and every seat ended up being sold. So you see, we have no more seats. They're all occupied. I'd be happy to try to accommodate you in some other way.

Ed: Jill, Max mentioned free tickets. Since we already have tickets, could they honor them for the 9:30 show?

Manager: I could certainly do that.

Jill: I don't want to go to the 9:30 show. Leslie, do you?

Leslie: Absolutely not.

Max: What if they gave each of us a free pass for a month? Ed, what do you think about that?

Ed: Works for me. Would you do it, Mr. Jenkins?

Manager: Well, uh, I don't know if I, uh . . .

Jill: Wait a minute. I want to see this movie now. I paid for it. I bought my ticket in plenty of time. I've been looking forward to it, and I intend to see it. A later show is not acceptable, and I won't be bought off with free passes. What's right is right.

Manager: Well, Ma'am, I'm not sure what I can do. There are no more seats. I can maybe give the four of you one pass to share.

Jill: Forget the pass! Now look, you told us that everyone who got in had a ticket and all the seats are taken, right?

Manager: Yes, Ma'am.

Jill: You know what that says to me?

Manager: Uh . . .

Jill: That tells me that people are sitting in my seat and Max's seat and Leslie's seat and Ed's seat. True, they may have tickets, but they don't have tickets to the 7:00 show in this theater. In fact, I'll bet if you look at every person's ticket, you'll find at least four people who have the wrong tickets. Maybe they have tickets to the 7:15 show in that theater next door. Maybe they have tickets to the 9:30 showing of this feature. But they don't have tickets to this show. We have those tickets; they don't.

Manager: What do you mean?

Jill: Let me spell it out for you, sir. They snuck in.

Manager: That's highly unlikely.

Jill: What's showing right now in that theater? Has the feature presentation started yet?

Manager: No, it's just the previews showing now.

Jill: Stop the projector and turn on the lights.

Manager: What? You have to be kidding. I can't do that.

Jill: I have four tickets here that entitle us admission into that theater. There are at least four people in there who are sitting in our seats. This ticket says I have a right to sit in this theater at this time. Now please do what you need to do to honor this ticket. Tell your projectionist to stop the projector, tell your usher to turn on the lights, and then you make an announcement that will correct this problem.

Max: Where's he going? Jill, this is really embarrassing. He'll never let us in. Let's just come back later.

Jill: You just wait. We are going to get in, I promise you.

Leslie: Look, the manager's going into the theater. I can't believe it, the lights just came on.

Manager: Ladies and Gentlemen. I'm terribly sorry to stop the projector and turn on the lights. We have mistakenly admitted some people into the theater who have tickets to another presentation. Please check your ticket stub. If your stub shows a time or a feature other than this one at this time, kindly leave the theater until your presentation begins. We appreciate your cooperation.

Leslie: I can't believe I'm hearing this.

Ed: Look, there must be twenty-five people getting up and leaving.

Jill: Max, don't just stand there. Give the ticket taker our tickets and let's go in.

Given that same situation, what would you have done? Most people who hear this true story are pretty impressed, yet they admit they probably would have just taken the free pass and come back for a later showing of the same feature. To get some insight into the decision-setting direction process of leadership, let's ask Jill what went through her mind when she and her party were denied admission. Then we'll try to find out how she made her decision to confront the manager with what she wanted.

Us: Jill, we're fascinated by how you handled that situation. Can you tell us what went through your mind when you first saw the "Sold Out" sign.

Jill: What immediately went through my mind was that the performance wasn't sold out. At least, not for us.

Us: But what about the sign?

Jill: The sign didn't faze me.

Us: Why?

Jill: Because we already had tickets.

Us: Okay, but then the ticket taker told you that you couldn't go in because the performance was sold out. What went through your mind then?

Jill: The performance was not sold out.

Us: Despite the sign that you saw and now despite what the ticket taker was telling you?

Jill: Sure. See, we had these four tickets. I'm no expert on movie management, but I didn't think they would sell more tickets than the number of seats in the theater.

Us: And so . . .

Jill: Simple. With that thought in mind, I knew that whenever the "Sold Out" sign went up, no more tickets to that performance would be sold.

Us: Okay.

Jill: Right at that point, everyone who had a ticket should also have a seat waiting for them. Remember, only one ticket per seat and a seat for every ticket.

Us: And . . .

Jill: Well, regardless of when we arrived, there should have been four seats left somewhere in the theater.

Us: But you certainly wouldn't expect that they would hold four seats all right in a row just for you?

Jill: Of course not. That's not the point.

Us: You mean, your group would have been willing to split up even if it meant sitting in individual seats at different spots in the theater?

Jill: That's not the point either.

Us: Where would you have sat?

Jill: Look, the issue is one of principle, not seating arrangements.

Us: Principle?

Jill: Sure. Because we had the four tickets and I knew they sold one ticket per seat, that told me that there should have been four seats left. The ticket taker told us that there were no seats left. The manager told us there were no seats left. It doesn't take a rocket scientist to figure out that the cashier either oversold, or at least four people purchased tickets to other shows, flashed the bogus tickets to the ticket taker, dodged their own movie, and snuck into our movie.

Us: How were you sure that they didn't oversell the seats?

Jill: I wasn't.

Us: But you said you knew they didn't oversell.

Jill: I never said that. I said I thought they wouldn't oversell.

Us: So you were gambling when you told the manager that people snuck in. You sounded so certain.

Jill: I don't think of it as gambling. I think of it as taking a reasonable risk. And in order to make it work, I had to sound certain. Besides, I was determined.

Us: You said to Max and your friends that you promised them you would all get in. How could you promise if you weren't sure?

Jill: By that time, I was 99 percent positive we would get in. And I said "I promise" as a way to help build their confidence. I was worried that the way Max and Ed were whining they could undo the whole thing. So I just wanted to straighten up their backbones a bit.

Us: Did you ever think that what you did was unethical?

Jill: Are you serious? The people who snuck in were the ones who tried cheating us out of what was rightfully ours. I was just protecting our interests. It was a matter of principle. The seats belonged to us, the logic told me that people took advantage of our not being there, and my own self-confidence and determination propelled me to take charge of the situation. Okay?

Us: Okay!

So how do leaders make decisions? In this case, Jill indicated that it was a matter of principle. That principle guided her whole outlook on the problem and guided the behaviors she used to deal with the problem. She also refused to accept at face value what she was told by an authority, namely that the performance was sold out and no more seats were left. She challenged that statement, and through her conviction and determination, she validated her beliefs and claimed what was rightfully hers.

The "Sold Out" sign and the barrier first imposed by the ticket taker presented Jill with the direction-setting opportunity. As the DSO occurred, Jill realized that she wanted to move in a particular direction. The direction-setting decision that flowed from the DSO was to move along a path that would get them into those seats. The path she chose included aligning the manager to her point of view and persuading him to grant her request.

Is Jill a leader? Certainly, at least she was a leader in that particular situation. The leadership process for Jill was that of first considering the different directions she could take as a result of the DSO, then purposefully choosing a particular direction (the DSD), and ultimately using behaviors to align and persuade others to produce change. That's leadership!

If what Jill did was leadership, could she lead an organization? Does she have what it takes to be a CEO, for example? Clearly, we don't know enough about Jill to form a conclusion. For all we know, based on the little information that we have, she might even already be a CEO. What we do know, based on what we observed, is that Jill effectively used the elements of leadership to achieve her objective.

What about CEOs or any other top executives in organizations? Is what they do all that different from what Jill did? Apart from professional training and technical experience, executives use the same basic leadership skills to lead their organizations as Jill used to deal with the ticket dilemma.

Directional Thinking in Organizational Leadership

Leadership in organizations usually begins with strategic management. Strategic management incorporates the use of both DSOs and DSDs. It sets the scope and direction of the organization and then frames the plans for how the organization will succeed. The process usually includes

Mission Statement—worthy goals and aspirations

Strategic Plan—how to accomplish the mission

Tactical Plans—what to do and who will do it

Let's take a look at these elements of strategic management in a bit more detail.

The Mission Statement

In its broadest sense, the mission statement gives the reason for the organization's existence. It either explicitly or implicitly expresses the organization's purpose, values, culture, and competencies. It clearly establishes the direction just as a leader proclaims a vision. In their book *Say It and Live It,* Patricia Jones and Larry Kahaner describe a mission statement as

> . . . *not simply mottoes or slogans, they articulate the goals, dreams, behavior, culture and strategies of companies more than any other document.*

Their book even goes as far as to say the mission statement is the most powerful tool that an organization can develop and use to implement change. It speaks to everyone about the organization, including customers, shareholders, competitors, suppliers, unions, reporters, and of course, managers and employees. An effective mission statement leaves no doubt in anyone's mind what the organization is trying to do and what it will do to get there. The substance of the Jones and Kahaner book is the set of mission statements that have been reprinted from fifty different corporations. To have been considered as one of the fifty entries, the mission statement had to pass two tests.

1. It had to be well written, well focused, and compelling.
2. The company had to demonstrate that it tries to live up to it.

As you consider the simulated mission statements developed from the Jones and Kahaner model, determine for yourself if they are simple, clear, and easy to understand and convey a sense of the company's personality. Notice how each sets a direction for the future.

Edwards Advertising, Inc. The reason we exist is to create the very best that advertising can be without exception.

International Home and Growth: To provide services that fulfill our customers' expectations for their real estate needs.

NutriSource: Everyone at NutriSource is dedicated to giving our customers wholesome, safe and satisfying foods at a fair price.

TransNational Airlines: To shrink the world through fast, comfortable and dependable airline services.

JetWay Taxis: We get people safely to the airport and back with on-time taxis operated by friendly drivers.

ClearSync Pagers: We know that getting messages can be the most important part of your day. We use the best equipment, the clearest signals, and the most reliable providers to ensure that you receive your message within seconds after it is sent.

Hansen Manufacturing: Customer Defined Quality, On Time Production and Delivery, Price Leaders—our watchwords at Hansen's.

Jensen Apparel: We are dedicated to offering our customers the latest international fashions and providing our employees with opportunities for career growth.

WhistWhile Entertainment: Our mission is to dominate the entertainment industry with megacomplex theatres that feature showings of all current movie releases, state of the art seating, the highest technological sound systems and an overall movie watching experience that is second to none. In the moviegoer's mind, there is simply no alternative to WhistWhile for watching a movie.

Like the leader's vision, an organization's mission statement establishes a direction. And like the leader who needs to lay a foundation for the new direction, the organization adds substance to its mission by developing a strategic plan.

The Strategic Plan

The strategic plan represents the part of the strategic management process that integrates the organization's projected direction with the steps that will be necessary to achieve it. According to Schermerhorn,

> *Strategy is a comprehensive plan that sets critical direction and guides the allocation of resources to achieve long-term organizational objectives.*

Planning and developing strategy often involves asking questions to help guide the process. One way of formulating the questions is through what's called a SWOT analysis: Notice how the SWOT analysis incorporates the concepts that we've discussed for DSOs.

What are our Strengths?

What are our Weaknesses?

What are our Opportunities?

What are our Threats?

Other useful questions include

What business are we in?

Where do we want to be in the future?

What do we need to do in order to get there?

What can we improve on?

By answering these types of questions, organizations can identify one of four directions called strategies that would make sense for them to pursue.

Growth Strategies—to increase the size of the operation through expansion either through *concentration* on a specific product line or through *diversification* into related or even unrelated product lines.

Stability Strategies—to maintain the current direction and continue an existing or a current pattern of operating the business. This strategy may be used to slow growth (that may be occurring too rapidly) or to create a block of time to evaluate the need for change.

Defensive Strategies—to protect the assets of the organization, which may include reducing the scale of operations through *retrenchment* or closing down operations through *liquidation*.

Combination Strategies—to address specific needs among different components within a large and multifaceted organization through strategies that could include growth, stability, and defense.

When put into words, strategies often include a statement about the direction intended (Grand strategy), the type of product line, a measurement of success, and a long-term estimate of how long it will take to get there. Here are some examples:

Concord Communications: To become the pre-eminent domestic print-based communications company by acquiring businesses that create and distribute news and information services.

General Glass: To deliver financial results that place us in the top 10% of the glass manufacturing industry within the next two fiscal years.

Delta Shoes: By the year 2000, we will lead the shoe distribution industry in operating profit, sales and customer satisfaction.

Southward Travel: We will increase revenues by expanding our business into all areas of passenger delivery.

A mission statement reflects the company's values and principles. It generally answers the question of *why* the organization exists. The strategic plan channels the mission statement into one of the grand strategies in order to give it direction and focus. The strategic plan generally answers the question of *what* the organization needs to do in order to bring its mission to life. The next step is called *tactical planning*. The tactical plan answers the question of *how* the plan will be implemented.

The Tactical Plan

Once the strategic plan is developed, then actions need to be specified in order to know how resources are to be allocated and who will be responsible for carrying them out. Compared to strategic plans which are written at an organizational level, tactical plans reflect how the individual units of the organization intend to achieve the organizational strategy.

For example, if a manufacturing organization has specified that it intends to capture 80 percent of the market share in its industry (a growth strategy), that organization will likely need to expand its manufacturing capabilities. To do so will probably require the purchase of new equipment (a tactical objective of the procurement division) that will be housed in new buildings (a tactical objective of the facilities division) that will be operated by new employees (a tactical objective of the human resources division), all of which will need to be budgeted (a tactical objective of the fiscal division). To achieve each of these tactical objectives, each division will need to develop a set of plans that detail the steps they need to accomplish and by when.

The process of tactical planning can be guided by several useful tools. The first steps and the most important, of course, are the company's mission statement and strategic plans. These tell the tactical planners the company's overall scope and purpose, the direction it intends to follow, and what it wants to accomplish. The tactical plan then is a natural outgrowth. To plan the steps in the tactical plan, the planner will likely specify all the tasks that need to be accomplished and then arrange them in a progressive sequence. As each task is accomplished, the planner can track progress by filling in the completion date next to the target date. This type of tracking process can quickly illustrate which of the steps have been completed on time, which are completed ahead of schedule, and which will require additional time.

Once the tactical objectives have been put into a plan and the plan is projected through a tracking system, the tasks can be assigned to workers for completion. One employee may be responsible for completing an entire tactical plan, or the tasks can be grouped and assigned to different employees.

The assignment of the plan to the employee is the final step in the process of communicating the goals that started way up at the highest levels of management.

Consider the following example:

Mission Statement—to be the airline of choice for business travelers.

Strategic Plan—to capture 33 percent of the market share in one year.

Tactical Plan—(human resources) to recruit 50 of the top ranked commercial airline pilots by the end of the first quarter.

This tactical plan reflects the roll-down of goals from the top of the organization down to the human resources function. As a member of the human resources division, the employee who will be held accountable for achieving the tactical objective is "carrying the torch" for the company's mission. If that employee succeeds, the tactical plan will be accomplished. If the tactical plan succeeds, it will contribute to the success of the strategic plan. If the strategic plan succeeds, the company will be more likely to achieve its mission.

To help ensure success, the employee conducts performance planning. Using the same types of tools for tracking tasks and completion dates, the employee specifies what needs to be done, who needs to be called, what resources will be required, and when each step needs to be sequentially completed in order to fulfill the assignment and meet the expectations of the tactical plan. When questioned for progress by supervision, the employee can review each task and its degree of completion. The employee and supervisor can then discuss problems, develop potential solutions, and create contingency plans as needed. While the performance plan is focused at the tiniest level of detail, the performance planning process equips the employee to reframe a discussion from the performance level back to the tactical level and as needed all the way up to the strategic plan and mission statement. As a result, employees can demonstrate to supervision how they are connected to the organization and how, as a result of their work, they are supporting the success of the enterprise.

Methods for Directional Thinking

The common thread that links personal and organizational leadership is the concept of directional thinking. Both Jill at a personal level and a CEO at an organizational level are able to quickly assess their direction-setting opportunity and then use directional thinking in order to make a decision.

If fast-paced directional thinking is the thread that unites the "Jills" and the CEOs as leaders, just how do they do it? What made only Jill use directional thinking while Max, Leslie, and Ed didn't? To understand how you can develop your own skills in directional thinking, we'll take a look at three methods: (1) paradigm shifts, (2) reframing, and (3) mind mapping.

The Concept of Paradigms

Joel Barker, the author of *Future Edge,* studied why people are resistant to change. Barker is a futurist, and what he studies are called *paradigms.* He begins his book with the following question:

> *Why is it that intelligent people with good motives do such a poor job of anticipating the future?*

To illustrate this apparent paradox, Barker describes what happened not too long ago in the watchmaking industry. He starts out by asking which country dominated the industry in 1968. The answer of course is Switzerland. The Swiss developed all types of innovations in watchmaking including the minute hand; the second hand; excellence in the manufacturing processes for gears, bearings, and mainsprings; and even waterproof and self-winding watches. When it came to watchmaking, the Swiss were the undisputed leaders. But something happened that changed everything as far as watchmaking was concerned. After it happened, the Swiss market share dropped from 65 percent down to less than 10 percent and fifty thousand Swiss watchmakers lost their jobs.

Barker asks an even more intriguing question. What country is the leader in the watchmaking industry today? It's no longer the Swiss. Now, it's Japan. Why? The reason boils down to the simple and clear fact that the Swiss were resistant to the idea of change. In Barker's terms, they suffered from "paradigm paralysis." To more completely understand what Barker is describing, consider his definition of a paradigm:

> *A paradigm is a set of rules and regulations (written or unwritten) that does two things:*
> *(1) it establishes or defines boundaries; and*
> *(2) it tells you how to behave inside the boundaries in order to be successful.*

Barker gives the example of tennis as a paradigm. Tennis is a game. A game is a paradigm. It has rules and boundaries. It is played for fun, for competition, or both. It can be played in or watched or both. Tennis itself is a paradigm. In this game, you hit a ball with a tennis racket. What would people think if you hit a domino with a tennis racket or if you hit a tennis ball across the net with a golf club? At the very least, they would laugh, and at worst you might get thrown off the court. You would be breaking the rules of the paradigm.

What about the Swiss and their demise as the preeminent watchmakers? Was a paradigm involved? According to Barker, there most certainly was. It was the watch paradigm. To the Swiss at the time, watches needed to have mechanical parts in order to make them work. Parts such as a spring, a bearing, a mainspring, and gears all went into manufacturing a watch and making it work. These parts, the manufacturing process, and the very act of winding a watch made up the watch paradigm. Anything else just wouldn't be a watch, right?

Not exactly. At least not according to Seiko of Japan who as of 1990 had captured well over 30 percent of the market share in the watch industry. With what, you ask? Why, with a watch of course. Admittedly, it was a very different kind of watch. It didn't have any of those parts such as bearings and mainsprings. In fact, you didn't even have to wind it to make it work. Inside of Seiko's watches was quartz technology and a little battery that supplied the power.

If the Swiss were so innovative as watchmakers, why didn't they think of it first? That's the irony. They did! A group of Swiss researchers invented the quartz movement technology right there in Switzerland and presented it to the Swiss manufacturers in 1967. The Swiss manufacturers weren't impressed. "It's not a watch," they may have shouted as they showed the researchers to the door. "It doesn't have springs or bearings or mainsprings," they surely reminded them as they chased them out of the building. Clearly, this newfangled contraption was not part of the watchmaker's paradigm.

Well, the Swiss researchers weren't to be discouraged. "We'll show them," they undoubtedly resolved. So, off they went to a worldwide watchmakers' convention to display their invention. Unfortunately, they neglected to patent it on the way there. Who strolled by their booth but none other than the Japanese who were interested in the future of watches. The rest is history.

The Swiss watchmakers, as mentioned earlier, suffered from "paradigm paralysis." They couldn't see beyond the boundaries of their paradigm. After all, a watch without a mainspring is as silly as hitting a tennis ball with a golf club. It doesn't fit the paradigm, so therefore it couldn't possibly work. It's ridiculous to even think about it, right?

For Barker, a "paradigm shift" is a change to a new set of rules. The new rules create a new set of boundaries. The Japanese created a new set of boundaries for watches. After all, some of us still wear watches with mainsprings. But now the boundaries are broader, and watches can be watches without having mainsprings.

A particularly useful concept that Barker describes is called "*going back to zero*." When a paradigm shifts, everything associated with that paradigm goes back to zero. Previous success guarantees nothing. As with the Swiss, once the watch paradigm shifted, their previous success guaranteed nothing.

What paradigms are operating in your life? Whether you are consciously aware of them or not, you can't see beyond their boundaries. Because for you, the boundaries of your paradigms are how you define reality. Let's take a look at some examples on the next several pages.

As you can see, the figure below has nine dots. Can you place a pen or pencil or other writing device on one of the dots and draw four straight lines through all of the remaining dots without lifting the pencil from the page or retracing any of the lines you have drawn? Go ahead, try it! You'll find one solution on page 111. Don't peek; try it first.

New Instructions: Connect the dots with three lines. Again, you'll find one solution on page 111.

Now try it with only one line. After you finish, turn to page 112 for a solution.

Here's a different problem. Below is a picture of a cake that you baked for eight guests. Can you cut the cake into eight pieces with only three cuts of the knife? Try it first, then take a look at one solution on page 112.

Here's one more. It's called the Farmer's Will. A farmer, who had three sons, died. His will stipulated that his seventeen cows be divided as follows: one-half to the oldest son, one-third to the middle son, and one-ninth to the youngest. Since the sons knew enough about arithmetic to recognize that seventeen cows could not be divided as stipulated, they discussed the problem and finally hit on the idea of seeking help from a Wise Old Soothsayer.

You're the Wise Old Soothsayer. What solution would you offer? If you have to peek, the answer is on page 113.

My solution is:

There you are, you experienced your own paradigms. Were you paralyzed? Did you have tunnel vision? Did your paradigms trap you? Did the solutions show you that by stepping out of your boundaries, there are some interesting possibilities? With paradigms in mind, let's go back to some of the examples from earlier in the book. Let's start with Mr. Stipple. Remember, think paradigms.

Mr. Stipple is the CEO of Stipple Manufacturing. His company has supplied products to support the use of paper supplies in offices. The problem for Mr. Stipple, his business, and the employees who depend on him is that because of new technologies in the area of electronics, the use of paper supplies in offices has been rapidly and significantly decreasing. People aren't using paper clips, staplers, and clipboards as much as they once did. The decreased usage poses a serious threat to Stipple's company and companies like his. Could he become more competitive and try to take whatever market share is left away from his competitors? Do his circumstances reflect a direction-setting opportunity?

Stipple's problem is that he is fenced in by his paradigm of how offices are supposed to work. He's still thinking in terms of paper. He needs to begin thinking like his customers—electronic solutions to their problems. People are sending fewer documents through interoffice mail. So, they don't need as many envelopes any more. What do they need? Can Stipple provide it? Message boards are being replaced by voice mail. Can Stipple provide it? Pens and notepads are being replaced by palm-top computers and pocket voice recorders. Can Stipple provide them? File folders are being replaced by electronic storage media such as removable hard drives and high-capacity diskettes. Can Stipple provide them? As long as Mr. Stipple is held captive by his paper paradigm, he will remain locked out of the future. His ability to shift paradigms could be the starting point for revitalizing his business. And shifting paradigms could steer his direction-setting opportunity.

What about Dr. Kramer? Is he locked into a paradigm? Absolutely. His doctor paradigm is that a doctor knows all, tells the patient exactly what to do, and then expects absolute compliance. Has the paradigm of doctor changed outside of Dr. Kramer's office? To find out, just ask Tina. Today, a doctor needs to specialize not only in medicine, but also in customer service. A patient is, after all, a customer. And we customers expect to be treated as though we are important people. Important people deserve to be treated with dignity, with respect, and most of all, as adults. Dr. Kramer treated Tina as though she were a child who was incapable of making independent and well-informed decisions.

What would Jill from the "sold out" movie have to say about paradigms? If we continue our conversation with her, it becomes clear. Her authority paradigm is clearly different from that of many other people.

Us: Jill, the manager told you that there were no more seats to be had. Why didn't you just accept those words as fact and move on? You have to admit that the manager was nice enough to try to accommodate you. If you had played your cards right, the four of you might have each gotten a free pass to any movie for a month.

Jill: The passes were not the issue. The issue was that the manager was trying to tell me something that simply wasn't true. I'm not accusing him of lying. He probably didn't even realize that people snuck in. In his mind, there were no more seats to be had. So, it's not like he's a bad guy or anything like that. Now maybe most people would just accept his words as "final" because, in fact, he is the manager. Don't question authority, right? Well, I don't buy that. I make decisions for myself. I try to get as much information as I can, consider the options, weigh the consequences, and then I make the decision that's right for me. If that decision happens to agree with the manager's decision, or the car salesman's decision, or the doctor's decision, or the lawyer's decision, or whoever, that's fine. But if not, I take a position and stand up for what I believe. An authority figure is only an authority figure for me if I decide to accept that person's statements as true. And if I don't, or if I question what they say, I either need to find a way for us to work together or else I do what I think is right. And if I am right, it's not because I'm hard headed or stubborn, though some people say that I am. It's because I've thought through the different parts of the issue, I've reasoned it out, and the decision that I end up making will stand the test of reason.

Before we move on, let's consider one more example about paradigms. Look back at your responses to the in-basket exercise. Chances are, your responses to each letter were specifically written to solve each problem. That is, you dealt with the barking dog problem in one way, and you dealt with the snow removal problem in a different way. On the surface, they didn't appear to be related.

The concept of paradigms effectively illustrates how we can get locked into particular ways of thinking and how we get blocked from seeing the possibilities that are all around us. In his book *The New Positioning,* Jack Trout argues that there are good reasons for paradigms. They help us filter out information in order to prevent what he describes as information overload. Is there such a thing as information overload? Trout (1996) gives some provocative examples.

In Shakespeare's day, the English language contained about 100,000 words. Today it contains roughly half a million.

Today, a Sunday edition of the New York Times weighs up to twelve pounds and contains more than ten million words. To read it cover to cover would require eighteen hours per day of reading for 18 days and by that time, you would have two more Sunday editions waiting to be read.

The number of television channels will soon increase from 50 to 500, and we now have over 7,900 on-line databases as compared with 300 in 1975.

In some parts of the world, children are exposed to a quarter of a million television commercials before they reach the age of twenty.

More than 4,000 books are published around the world every day.

The total amount of printed knowledge doubles every four to five years.

The mind can only take in so much information before it starts to selectively filter it. And like Barker, Trout also argues that we perceive best whatever fits most closely with the interests and attitudes we already have. Everything else is tuned out or ridiculed. Otherwise, we would get confused, right? The mind strives to keep things simple. Simon and Garfunkel said it simply in "The Boxer":

A man hears what he wants to hear and disregards the rest.

The ability to shift paradigms begins with an awareness of the paradigms that are operating in your own life to establish and maintain your boundaries. One way to find out what they are is to sensitize yourself to the judgments you make about other people and what they do. How often do you ridicule others? Why do you ridicule them? What is it that they do that upsets you? Another way is to look at what you don't want to do. If asked to read a particular book, listen to a certain kind of music, go to a particular movie, eat at a specific restaurant that you find objectionable, ask yourself why.

In his book *Quantum Leap Thinking,* James J. Mapes also describes ways to shift paradigms. For Mapes, quantum leap thinking is what happens when a sudden shift in thinking leads to a natural explosion of ideas that catapult you to

. . . a higher level, a level of increased energy, excitement, and options.

Just like Barker and Trout, Mapes argues that you must be willing to let go of your paradigms in order for the quantum leap to occur. To let go of them, you must first become aware of them. Mapes offers a couple of fun stories to illustrate the point.

The Corvette

One day a young man was moping around saying that he was depressed about his future. His friend suggested that he try to picture himself in a setting that would make him happy, whatever that setting might be.

"What would it look like and where would you be? Get as detailed as you can," the consoling friend suggested.

"I am sitting in a brand new, red Corvette convertible that is glistening in the sun. I'm looking at all the controls—my CD player, the five speed gear box, the power windows, the radar detector, the speedometer that goes up to 160 and my keys that I'm about to put in the ignition."

"Ah, that's a start, but you're thinking too small," his friend said wisely. "Who is sitting next to you?"

"She's incredible! She's wearing a white blouse that is tucked into blue shorts. Her eyes are hazel, her hair is long and swept down over her shoulders and her hand is resting on my arm."

"You're still thinking too small," the friend reminded him. "Where's the car parked? How about in the driveway of your new house?"

"Are you kidding? After paying for this car and taking care of this sweet lady, what makes you think I can afford a house!"

Thanksgiving Dinner

On their first Thanksgiving, these two newlyweds were preparing the turkey for the oven. Husband Randy removed the wrapper while his wife Susan got out the pot, picked up a serrated knife and proceeded to cut the tips off of the two drumsticks.

"What are you doing?," Randy asked.

"What do you mean, what am I doing? I'm getting the turkey ready."

"By cutting off the tips of the drumsticks? Why on earth are you doing that?"

"What are you talking about? Is this the first time you've made a turkey?"

"As a matter of fact, it is. But I've watched my mother make a turkey before and she never did that."

"Well, trust me, this is the way you make a turkey."

"But why are you cutting off the tips of the drumsticks?"

"Because that's just the way you do it, Randy—okay?"

"Look, Susan, I don't want to make a big deal out of this and I don't want us to get in a fight and ruin our first Thanksgiving together, but this is driving me nuts. Where on earth did you learn to do that?"

"That's the way my mother always did it. Hey, who are you calling?"

"I'm calling your mother. I want to get to the bottom of this. Oh, Hi Mom. Susan and I are making our turkey and I noticed that she cut the tips off the drumsticks. She said you always did that because that's just the way you make a turkey."

"Of course it is," Susan's mother insisted. "That is the way we've always made turkeys."

"Who did you learn that from? Who taught you how to make the turkey?"

"My own mother, Grandma Perkins."

"Do you mind if we call her? We've got 'Conference Calling' and we can get her on the line. Is that okay?"

"This is silly, Randy," Susan said.

"Hello Mother, I've got Susan and Randy on the phone here. Randy's got a question for you."

"Hi, Grandma Perkins, Happy Thanksgiving. We're looking forward to having you over later for dinner. We're making the turkey now and something came up. I noticed that Susan, just like her mother, cut the tips off of the drumsticks before she put the turkey in the pot. When I asked her why she did that she said that's how her mother made a turkey. When I asked her mother why she did it, she said that's how you always did it. Now I would like to ask you why you cut the tips off of the drumsticks."

"Lordy," Grandma Perkins said, "You mean to tell me they're still doing that? Sakes alive! The only reason I used to cut the tips off the drumsticks is because I never had a pot big enough to fit the whole turkey in. I had to cut those confounded tips off to get that big ole turkey in the pot. Otherwise, I would have needed to use two pots. No sense in doing that!"

Becoming aware of your paradigms is the first step in shifting them. Here are some other thoughts from Mapes:

Turning judgment into curiosity opens the channel for learning.
Breaking the routine is mandatory for the creative process.
You don't need to reinvent the basics, only rearrange them in a new way.
Commitment comes from "committere" which means "to ignite action."
J. J. Mapes

Creativity is first of all an act of destruction.
Pablo Picasso

In the beginner's mind there are many possibilities, in the expert's mind there are few.

Shunryu Suzuki

Every adversity carries with it the seed of an equivalent or greater benefit.
Napolean Hill

When you are committed to something, you accept no excuses, only results.

Ken Blanchard

And finally, Barker's suggestion for shifting paradigms is what he calls "the Paradigm Shift Question."

What is impossible to do in your business (field, discipline, department, division, technology, etc.—just pick one), but if it could be done, would fundamentally change it?

Reframing

Reframing is a second method for directional thinking that is closely related to that of shifting paradigms. In their book *Reframing Organizations,* Lee Bolman and Terrence Deal describe frames in ways that are very similar to the concept of paradigms.

Frames are both windows on the world and lenses that bring the world into focus. Frames filter out some things while allowing others to pass through easily. Frames help us to order experience and decide what action to take.

To illustrate, they offer a dialogue between the painter Cézanne and one of his critics.

Critic: That painting doesn't look like a sunset to me.

Cézanne: Then you don't see sunsets the same way I do.

Frames tend to limit the way people think. They impair the ability to see the world outside of those frames. One photographer looking through a wide-angle lens sees a very different view of the same scene than a photographer who uses a telephoto lens. The world is complex and ambiguous. Bolman and Deal suggest that to make sense of it, you should ask yourself the simple question:

What's really going on here?

To figure out what is really going on in a complex world is the heart of leadership. The lesson to learn is that there is always more than one way to think and act in any given situation. The leader's challenge is to develop the ability to reframe a problematic situation into one of opportunity by imagining new and creative possibilities.

The key to reframing is to remove one lens and replace it with another. To do so requires the belief that every set of circumstances is open to a wide variety of interpretations. By opening yourself up to these interpretations, your thinking expands and your ideas multiply. To illustrate, let's take a second look at the letter from Cheryl Sheathing that we first read back in the in-basket from Section I.

Mr. P. Franks
Twin Lakes Development

Dear Mr. Franks:

Permit me to introduce myself. My name is Cheryl L. Sheathing. I am the broker-owner of Sheathing Real Estate Development Corporation. I have just opened my offices here in town and would like an opportunity to meet with you.

A few days ago, while driving through various suburban developments as I routinely do when I move to a new location, I took the opportunity to familiarize myself with Twin Lakes. I understand from other real estate brokers that Twin Lakes has gone downhill in the last few years. Agents have trouble selling Twin Lakes homes at market value. Residents often overlook their lawns, many homes need maintenance, and in general, Twin Lakes is regarded by many of us as a plague to steer our clients far away from.

Mr. Franks, I see a gold mine in your subdivision. I have specialized in turning around neighborhoods like Twin Lakes. I see what once was a magnificent residential area now suffering needlessly. What the residents need is something to get excited about. We need to energize them and focus them to care about the beauty that is waiting just under the surface of Twin Lakes Development.

Imagine filling up Twin Lakes with vibrant neighbors that care about one another. The plans for the pool and tennis courts and golf course could be just months from ground breaking if we go about it in ways that I know can work. Think of the pride everyone will feel as Twin Lakes competes with other neighborhoods in swimming meets. Can't you just see the kids lining up to take tennis lessons, and even us older type kids driving our carts up and down the golf course? There's no limit to what we can do. Those lakes out in your back section will make for unbelievable sunsets, not to mention expensive homes we'll build right on their shores.

Mr. Franks, making Twin Lakes work is not just a matter of screaming at your residents to mow their lawns. It's not just a matter of plugging up holes in your streets. We need to build a community, a community that's filled with fun and with pride. Within a year, Twin Lakes homes could sell at premium prices. Who knows, we might even think of buying up that neighboring acreage to develop other sections.

Call me, Mr. Franks. Twin Lakes is waiting for us to meet and get down to business.

Warmest regards,

C. L. Sheathing, President
Sheathing Real Estate Development, Inc.

Sheathing's letter is an effective example of reframing problems into opportunities. What a clear and exciting vision for the subdivision. Her letter establishes a direction. She paints a picture that creates a sense of discovery and a sense of destiny. All of a sudden, the problems are transformed into a picture that most, if not all, of the neighbors would want to see themselves in. In effect, she shifted our paradigms by replacing our worn-out old glasses with kaleidoscopes of brilliant colors arranged in magnificent patterns.

Mind Mapping

A third method to help you develop the competency of directional thinking is called *mind mapping*. According to Gelb (1995), mind mapping was developed by Tony Buzan back in the 1970s as a notetaking system.

The way that most people take notes is through *outlining*. Outlining requires thinking in sequences. Mind mapping is different in that it uses a form of mental activity known as *associative thinking*. Let's illustrate the two approaches.

First, let's think about how we would outline this chapter. Not so easy, is it? What did we cover first? Obviously we have to remember that bit of information because it goes at the top of the outline. What was next? Then, what came after that? The reason that outlining is inefficient is that, as a process, it combines the content with the sequence. Why do that? It's unnecessary and cumbersome. It interferes with thinking, and it certainly encumbers creativity.

Now let's consider mind mapping. What's the first thing that comes to mind when you think about this chapter? For me, the first thing that comes to mind is Jill. I am now thinking about that entire story. The next thing that comes to mind is direction setting, then paradigms, then Cézanne, then Barker, then the corvette, then the girl in the next seat, and so on. On the surface, there is absolutely no logic to this train of thought. On the other hand, as a train of thought, I am rapidly reconstructing the major concepts of the entire chapter. True, they are in no particular order. Nonetheless, they are progressively emerging as scattered details that can later be pieced together to form a meaningful whole.

Mind mapping takes advantage of "thinking by association." That is, one thought triggers another thought that successively and relentlessly triggers yet another. The associations, while seemingly random, tend to free up the emergence of details that would otherwise remain "submerged" by logical or sequential methods of thinking.

The process of mind mapping differs from "free association" only in terms of how to record what you are thinking. The mind map is formed by drawing a picture or a key word in the center of a blank piece of paper. As you focus on that word or image, another word or image will soon come to mind. It may or may not seem related to the first. Whatever comes to mind, capture it by drawing a line from the center and then writing the word or drawing the image at the end of the line. As the next thought enters your mind, draw another line from the center and capture that thought by writing or drawing it at the end of the second line. If you find that any of your subsequent thoughts are related to an earlier one, capture those by drawing the line as a branch off of the earlier one. The following example illustrates the process.

Chapter Summary

Leadership begins with ideas about how to change the present by imagining the future. This ability was identified as the first of four competencies in this book—directional thinking. The process of directional thinking includes the awareness of direction-setting opportunities (DSOs) and the ability to carefully make direction-setting decisions (DSDs), both of which were discussed and illustrated as a way to establish the direction for that change. Three methods were presented to help develop the competency of directional thinking, including shifting paradigms, reframing, and mind mapping.

To help you strengthen your competence in directional thinking, complete the following exercise. Once you answer the questions, apply what you learned to each of your responses in the assessment from Section I.

— Exercise: A Visit to the Consultant —

| **Appointment** | **8:00–9:00** | **Sid Holten** | **President of Holten and Associates** |

Sid: Thanks for seeing me. I don't think I'll require a whole lot of your time. I just want to "touch base" with you and see if you can point me in the right direction.

You: Sounds interesting. I'll be happy to help in any way that I can.

Sid: Great. For the last ten years, I've been employed as a manager in the human resources division of a large organization. The company is operating in a very competitive industry, and the market for its products and services is shrinking. They have a great communications program and have told us now for at least two years that they will be shifting their corporate strategy from growth to retrenchment in order to conserve capital. As a result, we could expect staff reductions.

You: In other words, they would be downsizing.

Sid: Exactly, and I was just identified to be laid off.

You: I'm sorry to hear that, but it sounds like you have a plan.

Sid: That's right and that's what I'd like your opinion on.

You: I'm anxious to hear about it.

Sid: I have a graduate degree in the field of human resources, and as I mentioned, I have ten years of experience with this firm. I have worked in human resource positions previously in two other companies, but not at the management level. What I'm looking to do is to start my own HR consulting firm. What I need to do first is to scope out the mission for my company, the direction I want to move in, and the plans for how to make it a success.

You: What have you thought about so far?

Sid: I want to specialize in setting up human resource policies and procedures for small- to mid-sized companies. To me, a small-sized company would employ up to about 100 employees and a mid-sized company would employ anywhere from 100 to about 2,000.

You: The numbers sound right to me.

Sid: I feel that what I have to offer is to help these companies align their HR policies and procedures with the overall direction. What I mean by that is if a company is pursuing a growth strategy, their HR policies should be geared to support that growth. If their strategic objective is that of diversification, then their HR policies should reflect and support that.

You: You've apparently determined that there is a need for your services?

Sid: I believe there is. Through my membership in professional organizations and my knowledge of future trends in the workforce, I have reason to believe that most companies have personnel departments rather than true HR divisions.

You: Help me understand the difference.

Sid: A personnel department typically responds to the requests of the company's managers. For example, a manager may want six dozen insurance forms sent to his office. The personnel clerk is expected to send them. The accounting department may need a temporary worker for the next two weeks. The personnel clerk is expected to make the arrangements. By contrast, today's human resources division plays a key role in helping to shape and support corporate strategies. If the corporation faces stiff competition in a shrinking marketplace, the HR professional could help them develop strategies that could help to make them more competitive.

You: What kinds of strategies?

Sid: One of the first recommendations would be to do a SWOT analysis. Are you familiar with that?

You: Yes.

Sid: Once the company's strengths, weaknesses, opportunities, and threats are identified, the company would be in a good position to decide which direction it wants to pursue.

You: So an HR professional such as yourself might recommend a SWOT analysis and then offer your services to conduct it.

Sid: Exactly. See how high in the organization the HR professional can get involved?

You: Absolutely.

Sid: Depending on the outcome, the company could develop its mission statement and then choose the most logical strategy for achieving it. After the strategy is determined, let's say it's a growth strategy, the HR professional could help the company specify tactical plans for each of its operational and functional divisions.

You: What you're saying essentially is that the HR professional can guide the process for formulating strategy from the highest levels of the organization and then help to roll it down to the operational and performance levels.

Sid: Yes, and once that's done, to make sure measurement methods have been established so that the company can determine if performance at each level is meeting or exceeding expectations.

You: Besides facilitating the planning process, would you provide any other services?

Sid: My firm would be available to perform some or all of the HR work as needed. These services could include recruiting new employees; writing employee manuals; creating and maintaining benefits packages; conducting employee orientation sessions; assessing and developing candidates for management positions; investigating allegations of wrongdoing; establishing criteria for performance appraisals, raises, promotions, transfers, and layoffs; and conducting exit interviews. The key to making these services valuable to the organization is to link them with the mission and strategic objectives.

You: What do you mean?

Sid: For example, let's say the organization wants to be the premier bookmark producer in the U.S. It faces stiff competition and a shrinking market. Its key competitors have established a "niche" reputation in the industry. That is, when customers think of bookmarks, the name of the competitor comes to mind. And there is ample evidence that the market is shrinking because people are "reading" more books electronically through their computers or listening to them on tape. There is reduced demand for bookmarks. So, what can this company do in order to realize its mission? Well, there are many tactical plans it could develop. In the area of human resources, one tactical plan would be to identify and eliminate any jobs that aren't absolutely necessary to produce the product and thereby reduce the size of their workforce. Where there is a need to staff up, they should develop a recruiting policy that would go after the most qualified applicants, a salary policy that will pay them at the top of the wage scale, and a benefits plan that will be second to none.

You: Why should these organizations choose your services instead of services from your competition?

Sid: Good question. That's part of why I need your help. I can tell you that I have a pretty good idea about where the workforce is moving. I can bring this knowledge to my client prospects.

You: What do you mean?

Sid: Well, any organization that wants to survive needs to have its finger on the pulse of the U.S. workforce. They can't assume that just because their personnel policies have worked before, that they'll work five or ten years from now—or for that matter, even one year from now.

You: You mean because of the diversity issue?

Sid: That's just one element. There are clear themes and patterns that are emerging and these need to be seriously considered in developing HR policies. Organizations need to allow for more flexibility in working hours and schedules not only to accommodate parents of young children but also to attract and retain older workers who may not be able to sustain a full day's schedule. They need to recognize the impact of globalization and prepare themselves for foreign competition. This means increased travel, learning new languages, and getting comfortable and competent with new cultures. They need to bring themselves up to date and to anticipate the future with respect to the "electronic office" and its impact on company communication, working at home, and drastically reducing the cost of supporting full-time secretaries. They need to determine how they will pay for the cost of medical benefits, whether or not they want to use DNA testing to identify pre-existing conditions, and whether to increase or decrease salaries to replace the need for sick days or vacation days. They need to determine if they want to respond to government allegations of discrimination or take a stand that they promote diversity because they truly value people and their unique contributions. It is a confusing and complicated world out there. Unless an organization is aware of what is about to "hit them over the head," they will be unprepared and certainly strategically disadvantaged.

You: And that's where you can help?

Sid: That's where I can help.

You: What would you like from me?

Sid: I think I'm too close to all of this to pull it all together. I have to admit that I'm a bit wounded by my recent layoff. I have to wonder that if I can do everything that I've told you, why was I laid off? I would like you to develop a plan for me that starts with my mission statement, establishes my strategic objectives, lays out my tactical plans, and even specifies my performance objectives complete with tasks and milestones.

You: Fair enough. It will take me a few days, but I'll send you a draft within a few days. Once you receive it, call me and we'll set up another time to discuss it.

Consultation Guide

This chapter has concentrated on the first of our four leadership competencies, directional thinking. Directional thinking is the thought process a leader goes through, whether individually or within an organization that ultimately produces a vision or establishes a direction. The process consists of two major steps: (1) a direction-setting opportunity (DSO) and (2) a direction-setting decision (DSD).

Now you will have an opportunity to prepare the consultant's analysis and recommendation for Mr. Holten. To help you get started, write out answers to the questions on the following pages as completely as you can.

Question 1

It seems that Mr. Holten is doing a good deal of directional thinking. The first question for you to consider in addressing his concerns should be

What was the direction-setting opportunity that propelled him into his directional thinking?

Question 2

Mr. Holten is trying to make a direction-setting decision. He has taken the first step by deciding to launch his own business as a human resources consultant to small- and mid-sized companies.

In Mr. Holten's opinion, what is the current paradigm for human resources departments? How should that paradigm shift?

Question 3

The chapter indicated that a leader is different from a visionary. Visionaries look back only to find they are alone, and their visions often die. Leaders lead the followers to make the vision part of reality.

What is Mr. Holten's vision? Is he a visionary or a leader? Give reasons.

Question 4

Mission statements indicate why an organization exists and what it stands for by describing its principles and its values.

What is a possible mission statement for Holten and Associates?

Question 5

Strategic plans describe what the organization is trying to accomplish in terms of growth, stability, defense, or a combination strategy.

What direction do you think Holten and Associates is moving in? Can you offer a statement for a strategic plan?

Question 6

Tactical plans specify how the organization can achieve its strategic objectives. Clearly, Holten and Associates needs to make itself visible among the companies it wants to solicit.

Can you suggest a marketing approach that Holten could use as one of his tactical plans? Make sure the approach aligns with the strategic objectives and the mission statement.

Question 7

Performance plans delineate a "road map" to guide each employee's daily work. The performance plan tells employees what to do, when to do it, and what to do if problems arise. It also helps them communicate with their supervisors and provides direct evidence of how their work is linked to corporate objectives.

Write a sample performance plan for Mr. Holten that he could use as a model for how to structure his daily activities and align them with the higher-level plans of his company.

Question 8

As you consider the issues that Mr. Holten raised, think about the concepts of paradigms and reframing.

What frames might be limiting his views and inhibiting his ability to move forward? How might you reframe them from limitations to opportunities?

Question 9

Draw a mind map using "Mr. Holten" as the key word.

Based on the results, what is your analysis of his problem and what recommendations would you offer?

Question 10

Using your answers to these discussion questions, prepare a response to send to Mr. Holten. Make sure you incorporate the key terms and ideas from this chapter to demonstrate your ability to apply the concepts of directional thinking.

Consultation Report

To: Mr. Sid Holten
        Holten and Associates

Statement of the Problem:

Major Areas of Concern:

Recommendations:

Nine Dots—Four Lines

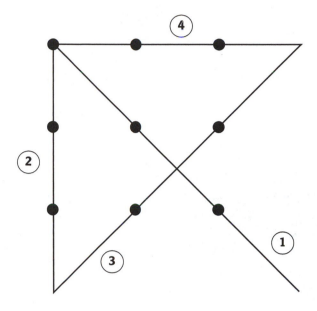

Nine Dots—Three Lines

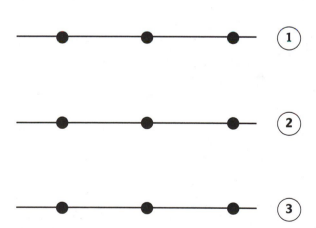

Nine Dots—One Line

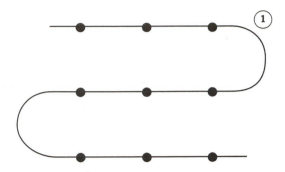

Cake-Cutting Puzzle
(three cuts into eight pieces)

Cut 1: Cut the cake into a top and bottom half.

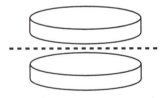

Cuts 2 and 3: Stack the top half on top of the bottom half and cut as shown: Serve the four pieces from the top half, then serve the four pieces from the bottom half.

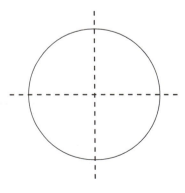

The Farmer's Will (*The Soothsayer's Reply*)

Your problem is that you must divide 17 by 3 so that half of the 17 cows can be given to the oldest son, one-third to the middle son, and one-ninth to the youngest. Here is my solution.

I will lend you one of my cows so that you have 18 to work with. Now you can make your division. You will find that the number 18 breaks down into 9 (one half), 6 (one third), and 2 (one ninth) just as your father's will requires. I see by your looks that you are satisfied.

Now, you will realize that 9 plus 6 plus 2 is 17, not 18. Since you are satisfied, you don't need my cow any longer, so I will take him back.

The Soothsayer's Magical (#18) Cow

Bibliography

Barker, Joel, *Future Edge* (New York: Morrow, 1992).

Bennis, Warren, and Joan Goldsmith, *Learning to Lead* (Reading, MA: Addison-Wesley, 1995).

Blanchard, Kenneth, and Norman V. Peale, *The Power of Ethical Management* (New York: Fawcett Crest, 1988).

Bolman, Lee, and Terrence Deal, *Reframing Organizations* (San Francisco: Jossey-Bass, 1990).

Clark, Kenneth, and Miriam Clark, *Measures of Leadership* (Greensboro, NC: Center for Creative Leadership, 1990).

Coates, Joseph, Jennifer, Jarrett, and John Mahaffie, *Future Work* (San Francisco: Jossey-Bass, 1990).

Eitington, Julius, *The Winning Trainer* (Houston: Gulf Publishing, 1989).

Fear, Richard, and Robert Chiron, *The Evaluation Interview* (New York: McGraw-Hill, 1990).

Gelb, Michael, *Thinking for a Change* (New York: Harmony Books, 1995).

Hamel, Gary, and C. K. Prahalad, *Competing for the Future* (Boston: Harvard Business School Press, 1994).

Jones, Patricia, and Larry Kahaner, *Say It and Live It* (New York: Doubleday, 1995).

Kotter, John, *A Force for Change* (New York: MacMillan, 1990).

Mapes, James, *Quantum Leap Thinking* (Beverly Hills, CA: Dove Books, 1996).

Rosen, Robert, *Leading People—Transforming Business from the Inside Out* (New York: Hudson Press, 1990).

Schermerhorn, John, *Management for Productivity* (New York: Wiley, 1996).

Trout, Jack, *The New Positioning* (New York: McGraw-Hill, 1996).

CHAPTER 6

Consequential Thinking

We now know that leadership begins with vision, and its purpose is to produce change. Through such concepts as paradigm shifts, mind mapping, and reframing, we've seen how leaders create their visions. By considering the leadership of John F. Kennedy, Martin Luther King Jr., Cheryl Sheathing, and others, we've seen how leaders produce change. We also now know that management, unlike leadership, focuses on predictability and stability. The manager wants to maintain control over the flow of activities to ensure that their completion results in achieving a particular objective in a predictable way.

By contrast, leadership is about carving out new frontiers. And as with any new frontier, the pathways for getting there are often filled with risk. The wise leader contemplates the risk. Based on careful judgment, that leader either proceeds carefully or judiciously abandons the journey. The foolish leader is seduced by self-gratification and proceeds impulsively without due consideration for the dangers that can potentially bring defeat, humiliation, and harm.

> *Life requires choices; choices require risks.*
> Kenneth R. MacCrimmon and Donald A. Wehrung

> *A life without adventure is likely to be unsatisfying,*
> *but a life in which adventure is allowed to take whatever form it will,*
> *is likely to be short.*
>
> Bertrand Russell

This chapter is about considering the consequences that may result from change or even as a result of the process used while trying to create it. Once considered, the consequences may either deter the leader or inspire the leader to proceed. Consequential thinking is the process of identifying the risks associated with a particular action and then determining whether to continue in pursuit of a goal.

No one is immune from risk. Choices create risks. As long as we make choices, we cannot avoid risk. Just as each of us lives with risk on a daily basis,

115

leaders encounter risks with every decision they make and every action they pursue. The difference between an individual's decisions and the decisions made by leaders is the number of people affected. If I as an individual choose to walk on a wet floor with bare feet, then fall and injure myself, I and perhaps a few others are impacted. If a leader chooses to change the direction of a business and fails, hundreds and perhaps thousands of workers and their families will be impacted. Let's first consider risk as applied to an individual.

A driver stopped at a local bar on a dark and rainy night. He has had a particularly frustrating day at work and thinks that his stress may be eased by three stiff drinks. He then leaves the bar and speeds away down the rain-slicked road now in a rush to get home because he promised his wife that he would be home early. His tires are nearly bald, though he intended to get new ones when he could find the time. His windshield wipers are worn out, thus badly blurring his view. Winding a flat curve that he failed to spot in enough time, he careens, skids, and slams into a tree. He is killed instantly. Ask his widow why he died. She'll tell you it was an accident.

In his book entitled *Managing Risk*, Vernon L. Grose argues that there's virtually no such thing as an accident. We often attribute accidents to such things as fate, bad luck, or "his time was up." Says Grose, nothing could be further from reality. What we call "accidents" are caused by choices. In the example, due to his difficult day, the man was frustrated. Frustration often causes thinking to become irrational, and irrational thinking causes impulsive behavior. He had been drinking. His tires were bald. His windshield wipers were deteriorated. It was raining. It was dark. He was speeding. His death was caused by the car slamming into the tree, but the crash was caused by the driver's choices. He could have made alternate choices that could have prevented his frustrations, avoided his drinking, and resulted in new tires and wipers. Ultimately, these choices would probably have gotten him home after safely driving through the dangerous curve and past the ominous tree.

Now consider a set of choices that initially affected seven people but ultimately impacted millions. Roger Boisjoly was an engineer with Morton Thiokol who tried to convince NASA not to launch the Challenger on the morning of January 28, 1986. If you were to ask Roger Boisjoly what he thinks of the phrase "the Challenger accident," he would argue that the explosion was no accident. It was a terrible disaster. It was a tragedy that didn't have to occur. It should never have happened, and it could have been prevented. But under no circumstances was it an accident. Just as in the example of the car crash, there were hundreds of precipitating causes related to Challenger. NASA's designation for a level of danger is called "criticality." The most severe rating is that of Criticality 1. This level designates that failure would result in loss of the crew, loss of the vehicle, and certainly loss of the mission itself. The presidential commission that investigated Challenger determined that a set of rubber O-rings in the solid rocket boosters failed to contain hot gases. The gases escaped and burned a hole in the center fuel tank causing a massive explosion. Years before the catastrophe, NASA had designated the rubber O-rings as a Criticality 1. Incredibly, there were 828 other items on the shuttle that had the same Criticality-1 classification.

For leaders, the question before proceeding with their vision should not be "How likely is an accident?" Instead, the questions should be "What are the risks associated with my choices, which risks can I eliminate, which risks can I avoid, which risks can I sufficiently control in order to proceed safely, and which risks if any are so formidable that I should consider abandoning my vision at this time?"

Since leadership involves changing things from the way they are to the way the leaders thinks they should be, the process for creating change and the outcome associated with that change should be considered very carefully. When the stakes are high and the losses could be great, the process for consideration should be done painstakingly.

Obviously, there is no way to guarantee that consequential thinking will eliminate all risks. But by carefully and diligently trying to anticipate the consequences of a projected course of action, the leader could alter the vision and the plans for achieving it in ways that could produce the benefits without the high probability of danger, harm, and loss.

For leaders in business, the consequences of unmanaged risks can be severe. Since 1991, the business practices of virtually every size business have been closely scrutinized under the Federal Sentencing Guidelines.

The guidelines are comparable to the old saying "Throw the book at him." The "book" so to speak, is a set of guidelines that a judge uses to determine the appropriate sentence to fit a particular crime. Most crimes have a range of sentences that a judge can use for the purpose of punishment. Depending on the nature and severity of the crime, the judge might sentence a first offender to probation or community service. A criminal guilty of repeat offenses might be sentenced to long-term imprisonment for the same offense. Federal judges turn to the Federal Sentencing Guidelines to help them determine the type of sentence to administer to a business that violates federal laws.

As an example, consider a company that processes and cans food, then distributes the cans to the public through national grocery store chains. That company would be subject to the laws overseen by the Food and Drug Administration or FDA. If the company mislabels its products, it would be violating a federal law and, as such, could be tried and convicted in a federal court by a federal judge under the Federal Sentencing Guidelines. The Guidelines permit the judge to determine the sentence based on a number of extenuating circumstances. If the judge determined that the company knew about the laws and willfully used its resources to break the laws, the judge would likely sentence the company with the maximum penalties (compensation for loss to the victim) and fines and/or jail time for the responsible parties (punishment for the crime). In the future, the company would be much more likely to comply with the law because it would then anticipate the consequences of any further misconduct.

Let's take the example a bit further. Suppose the judge determined that the company had taken measures to educate all of its employees about the federal laws long before any crime was committed. And suppose that those who committed the crime, even though they had been educated by the company and warned of personal consequences if they broke company policies and federal laws, decided to take matters into their own hands and mislabel the products in order to meet their own cost and schedule requirements. When the company discovered this misconduct based on an anonymous allegation, the company conducted an investigation, disciplined the employees, recalled the defective products, and notified the FDA. Considering the circumstances, could the judge sentence the company differently than in the earlier example?

Under the Federal Sentencing Guidelines, the judge would be so permitted. The extenuating circumstances are represented by the company's actions both before and after the misconduct. By conducting an educational program, the company set up expectations regarding its views of right and wrong and notified all of its employees of the behavior and standards they were expected to uphold. By responding to the anonymous allegation, investigating it, disciplining the culprits, addressing the public's concerns, and notifying the government, the company demonstrated its commitment to uphold its values and comply with the laws. The judge may require the company to make whatever restitution is appropriate to compensate the public for any remaining damages. However, the fine is minimal because of the company's adherence to its values and its consistency in implementing them.

Is there a lesson to be learned from the Federal Sentencing Guidelines with respect to consequential thinking in leadership? Yes, in that the Guidelines provide an incentive for avoiding behavior that will result in painful consequences. In essence, the Guidelines say

Think about the consequences before you engage in the behavior.

Is there a process for thinking about the consequences before transforming an idea into an action? There are many. For our purposes, we'll consider two approaches. The first is *ethical decision making*. The second is *analytical decision making*. While they are related, they are sufficiently different to warrant separate consideration.

Ethical Decision Making

The word *ethics* means different things to different people. For some it means right versus wrong. To others it relates to morals and values. And for others, it is a subject for discussion by members of the clergy and their congregations or by students of philosophy. Some even argue that "ethics" is certainly not a subject for discussion in the business arena (see Pava). According to this notion, ethics is about moralism, whereas business is about the management and creation of profits. Whatever works to create a profit is acceptable as long as laws are not violated.

Can ethics be taught? If so, should it be part of a curriculum in an elementary school? What about offering it in a business school? Should corporations teach their employees how to be ethical? Most experts and preschoolers agree that ethics is learned early in life and is conveyed rather than taught by one's parents, relatives, and clergy. What we learn in a classroom setting or among fellow adults in the midst of a group discussion is not how to be ethical, but rather how to use a thought process as a means of avoiding or solving an ethical dilemma.

A simply written and clearly presented book that illustrates this thought process is called *The Power of Ethical Management* by Ken Blanchard and Norman Vincent Peale. The book describes an ethical dilemma that a middle-aged manager faces as he struggles to save his company from going out of business. It seems that while the company is in financial trouble, the manager needs to hire an employee for a special project. After interviewing a number of candidates, the manager makes his selection and is about to offer the position to one of the candidates. Just before he can make the offer, the candidate takes a computer disk out of his shirt pocket. In a secretive voice, he informs the manager that the disk contains confidential information about the company's major competitor of which he is a current employee. As a gesture of good faith and a sign of his intense desire to join the new company, the candidate offers the disk to the manager. Confronted with the immediate decision of whether to take the disk or hold up his hand to refuse it, the manager is faced with an ethical dilemma.

On the one hand, he is painfully aware that his company is on the brink of financial ruin. At a phase of his life in which he must pay on his mortgage, keep his kids in college, and figure out how to provide an income for himself and his wife during retirement, he worries about his own financial security. If his company goes out of business, he doubts whether he could find another position that would enable him to pay his bills much less to build a secure future. By accepting the disk, he could virtually ensure the health of his company which in turn would keep him financially sound.

On the other hand, he is also painfully aware that to accept the disk is probably illegal. What does the very offer of the disk say about the integrity of the candidate? Yet if he refuses the disk, he would likely insult the candidate, thereby losing the prospect of gaining his considerable talent and skill within the company. What should he do? How should he make a decision?

Blanchard and Peale offer an ethical decision-making checklist to think through ethical problems. The checklist consists of three questions: (1) Is it legal? (2) Is it fair and balanced? and (3) Will it pass a test of public scrutiny?

Is It Legal?

This question is the most direct and easiest to answer of the three. If the action that you are considering violates a law, the answer is simply—*don't do it*. In this respect, the word *law* also encompasses the rules and regulations of any organization.

In terms of consequences, laws, rules, and regulations often are accompanied by what will happen to an individual or a company if violations occur. For example, consider a speed limit of 55 miles per hour. The signs are clearly posted in driver's manuals and on streets and highways so that all drivers are made aware of the law before and while they drive. If they obey the law, there will be no consequences. Of course, most drivers contemplate whether they should exceed the speed limit. They know that to do so is illegal. However, some drivers are not concerned about the consequences. Either they believe that no one will catch them, they can talk their way out of a ticket, or the consequences are no big deal ("I'll just put the ticket in my glove compartment and forget about it"). Accordingly, they may choose to ignore the law and drive 80 miles per hour. If they avoid detection, they will in fact escape the legal consequences. But if they do get caught, they will likely suffer from not one, but three consequences. First, they will get a ticket for a moving violation which involves a monetary fine, possible court time, and perhaps even a mandatory class in driver safety. Second, they will accumulate points on their driver's license. Third, most insurance companies raise auto insurance rates when the state notifies them of their client's moving violation. After someone experiences these types of consequences, they will likely think twice before violating the law again.

Will the anticipation of consequences always, usually, or seldom deter someone from breaking the law, rule, or regulation? The answer depends on the severity of the consequences as well as the likelihood that they will actually be administered. Consider another example.

Suppose I go to a local music store and buy a CD for $15. After sampling tracks from the CD at home, I decide that I do not want to keep it. The music store has a liberal return policy and refunds my money without question. No problem so far. Next I buy a second CD from the music store for $15, and I also buy a premium quality blank audio cassette tape for $3. This time when I return home, I copy the CD onto the tape. I put the copied tape into my collection and return to the music store with the CD for a refund. They ask no questions and cheerfully return my $15. Is that legal?

Some people actually believe that no laws have been broken. To their way of thinking, you are entitled to make a copy of a tape or CD. This is not the case. They are confusing the idea of copying music with the legal right to make an archival (backup) copy of software. The software license grants this privilege in the event the computer damages the original copy. While the software license legally permits making the copy for safety purposes, it specifically restricts the loading or running of the software on more than one machine at one time. In the case of music, copyright notices are posted within the packaging thus making it illegal to copy the music.

In the example, we've clearly gone beyond making a copy for backup purposes. Consider what occurred: (1) I paid $15 for the CD; (2) I paid $3 for the tape; (3) I copied the music from the CD onto the tape; (4) I returned the CD for a refund of the $15. The outcome is the music is in my possession for a cost of $3 instead of $15. In the eyes of the law, that action is considered stealing.

What about consequences? If while in the music store I put the CD into one of my shopping bags without paying for it, there's some chance I'll get caught. And if I do get caught, the consequences will be fairly severe. If, however, I steal the music another way by copying it onto a tape and then returning the CD to the music store for a refund, I will probably not get caught. And since I would not get caught, there will be no legal consequences. The bottom line is that legal consequences usually only deter illegal behavior if there is a good chance that the perpetrators will be detected. If there is a good chance of escaping detection, the perpetrator probably doesn't care about the consequences.

The first question in the ethics checklist—"Is it legal?"—is only powerful if the one who asks the question thinks there is a reasonable chance of getting caught. Beyond this level, the question by itself has limited power to deter unethical behavior. In other words, the logic would be as follows:

> Is it legal?
> No.
> Am I likely to get caught?
> Probably not.
> Then I am not deterred by the consequences.

Leaders in a business situation would be well advised to familiarize themselves with laws that govern the treatment of people in the workplace. The costs of lawsuits can easily run into the millions of dollars, are often paid for directly out of profits, or worse yet, cause losses and in some cases can even close down the business. It is beyond the scope of this book to present a thorough coverage of business laws in detail. It is also not the intention of the book to provide legal advice. However, to assist you in developing skills in consequential thinking and as a useful reference, a summary of relevant laws is included at the end of this chapter.

Is it Fair and Balanced?

This question gets at an issue in the study of ethics called a *benefits-harm analysis*. In other words, will someone else be harmed as a direct result of my receiving the benefits? Let's return to the example of the CD. Recall that I purchased the CD, copied it onto an audiotape, and then returned the CD to the music store to get a full refund. We discussed that the practice is illegal. However, if I'm not deterred by the prospect of getting caught, then the first question probably would not deter me from making the illegal copy. In other words, the question has limited power as far as consequential thinking is concerned. What about the second question? Is it fair and balanced? My action certainly benefits me. I get $15 worth of music at a cost to me of only $3 for the blank tape. Do the benefits that I receive cause harm to any others? Let's check it out by asking a manager in the music store.

Me: You have a very liberal return policy in your store. Not that I would ever do this, but aren't you concerned that someone might make a tape of a CD and then just return the CD?

Manager: We know it happens.

Me: Aren't you concerned? Don't you lose money?

Manager: Actually, it's just the opposite. We make money.

Me: You make money if someone returns a CD that they've copied?

Manager: Maybe not on that particular transaction, but in the long run we do. You see, our aim is to get as much traffic in the store as we possibly can. If you return a CD, that means you've now been in the store at least twice.

Me: Yes, but I got my money back. I didn't spend anything here.

Manager: Not yet. But consider for a moment that we haven't lost any money on the CD. When we get it back from you, we repackage it and put it back out for sale in new condition as long as it isn't damaged.

Me: Suppose it is damaged?

Manager: Then we return it to the distributor for credit or replacement.

Me: I see how you break even, but how do you make money?

Manager: Since you're in the store again, look around. Our merchandising plan presents you with literally hundreds of opportunities to spend money. See that bin of tapes?

Me: Yep.

Manager: Those are the best-selling singles from last year that we're selling for 79 cents each. You can't go anywhere else and even buy a blank tape for that amount. Look up on the wall and you'll see some portable tape players. There's tremendous profit in those. And when you buy anything, we'll try to convince you to join our "Frequent Buyers" club. We make a bloody fortune on that. So everyone comes out ahead!

Everyone that is but the artist. How much does an artist stand to lose on any one CD? Maybe it's three dollars or maybe it's only one dollar. In fact, it doesn't matter if it's only one penny. The fact is that if it is a penny, that penny belongs to the artist. It doesn't belong to the music store, and it certainly doesn't belong to us. We benefited. The artist was harmed. Certainly the harm may not be of significant value. However, value is not what this question (Is it fair and balanced?) is about. What the question focuses on is fairness, balance, and keeping promises. True, promises were not explicit. But there is an implicit promise between the artist and the consumer of the music.

Artist: I will produce this music for your enjoyment if you will pay me what I'm due.

Consumer: Okay, that's reasonable.

In the case of the CD and the music store, the artist lived up to his part of the agreement. The consumer did not. So set aside the issue of legality and set aside the issue of value. The answer to the question is "No, it is not fair and balanced."

Will It Pass a Test of Public Scrutiny?

An easy way to remember this question is to think of it as "the Mother Test." How would your mother feel about you if she found out what you did? Suppose you were caught doing something you shouldn't have been doing and a picture of you doing it ended up on the front page of the newspaper. How would your mother feel? How would your grandparents, aunts, uncles, clergy, or friends feel? What would you say to your children? How would you feel about yourself? If the answers to these questions trouble you, then you should probably avoid the behavior.

In the case of the CD and its audiotaped counterpart, this is probably not a very powerful question. Why? Because if one of my friends asked me where I got the tape and I said I made a copy of it, no big deal, right? Why? Because "everybody does it." So of the three questions, in this case the second question is the most powerful and would likely be the most useful to help facilitate the process of consequential thinking. On the other hand, if I am thinking about putting the CD inside my shirt and walking out of the music store without paying for it, questions 1 (legal) and 3 (public scrutiny) become extremely powerful.

Me: Is it legal?

Myself: No!

Me: What if I get caught?

Myself: I would probably go to court and maybe even to jail.

Me: What else?

Myself: When others found out what I did, I would be ashamed, embarrassed, and I could never show my face in public again. It would be horrible. People like me just don't end up in the newspapers for stealing.

Many businesses provide materials such as the three-part checklist we've been discussing. They may also publish and distribute a Code of Ethics, Standards of Behavior, Rules of Conduct, and various policies regarding the company's position on illegal discrimination and sexual harassment. These kinds of resources not only inform employees as to the company's position on the issues, but they also serve as resources to help them through the process of consequential thinking. By taking the time to clearly think through the potential consequences of their decisions, employees (including leaders at all levels within an organization) can avoid costly mistakes that could ruin their careers, tarnish their personal credibility, and potentially bring significant harm to the business itself.

Let's apply the ethical decision-making checklist to one of our cases from the assessment, that of Mrs. Collins and John, the store manager. John increased the profits of the business in many ways, not the least of which was through the sale and rental of pornographic videotapes. Mrs. Collins was appalled by John's practices and instinctively wanted to terminate his employment. To do so, however, could mean the end of her business owing to the absence of a strong-willed, determined, and otherwise competent manager. She certainly wasn't capable of running the store herself, and she felt unprepared to find anyone to replace John. Her dilemma—should she fire John, should she retain him conditionally pending his acceptance of her guidelines, or should she overlook her concerns and allow him to continue his policies?

The first question for her to consider is "Is it legal?" After a bit of research, she discovered that the sale, rental, and/or distribution of pornographic videotapes is illegal in her county. If convicted of the offense, the business and its executives are subject to fines and penalties of up to $5,000 and revocation of the license to do business in the county.

The second question to address is "Is it fair and balanced?" Profits are up, vendors of the tapes are making money, and consumers of the pornographic tapes are undoubtedly happy. On the surface, the answer to this question seems to be "yes." On closer inspection, however, the answer may not be as definitive. While certain of the store's clientele may be happy with the merchandise, others might be offended. They may feel that the store has broken a promise to them based on the reputation that the store's original owner, Nathan Collins, had established. That reputation was based on providing "good, clean entertainment through video rentals and sales for the entire community." If clients who are neighbors and friends are offended, then certainly there is a question of balance. Using this perspective, the answer to the question would be "no."

The third question is "Will it pass a test of public scrutiny?" To address this question, Mrs. Collins might imagine what the headlines might look like: "Widow Collins Peddles Porn" or "College Lust at Collins Video." No fuzz on the answer to this question.

Analytical Decision Making

Related to considering the ethical impact as a process for consequential thinking is a type of tool called analytical decision making. The method usually involves drawing a "T-chart" which allocates space for the proposed action at the top, the pros in one column, and the cons in another column.

Proposed Action	
Pros (+)	Cons (−)

To get some experience using this chart, let's apply issues from the case of Lester Stipple. Recall from Section I that Mr. Stipple is the CEO of Stipple Manufacturing who is trying to decide whether to maintain his current business focus as a supplier of materials in the office supply industry. Since many of Stipple's products such as staplers and clipboards have decreased in consumption due to their replacement with by-products of the electronics industry, Stipple Manufacturing is faced with possible bankruptcy or buyout. Mr. Stipple could use this decision chart to help him "think through" a solution to his problem. A question for him to address is "Should Stipple Manufacturing refocus its distribution to products from the electronics industry?"

Should Stipple's Shift Production and Distribution into Electronics?	
Pros (+)	*Cons (–)*
Products for today's office needs	No experience with new products
Maintain current customer base	Might lose current customer base if we drop current lines
Attract & expand new customer base	"New" customers already served by competitors we know nothing about at this time. We may not be able to "sell" them.
Raise employee morale new and exciting venture training opportunities sense of hope	Unknown start-up costs, tooling, training, technology, machines, entire infrastructure
Could save the business	Could go bankrupt and lose what assets we have and our ability to maintain even a smaller version of our current business
Could radically improve profits	

By using this simple chart, Mr. Stipple has been able to think through some of the advantages and disadvantages of moving into a new line of business. The risks are inherent in the "Cons" column of the chart. Mr. Stipple's ability to reach a decision depends on whatever items are the most "salient" or powerful to convince him one way or the other.

The advantage of the pro/con approach is that it offers a chance to view the decision from two perspectives—almost as though one were having a discussion with another person. Of course, the tool need not be limited to a "one-person" thought process. An alternative would be for a team leader to facilitate a session whereby a decision could be developed using the chart as a discussion guide.

The disadvantage of this approach is that the thought process is limited by the two columns, that is, the pros and cons. And the contrast between them is limited to one idea per chart.

As a more powerful alternative, consider a thought process that would simultaneously consider two choices. The first choice would be the current way of doing things. The second choice would be the new way of doing things. Applied to each choice would be a pro–con analysis or, to say it a different way, the benefits and the risks. This approach is called a "double T-chart." Here's how the chart would look:

Current Way		New Way	
Benefits	Risks	Benefits	Risks

The thought process would include the following steps:

1. What is the proposed idea?
2. What is the current way of doing things?
3. What benefits can be gained from the new idea?
4. What are the risks, what could be lost if the new idea succeeds or fails?
5. What are the benefits of keeping things as they are now?
6. What could be lost if the current way is retained?

Any idea brings with it the risk of loss. If it fails, all kinds of things could be lost including money, reputation, opportunity, and physical and/or mental health. An equally important aspect to consider is the potential for losses associated with the success of the new idea. For example, the whole family may agree that they want a new car. In order to afford it, however, they have to give up some "extras" such as eating out one night per week.

Along with the consideration of a new idea, it is also useful to consider the idea that the new one would be replacing. For example, *Do we really want to give up that old car? Certainly there are some headaches with it, but there are many comforts and conveniences it provides including the fact that it's already paid off.*

Let's consider how the double T-chart might look if completed by Lester Stipple.

Manufacture/Distribute for Paper Only		Expand/Specialize for Electronics	
Benefits	**Risks**	**Benefits**	**Risks**
Keep current customers happy.	Risk buyout from larger companies.	Make products that meet customers' needs.	A great deal of capital needs to be invested in a start-up venture— new machines, work processes, training, marketing, equipment.
Retained employees do what they have always done which avoids stress associated with change.	Competitors may expand and take away our current customers.	Build on our reputation among our current customers.	I currently know little about the new products and markets.
I continue to be the expert and in control of the entire operation.	Market will likely continue to shrink.	Expand into a company of the future with new technologies and work processes to produce the best "electronics" for office use in the world!	I need to work with people I don't even know yet.
Maintain relationships with current suppliers including cost advantages and preferred delivery schedules.	Operating capital would dry up.		Current production, customers, profits could dry up while we convert to the new system.
	Stipple's would need to lay off loyal employees.	Give our loyal employees something to hope for— new and exciting work, the chance for job security.	
Continue to use existing manufacturing machines and equipment.	Production schedules could be delayed.		Stipple's would be competing with companies already established in the industry; they could eat us alive.
Overall costs are predictable; new expenses are kept to a minimum.	We could lose even more customers.	Share the burdens with business associates from the executive staff rather than retain all the burden myself.	
	Face even greater losses and spiral into bankruptcy.		We would need enough funds to meet our costs for at least two years which could erode our economic base if we don't make a profit by then.
	Market is rapidly drying up which means less and less need for Stipple's as we now are.	Keep the company alive & prosperous.	
Status quo	**Lose everything**	**Build a future!**	**Lose everything**

What would you do if you were Mr. Stipple? Or, going back to the assessment, how would you advise Mr. Stipple as his consultant? The use of the T-chart or the double T-chart ensures that a logical thought process would guide your decision. The very process of using either chart minimizes the risk that a leader will make a decision impulsively. Remember that impulsive decisions often create more problems than they solve.

Using the double T-chart as a guide, here's how a consultant might draft a letter to Mr. Stipple:

Mr. Lester Stipple, CEO
Stipple Manufacturing

Dear Mr. Stipple:

Thank you for the opportunity to consider the problem you are trying to solve at Stipple Manufacturing. I have weighed the options and would like to offer my assessment.

As I see the problem, you have two options to consider. The first option is to continue to manufacture only products that would support the paper goods industry. By doing so, you could continue to enjoy certain benefits, but you also face certain risks.

The benefits of maintaining your current focus is that Stipple's will remain as it always has been—a source of comfort, security, and satisfaction to you, your customers, and your employees. The risk you face stems from the new trends and products in the office supply industry. If you choose not to change your product line, your market will likely continue to shrink, which means your customers will go elsewhere for their product needs. That means you will lose revenue and may not be able to meet your operating expenses. You could be a target for a corporate takeover or you could face bankruptcy.

The benefits of expanding and specializing in "electronics" for office supply revolve primarily around making and distributing products that are in demand by today's customers and customers in the future. By providing these products, you will be entering into a market that can help restore your profits. With a strong profit base, you will be able to meet your operating expenses which means that Stipple's will be able to provide jobs for its employees and security for their families. A new line of products will also likely build morale through a sense of excitement and vitality. Also, since you will no doubt need assistance from your associates, they can share some of the burden and pressures of the business, which will help you enjoy peace of mind and perhaps even more time with your family. Of course, there are risks associated with this new venture. The start-up capital will be heavy and you will be relying on others who you have not yet come to know and trust in order to help you succeed. In the end, you could lose Stipple's and many of your assets.

Ultimately, the decision is yours to make. A consultant can and should only advise. What is most intriguing to me is that the ultimate risk in either case is losing your business. On a personal note, if I faced that risk, I would rather take the path filled with promise, hope, excitement, and vitality. Stipple's has been the foundation of the business office for the last fifty years. With your integrity, customer loyalty, and keen sense of business, Stipple's could build the electronic office of the future.

Sincerely,
Your Consultant

Chapter Summary

Consequential thinking is a logical extension of directional thinking. Is it absolutely necessary that you weigh each decision by using a structured process such as the ethical decision-making checklist or either of the T-charts? The answer depends on the potential consequences as well as your own ability to have presence of mind. The greatest enemy to a successful decision is your own impulsivity. At some level, whether through a structured process or through an "instantaneous" analysis, leaders should consider the consequences before they make a decision and certainly before they implement it.

One way to consider consequential thinking is to imagine that you are bouncing a basketball. As you are actively bouncing the ball, you are in control. You control how fast it bounces, how high it bounces, and whether or not it moves up and down in the same spot, forward or backward. As long as you control it actively, it will not bump into anything and cause harm unless you aim and propel it. But if at any point you lose control, it becomes an unguided missile on its own trajectory, striking and perhaps harming whatever lies in its path.

To illustrate this concept of losing control, consider the following true story.

An employee of a large defense contractor (we'll call the company Advanced Avionics and we'll call the employee Pete) was discussing the subject of abortion with his friend who worked for a different company (we'll call the friend Al). Pete's position on abortion was "pro-choice" and Al's was "pro-life." One day, Pete read a "pro-choice" article in a popular magazine. He thought the article was so interesting that he wanted to send it to Al. He brought the article into work at Advanced Avionics. (Picture Pete bouncing a basketball—so far, he's in control.) He made a copy of the article using one of the company's copy machines. (He's still in control—the ball is bouncing where he wants it to bounce.) He took the copy and put it into one of the company's fax machines and dialed Al's number in another city. (So far, the basketball bounces only where Pete directs it.) Then, he dialed Al's number and the paper goes through the fax machine. (That's the end of Pete's control—he has no control over where the fax will end up, who will read it, or what they will do with it. The basketball is now an unguided missile.) What happened was that Al did receive the fax and read it just as Pete had hoped. Only what Pete didn't count on was that Al put the fax down on a table in his barber shop later that afternoon. He intended to retrieve it after his haircut, but forgot about it. Later, another customer picked it up with some interest. He read the article, but also noticed something interesting at the top of the article. What appeared was something Pete had never anticipated—the words "A Fax From Advanced Avionics." The person who now possessed the fax happened to be a reporter for a local newspaper. The headline on the front page of the next edition read "Advanced Avionics Advocates Pro-Choice for Abortion."

Had the defense contractor ever intended its position on abortion to be published? Of course not, because it never had a position on abortion. That's not what its business was about. But through the carelessness of one of its employees, the company suffered great embarrassment and some degree of harm. The idea behind the bouncing basketball, just like the idea behind the ethical decision-making checklist and the analytical decision-making charts is "take the time to think."

As we discussed at the beginning of this chapter, leadership is about carving out new frontiers. And as with any new frontier, the pathways for getting there are often filled with risk. The wise leader contemplates the risk. Based on careful judgment, that leader either proceeds carefully or judiciously abandons the journey. The foolish leader is seduced by self-gratification and proceeds impulsively without due consideration of the dangers that can potentially bring defeat, humiliation, and harm.

Through the process of consequential thinking, leaders can (1) anticipate, avoid and manage risk and (2) avoid, minimize, and manage the consequences. The thought process may require days or hours. In some cases, leaders can accomplish it in only seconds. Regardless of the time required, the very act of considering the risks and the potential consequences can almost always minimize harm and help ensure that the outcome is consistent with what the leader intended.

— Summary of Selected Employment Laws and Topics —

The At Will: Doctrine

The term *at will* refers to an implied understanding between a prospective employee and employer. The understanding relates to an agreement that they reach regarding the nature of the employment, that is, the wages, where the employee will perform the work, what work the employee will perform, and how long the work (job) will last. As long as the agreement is reached verbally and without reference to the duration of time that the job will last, that agreement is often considered by a court to be "at the will of the employer." Under this *at will* arrangement and as long as no other laws are violated, the employer can dismiss the employee with no other reason other than "your services are no longer required."

To avoid a possible interpretation by a court that a different understanding occurred between the employer and the employee, the employer should take great care in what is said to the prospective employee. For example, a phrase such as "your annual salary will be . . ." could be interpreted by the employee (and later by the court) as implying that the employer is promising that the employee will have a job for a least one year ("annual"). If the employee is dismissed before that time, the employee might consider the dismissal to be a breach of contract and sue the employer. The good intentions of the employer could also cause problems if interpreted by the prospective employee as part of the job offer ("you'll have a job here as long as we're profitable."). If the employer terminates the employee for any other reason besides poor profits, the court may interpret the dismissal as a violation of an implied contract and could subsequently penalize the employer.

To summarize, the *at will* concept means that the employer can dismiss the employee for any reason as long as that reason does not violate any law. By the same token, the employee can choose to quit for any reason as well.

Employee Handbooks

Remember that the *at will* concept essentially says that there is no legally binding relationship between an employer and an employee. This concept may be superseded by the written documentation that is contained in an employee handbook. Yet the employer may not realize the binding nature of the handbook until the company is sued and penalized.

For example, if an employee handbook says that an employee will receive three warnings for misconduct before termination, that employee handbook could be viewed by a court as an enforceable contract that supersedes the *at will* doctrine. An employee who is fired prior to getting a third warning could claim that the employer breached the contract documented in the employee handbook.

Employers should use great care before writing and distributing an employee handbook. Courts have regarded these handbooks as information that the employer wants the employee to know, understand, and be guided by. Why would the employer provide the employee with such information if that employer doesn't intend to abide by it? Interestingly enough, the test that the courts use is comparable to a test for insanity or retardation. In other words, judges recognize that they should not hold insane or retarded people to promises they are incapable of keeping. To apply the same logic to an employer, some judges have reasoned that if the employer is insane or retarded, he or she probably shouldn't be held liable for the information written in an employee handbook. Since the employer is probably not insane or retarded, then the words in the employee handbook can be regarded as good faith and reasonable promises to the employee and are therefore enforceable. The lesson for the employer is to first think carefully as to whether the company really wants to provide its employees with an employee handbook. If so, they should choose carefully what words will appear in that handbook. Otherwise, those words will likely come back to haunt them.

The Fair Labor Standards Act (FLSA)

Passed in 1938 and administered by the Department of Labor, the Fair Labor Standards Act contains provisions regarding child labor laws and regulations that govern the payment of the minimum wage and overtime. The law is set up to cover all employees. It does not cover independent contractors. Generally, independent contractors are any workers who set their own hours, determine their own sequence of work, work by project instead of having a continuous relationship with an employer, get paid by the job rather than for a position, and are considered to be self-employed or employed by a company that supplies such personnel.

Under the child labor portion of the law, employers are prohibited from employing children under age fourteen in most types of jobs. Between the ages of fourteen and fifteen, children cannot work more than three hours per day during the school year or forty hours per week during school vacations. Their hours are restricted from 7:00 A.M. to 7:00 P.M. during the school year, but they can work up until 9:00 P.M. during summer vacations.

The overtime portion of the law established the two categories of *exempt* and *nonexempt* workers. The law protects nonexempt workers, but offers no protection for exempt workers. In general, employees are considered exempt (not protected by the law) if they use analytical judgment for which they have been professionally trained in order to perform work as opposed to performing the work through the use of a technical skill. Typical categories to qualify a worker as exempt include those of (1) executive with the primary duty of management, (2) administrative with the primary duty of managing office policies where discretionary judgment is required, (3) outside salespeople who sell or take orders for the company's products and spend less than 20 percent of their workweek in nonsales activities, and (4) professionals whose work requires advanced knowledge that results from specialized study and the use of discretion and independent judgment.

The outcome of classifying an employee as exempt or nonexempt determines whether or not the worker will be paid overtime. By law, the employer must pay nonexempt employees time and one-half the hourly pay if they work more than forty hours in any given week. For example, if an employee makes $8 per hour, he would earn $320 for a forty-hour week. If she worked forty-five hours, she would earn $12 for each of the five hours worked past forty to equal $60. The weekly total would then be $380.

Suppose a secretary who works for one of the company's executives decides to catch up on typing and decides on her own to work four hours of overtime. Does the company have to pay her even if her boss did not require the overtime to be worked? The answer is an absolute and unqualified "yes." Whether or not the overtime is necessary and regardless of who made the decision for the overtime to be worked, the law requires overtime pay for overtime worked.

Suppose a departmental assistant helps to host a company party for new hires on a Sunday afternoon. Does the assistant need to be paid overtime if he works more than forty hours in that week. Yes! Suppose a computer service technician completes a required self-study manual at home during one-hour blocks after dinner for five consecutive nights. Does he need to be paid overtime? Once again, the answer is "yes."

The challenge for employers is not only to ensure that overtime is paid for overtime worked, but also to ensure that they discover any overtime worked that they did not authorize. If the Department of Labor discovers that overtime is being worked by nonexempt employees who are not being paid in accordance with the law, it can investigate, fine, and penalize the employer. Fines and penalties can include not only the retroactive payment for overtime hours, but also the reclassification of exempt workers who should have been classified as nonexempt.

For example, if a group of graphic artists was classified as exempt and the Department of Labor determines that their work is more *technical data entry* than *professional judgment*, the workers can be reclassified from exempt to nonexempt. The outcome would mean that any overtime they had worked as exempt employees would retroactively be paid to them at the nonexempt rate as a result of their reclassification to the nonexempt status. The penalty could cover a period of several months preceding the effective date of reclassification.

Do exempt employees get paid overtime? Suppose a group of accountants worked eighty hours per week for six consecutive weeks during tax season. How much overtime does the Fair Labor Standards Act require the employer to pay? The answer is none. Exempt employees are not protected by the law. If the company does pay them overtime, it is because of company policy, not because of the law.

Equal Employment Opportunity (EEO)

Equal employment opportunity represents both a collection of laws and an employment philosophy that protects an employee's right to equal treatment in all employment-related actions. The laws specify the nature of this treatment and prescribe penalties for organizations that violate them. The laws include:

The Equal Pay Act	1963
The Civil Rights Act (Title VII)	1964
Executive Orders 11246 and 11375	1965, 1967
Age Discrimination in Employment Act	1967
Executive Order 11478	1969
Vocational Rehabilitation Act	1973
Rehabilitation Act	1974

Vietnam-Era Veterans Act	1974
Pregnancy Discrimination Act	1978
Immigration Reform and Control Act	1986, 1990
Americans with Disabilities Act	1990, 1994
Older Workers Benefit Protection Act	1990
Civil Rights Act	1991
Family and Medical Leave Act	1992

These laws are designed to protect people from illegal discrimination in areas of employment. Not all discrimination is illegal. To discriminate simply means to "separate by difference." The ability to discriminate is essential to perceive and recognize information as meaningful. We discriminate thousands of times in any given day in virtually everything we do. Discriminating between red and green traffic lights, the up and the down buttons on elevators, the keys on a keyboard and the items on a menu are just a few examples of how we perceive differences between things in order to conduct our lives. With respect to employment, discrimination is essential for many practices including selecting and choosing people for various job functions and even for termination as long as the discrimination is done on the basis of business criteria. Discrimination can become illegal when certain groups of people are denied equal opportunities. Discrimination can be determined to be illegal when it can be established that (1) two different standards are used to judge two otherwise equally qualified people or (2) the same standard is used but it is not related to the requirements of the job.

Collectively, the laws have established groups known as *protected classes*. A protected class is regarded as a group of people who are identified for protection against discrimination under the equal employment laws. The classes are comprised of individuals who have typically been subjected to illegal discrimination. Currently, the protected classes include

- Race, ethnic origin, color (Asian Americans, African Americans, Native Americans, Hispanics)
- Gender (females, including those who are pregnant)
- Age (people over the age of forty)
- Religion (including special beliefs and practices)
- Military experience (Vietnam-era veterans)
- People with disabilities (physical or mental)

To oversee the administration of the laws and to ensure that they are properly enforced, two federal enforcement agencies have been established. The Equal Employment Opportunity Commission (EEOC) was created by the Civil Rights Act of 1964 and has enforcement authority as an independent agency of the United States Government. The Office of Federal Contract Compliance Programs (OFCCP) is part of the Department of Labor and operates under executive orders to ensure that discrimination does not occur among the employment practices of contractors and subcontractors that do business with the federal government.

To prove that discrimination has occurred illegally, the individual must first of all be a member of a protected class. There are other issues to be considered as well. Two such issues are *disparate treatment* and *disparate impact*.

Disparate treatment occurs when members of a protected class are treated differently from other employees. For example, an organization may openly restrict pregnant women from applying for certain positions. Or, people over the age of forty-five have to pass a medical exam in order to operate a forklift.

Disparate impact occurs when the members of a protected class have substantially less representation in an employment area as compared with nonprotected class members. For example, consider a case in which an equal number of African American and Caucasian applicants are considered for promotions. An investigation of the results reflects that 80 percent of the Caucasian applicants were promoted compared with only 10 percent of the African American applicants. The process for granting the promotions is said to have had disparate impact on the African American applicants.

To determine if disparate impact has occurred, an EEOC investigator could apply what's called the Four-fifths Rule. This rule states that discrimination generally has occurred if the selection rate for a protected group is less than 80 percent of their representation in the relevant labor market or less than 80 percent of the majority group. Here's an example of how it can be applied:

A. Selection rate for men
$$\frac{\text{Number of men hired}}{\text{Number of men applied}} \quad \frac{20}{50} \quad = 40\%$$

B. Disparate impact determination
$$80\% \text{ of } 40\% \quad = 32\%$$

A selection rate below 32% for women would indicate disparate impact.

C. Selection rate for women
$$\frac{\text{Number of women hired}}{\text{Number of women applied}} \quad \frac{9}{36} \quad = 25\%$$

D. Result: Disparate impact?
Yes, since 25% is less than 32%

Would an agency such as the EEOC contend that the disparate treatment or the disparate impact establishes proof that the organization has illegally discriminated against the member(s) of the protected class? Not necessarily. In fact, the burden of proof is on the organization to demonstrate that there were business reasons for the discrimination, and therefore it was legal rather than illegal. Two reasons that the organization can offer are (1) business necessity-job relatedness and/or (2) bona fide occupational qualification (BFOQ).

Regarding a business necessity or a job-related skill, it is entirely appropriate and legal for an organization to require that employees possess certain qualifications in order to be considered able to perform a job. Clearly, a keyboard operator must be able to type. Suppose, however, that 80 percent of the applicants for the position of keyboard operators did not know how to type, and they happened to be members of a class protected for ethnic origin. The company rejected their application and instead selected all the applicants from the other 20 percent of the applicant pool because they did know how to type. It so happened that all of these selected applicants were Caucasian. In response to an investigation by the EEOC, company representatives agreed that while they could have trained the nonselected applicants to type, their immediate need was to hire keyboard operators to finish a critical project within two weeks. Under the circumstances, the company would likely be able to defend its decision as a "business necessity."

A bona fide occupational qualification (BFOQ) is what the EEOC considers a legitimate business reason for excluding an individual for an employment consideration. The exclusion often singles out one or more of the protected classes. For example, should men over age forty be given consideration for parts in a play? On the surface, of course, they should. However, think of the part of *Moses* as he nears the end his life if that part were played by a fifteen-year-old actor. Theater makeup can no doubt work wonders, but the characterization would undoubtedly be more convincing if cast with someone closer in age to that of the actual character. On the other hand, should a sixty-year-old male be considered for the part of Dorothy in *The Wizard of Oz*? That would make no sense. The part calls for a girl in her early teenage years. Is it discriminatory to deny a sixty-year-old male the opportunity to try out for the part? Yes. Is it illegal? No. It is legal to discriminate on the basis of a bona fide occupational qualification. Is it illegal to require rabbis to be Jewish or priests to be Catholic? Of course not. Can women be legally excluded from consideration for positions as prison guards in an all-male prison? Probably so.

Once again, it is up to the employer to prove that its practices do not illegally discriminate against members of a protected class. If disparate treatment or disparate impact occurs, the employer will probably be able to defend the practice if a business necessity and/or a bona fide occupational qualification can be demonstrated.

Some of the most recent employment laws pertain to (1) Americans with disabilities, (2) employees who request leaves to be with members of their families during times of hardship, and (3) sexual harassment. Leaders should familiarize themselves with these laws if their leadership involves decisions and practices that are related to these types of issues.

Of these issues, perhaps the most sensitive is sexual harassment. The word *harassment* lies at the core of an employee's basic rights in the workplace. We mentioned earlier that an employer is "at will" to dismiss an employee without giving any specific reason. Even though the At Will doctrine acknowledges the power of the employer, that doesn't mean that the employee is without rights. Within any organization, an employee has the right to a wage for work performed as well as the right to a safe and comfortable workplace. If those rights are taken away or threatened, the employee is said to be harassed.

Sexual harassment is a behavior or practice of a sexual nature that makes an employee feel uncomfortable or threatened by danger. There are two types of sexual harassment: (1) quid pro quo and (2) hostile environment.

Quid pro quo is a term that means "an equal exchange" or "something for something." In the workplace, it refers to doing something for someone as a repayment for something they've done for you ("If you do this for me, I will try to help you" or "If you won't do this for me, then I will try to harm you"). Applied to sexual harassment, quid pro quo refers to a situation in which someone in a position of power offers to do something good (a promotion) or threatens to do something bad (a demotion, termination, vicious gossip) in exchange for a sexual favor from a person without such power.

A hostile environment occurs when unwelcome and discouraged sexual behavior (pictures, jokes, staring, touching) interferes with a person's ability to perform his or her work. In other words, the right to a safe and comfortable work setting has been violated.

Employers have two responsibilities with respect to sexual harassment. First, they must publicly advise everyone in the workplace as to what it is and that if it occurs, the harasser will be disciplined. Second, the employer must follow through with the policy by aggressively investigating allegations of sexual harassment, effectively stopping it if is found to occur, and disciplining the offender based on preestablished levels of discipline.

The consequences for illegal employment practices can be severe. In the case of copyright violations, Kinko's corporation paid over half a million dollars in penalties. Shoney's, Inc. paid over 132 million dollars to settle a claim of racial discrimination. State Farm Insurance paid over 157 million dollars to settle claims of sexual discrimination. Staggering sums have also been assessed against corporations for infringements of overtime, patent claims, and nearly countless other allegations.

The lesson is clear and simple. In developing their vision and considering how to implement it, leaders should be well aware of the applicable laws and the consequences if their leadership practices violate them, even if those violations were absolutely unintentional. The law doesn't care.

Bibliography

Blanchard, Kenneth, and Norman Vincent Peale, *The Power of Ethical Management* (New York: Fawcett Crest, 1988).

Cheeseman, Henry, *Business Law—The Legal, Ethical, and International Environment* (Upper Saddle River, NJ: Prentice-Hall, 1992).

Grose, Vernon, *Managing Risk—Systematic Loss Prevention for Executives* (Upper Saddle River, NJ: Prentice-Hall, 1987).

MacCrimmon, Kenneth, and Donald Wehrung, *Taking Risks—The Management of Uncertainty* (New York: MacMillan, 1986).

McWhirter, Darien, *Your Rights at Work* (New York: John Wiley & Sons, 1989).

Pava, Moses, *The Talmudic Concept of "Beyond the Letter of the Law": Relevance to Business Social Responsibilities (Journal of Business Ethics,* 15: 941–950, 1996).

Walsh, James, *Mastering Diversity—Managing for Success Under ADA and Other Anti-Discrimination Laws* (Santa Monica, CA: Merritt 1995).

Weiss, Donald H., *Fair, Square, and Legal—Safe Hiring Managing and Firing Practices to Keep You and Your Company Out of Court* (New York: American Management Association—AMACOM, 1991).

CHAPTER 7

Influence Strategies

At the very core of leadership is the ability to influence people. The importance of this ability is reflected in most definitions of leadership. Consider just a few.

According to Ken Blanchard, author of *Leadership and the One-Minute Manager*,

Any time you try to influence the behavior of another person, you're engaging in an act of leadership.

In their book entitled *Learning to Lead*, Warren Bennis and Joan Goldsmith say,

What leaders do is inspire **peo**ple, empower them. They pull rather than push. If you want to lead people, the first thing you have to do is get them to buy into shared objectives.

Kenneth and Miriam Clark in *Choosing to Lead* indicate that

The leader persuades, the leader does not coerce.

And in their book *Measures of Leadership*, the Clarks say that leaders

. . . increase the energy in the system.

Robert Rosen in *Leading People* writes,

Leaders must create healthy environments where people are excited about their work, take pride in their accomplishments, and contribute to their colleagues doing the same. Their task, in short, is to foment ideas, skills, and energy.

Noel Tichy and Mary Anne Devanna in the *The Transformational Leader* advise that

Leaders . . . mobilize commitment.

In *Leadership—A Force for Change*, John Kotter says that a primary function of leadership is

> .... being able to generate highly energized behavior . . . not by pushing people but by satisfying very basic human needs: for achievement, belonging, recognition, self-esteem, a sense of control over one's life, and living up to one's ideals.

And according to Jennifer George and Gareth Jones in *Understanding and Managing Organizational Behavior,*

> Leadership involves exerting influence over other members of a group or organization.

If an important part of leadership is influencing people, just how do leaders do it? What makes them so effective in getting people to do something they either don't want to do or may never have even thought about doing?

How was Jill able to convince the theater manager to stop the projector and get people to virtually admit that they had entered the movie under false pretenses? What was it that John Baker said or did that convinced Mrs. Collins to entrust him with the management of her husband's business and personal reputation? What did John Kennedy or Martin Luther King, Jr. or Louis Farrakan do or say to move thousands of people toward supporting a cause they either didn't know about or care about or felt too powerless to make any difference about? In each case, the leader knew how to use influence strategies.

The purpose of this chapter is to help you learn several basic influence strategies. As a result, you'll begin to recognize how others use these strategies to shape how you think and to gently and in some cases aggressively determine what you do. As you learn to use the same strategies, you will be better able to persuade people that because it is in their best interests to support your vision, they should follow your lead.

The chapter is organized around four major topics. The first is why people resist change. In this section, we'll consider the concepts of inertia (how habits and routine block new ideas) and resistance (why people actively block attempts to change their thinking). The second topic is how and why influence strategies neutralize the barriers to change. Here, we will primarily look at the "Theory of Needs" developed by Abraham Maslow and use it to determine why and how influence strategies can be so powerful. The third topic presents a series of gambits and "dirty tricks" to illustrate how some people try to influence others unethically through pressure tactics, subterfuge, and other forms of manipulation. The fourth topic discusses more principled methods for influencing people that are based on fairness, logic, reason, and the satisfaction of mutual needs.

Inertia and Resistance as Barriers to Change

The two objectives of influence strategies are

1. To replace inertia with saliency
2. To replace resistance with cooperation and commitment

Inertia refers to a person's attitude about change. Unless stimulated or provoked, the person remains blissfully unaware that things could or should be different.

Routine patterns govern thinking and habits drive activity. There is no particular pleasure associated with this type of behavior. On the other hand, there is no particular pain either. In short, the person believes there is no reason to change. In fact, the prospect of change is largely never even considered.

Resistance is also an attitude about change. Unlike inertia, however, the person resisting clearly is aware that he does not want to or intend to change. In fact, he actively opposes attempts to modify his attitudes, beliefs, and behavior.

Let's consider a few examples.

Parker Hastings: Hello there, beautiful afternoon isn't it?

Joseph Metler: Would be if I didn't have to rake up all these leaves.

PH: Sir, my name is Parker Hastings and I'm running for councilman of the 5th District.

JM: That so? Would you mind moving over a bit to your right, young man? I need to scoop up these leaves in that there can.

PH: Oh, uh, sorry. I'd like to ask for your support in the next election.

JM: No offense, but I don't much care about, where'd you say you're from?

PH: The 5th District.

JM: Uh huh. Don't much care about the 5th District.

PH: Can I leave one of my brochures with you?

JM: S'up to you. Can't guarantee this ole north wind won't blow it away though.

PH: Could I hammer one of my wood signs in your lawn so all your neighbors will see it and think about voting for me?

JM: 'Fraid not, son. 'Sides, most of the neighbors can't see all that well anyway. Move along now. I've got to finish up my chores here. S'pect it'll take most of the afternoon as it is. Nice talkin to ya.

Poor Mr. Hastings. He really didn't make much of an impact on neighbor Metler. It's probably not very easy to carry that sign against a strong north wind either. Unfortunately, he had no luck in convincing Mr. Metler to vote for him. In fact, he was pretty sure that Mr. Metler wouldn't even vote at all in the election for the 5th District.

Mr. Metler's lack of interest reflects the concept of inertia. He was resistant to voting because he saw no reason to vote. As far as he knew, the "5th District" had no relevance for him. He'd lived very nicely without concerning himself about it before, and it would make no difference to him in the future. At least, that's how he viewed it. Mr. Hastings did nothing to change his point of view. The only thing Mr. Hastings knew about Mr. Metler for sure is that he didn't want to spend one more minute raking leaves than he had to.

Is there anything else Mr. Hastings could have done to have gotten Mr. Metler interested? Are there issues he might have raised that could have virtually guaranteed Mr. Metler's vote? The answer lies in the concept of saliency.

The word *salient* means "conspicuous" or "prominent." To illustrate, notice the feeling of the watch around your wrist. That feeling wasn't salient until I just called your attention to it. While the actual sensation was present all the time, you probably only notice it when you put the watch on, take it off, or have someone comment on it as I just did. In contrast, imagine that you slammed your finger in a door. The pain would be salient. It would be hard to ignore. The saliency would remain for as long as the pain continued.

For Mr. Metler, there was no saliency in the 5th District. Just the opposite was true—in other words, there was inertia. And Mr. Hastings did nothing to replace the inertia with saliency. What was salient to Mr. Metler was his aggravation and perhaps even physical discomfort with having to rake leaves. Could Mr. Hastings have brought saliency to his meeting with Mr. Metler? Consider this:

Parker Hastings: Hello there, beautiful afternoon isn't it?

Joseph Metler: Would be if I didn't have to rake up all these leaves.

PH: What a waste of a beautiful afternoon. Hi, my name is Parker Hastings and I'm running for councilman of the 5th District.

JM: That's nice. Would you mind moving out of the way? I need to scoop up these leaves into that can.

PH: What would you say if I could cut your job in half?

JM: I'd say if you want to help, there's an extra rake up there in the garage.

PH: Sure, I'd be happy to help you, but that's not what I mean.

JM: You gonna help or not?

PH: As councilman in the 5th District, I would propose a leaf vacuuming service. Sure, you'd still have to rake the leaves from the lawn down to the curb, but you'd never have to scoop them up. Once you rake them into a pile, you'd wet them down with a fine spray of the hose and just walk away and have the rest of the afternoon to yourself.

JM: Who'd pick them up?

PH: The 5th District. That's the beauty of it. They would come by once a week with a huge truck that sucks up the leaves from the curb. Imagine, you'd never have to bend down and pick up another leaf again.

JM: It'll never happen.

PH: It's already happening. Look at this picture in my brochure. Every one of our surrounding districts is using this service. Sure, there's a slight tax increase. But with the cost defrayed among the five districts in this county, it'll be just a few pennies per month. Interested?

JM: You betcha!

PH: Could I post this sign in your yard?

JM: I'll hammer it in for you!

To summarize so far, the working principle for overcoming inertia is to replace it with saliency. Let's consider an example that involves resistance.

Sherry Walker: Peter, do you have few minutes?

Peter Manchester: Okay, what's up?

SW: Peter, ever since we hired you, I've been pretty upset that you haven't been carrying your weight on the staff.

PM: Whoa, what are you talking about?

SW: Our job in this department is to deliver training programs for our newest managers. We have over twenty-one new programs. Everyone else on staff is delivering at least five of the programs. You've taken only two.

PM: Sherry, I thought I was hired to develop the Contracts course. That's my expertise. That's what my book is about. That's what you guys interviewed me on, and that's why I said yes to the job. You know the development of that course is labor intensive. As it is, I'm working overtime, and I'm just barely able to squeeze in the Cost Accounting class. I don't understand why you're bringing this up.

SW: Peter, I don't mean to upset you. But since I've taken over as manager to replace Fred, I've also changed our priorities. Contracts is an important course, but it is certainly not our only concern. The rest of the staff is stretched thin, and we need you to pitch in and carry your fair share. So you'd best figure out a way to pick up at least two more classes to deliver this quarter. By the beginning of next quarter, I expect you to be up to five classes.

PM: Look, Sherry, the CEO has made it clear that he wants this course on line by the end of this month. If you want to reallocate my time, you're going to have to take it up with him.

SW: Be careful, Peter. Remember, I'm your manager. Please think about it and do what you need to do in order to adjust.

Clearly, Sherry is in a power struggle with Peter. Of course, as his manager Sherry has the authority to make Peter comply with her direction. She can obliterate his resistance with the force of her position. Were she to do so, however, Peter will likely try to "even the score" by resisting in some other way. Perhaps he will hold back his best effort. Maybe he'll talk about her behind her back. He might even go directly to the CEO. Regardless of her power, this kind of forceful approach fails to replace resistance with cooperation and commitment. Let's consider an alternative approach.

Sherry Walker: Peter, do you have few minutes?

Peter Manchester: Okay, what's up?

SW: Remember during your interview you suggested that we consider offering our courses in the local business community?

PM: Sure. I still think there's a tremendous market out there and with it a potential to bring in large profits for the company.

SW: You may be on to something. I've bounced the idea off of our director. The good news is he really likes it.

PM: Is there bad news?

SW: It's not bad news at all. Just a bit of work we would need to do in order to position the idea to our senior managers.

PM: What kind of work?

SW: Let me ask you a question first. Would you want to be the one to develop the profit center and propose it to management?

PM: Absolutely. I believe in it strongly, and I'm convinced I could present it effectively.

SW: I agree and I thought you would want to be the one to champion this. Okay, here's what we need to do. First, since you're still fairly new to the company, most of the senior managers don't know you yet. It's true that you joined at about the same time Jill and Mike did, but since they've delivered classes to senior managers, they're already known commodities. We need to make you more visible.

PM: I know. I'm just teaching two classes now and neither one is delivered to senior management.

SW: That's true. What's your time line for finishing up the development of the Contracts course?

PM: About another 120 hours. I'd say that's four to six weeks.

SW: And how quickly do you think we should move on the profit center idea?

PM: If we wait much longer, the national sales vendors will come to town and soak up the market.

SW: I see. What do you think we should do? Seems like your time is all tied up with your two courses. In order to build our profit center, we need to get you in front of senior management and your current classes don't do that.

PM: I could probably pick up the Negotiations course and the Government Liaison course within the next few weeks. Those are both courses that would be delivered exclusively to senior management.

SW: That way you certainly would get visibility with them fairly quickly. And once they'd see you in front of a classroom, you would develop credibility with them in no time.

PM: Would you want to copresent the profit center proposal with me when I do present it to senior management?

SW: I'd be happy to. I think it's a worthwhile project that could make a real difference for our company.

Inertia and resistance are two barriers to convincing people to change. In each of the earlier examples, we've noticed that the leader's first attempt to influence the follower is blocked. The follower is either not interested or else blatantly opposed to making any kind of change. The leader's second attempt is entirely different. While the interaction begins in much the same way as the first attempt, this attempt results in the follower agreeing to do what the leader wants him to do. Why? What happened? What was it that the leader did that pierced the barrier and persuaded the follower to change? The answers of course pertain to influence strategies.

How Influence Strategies Neutralize Barriers to Change

The first step in learning to use influence strategies is to determine how influence strategies attempt to neutralize inertia and resistance. To begin, let's consider another example that should help illuminate the reasons that make influence strategies so effective.

Janet: Phil, how did the interview go today for the director's position at Alliance Chemical?

Phil: It couldn't have gone better. The responsibilities are exactly what I've been looking for. They make great use of my skills and will even cause me to stretch a bit. But that's okay because I'd be working in an area of the field that's rapidly growing.

Janet: And you could grow right along with it.

Phil: Exactly.

Janet: Did you get the salary we talked about? With the baby coming, I don't think we can afford a drop in income.

Phil: Janet, they not only offered more than we were hoping, but there's a $5,000 sign-on bonus.

Janet: That's wonderful. I'm so proud of you! What about their health care package? How much do they contribute, and how much do we have to pay each month?

Phil: They offer a list of health benefit providers that have agreed to service company employees at a discounted rate.

Janet: I'm not thrilled about that, but does that mean we don't have to make monthly contributions?

Phil: Not exactly.

Janet: Well, how much do we have to pay, like $25 to $50 a month?

Phil: A bit more than that.

Janet: How much more?

Phil: Our contribution rate is $800 a month.

Janet: You've got to be kidding. Phil, we can't afford that. What about coverage for "well baby care" and catastrophic illness? Is that at least included?

Phil: I don't know. I didn't ask.

Janet: Phil, if we don't find out the answers to these questions before you take the job, we could end up in financial ruins. "Well baby care" alone will totally wipe out the effect of any raise or sign-on bonus you get, not to mention what a catastrophic illness could do to us.

Clearly the tension between Janet and Phil is overshadowing the excitement about the job offer, the raise and the sign-on bonus. The issues that Janet raised are extremely important to her, so much so that she might even express to Phil that he should pass on the job entirely. Why is Janet making such an issue over her concerns? Why not just let the chips fall where they may? One answer of course is to return to our discussion of consequential thinking. Janet is obviously worried about the financial impact of being underinsured. She and Phil are not prepared to handle an $800-a-month coinsurance payment much less pay for medical expenses out of pocket. Based on her use of consequential thinking, she is worried about the risk of "making ends meet" and going into debt on the one hand versus disappointing Phil on the other hand.

From Janet's perspective, then, Phil should either negotiate the benefit structure of the job offer or go for a higher salary. If he is unsuccessful, he should turn it down.

From Phil's perspective, it's the job of a lifetime. To turn it down would set his career objectives back at least five years. What should they do?

The solution to the dilemma lies not in impulsive bickering. The stakes are too high. If they don't resolve the conflict to their mutual satisfaction, one will "win" and the other will "lose." As a result, their relationship will be burdened with tension, mistrust, and resentment. Instead, the solution to the dilemma should be regarded as a process rather than as an outcome. The process should begin by trying to discover and understand each other's objectives. What forces are motivating them to hold fast to their respective positions? Why is Janet so concerned about the finances almost to the exclusion of Phil's excitement about career advancement? Why is Phil focusing on his career goals without apparent concern for the financial implications of an insufficient benefit package?

These are the types of questions that an influence strategist would raise as a first step toward what could be said to Janet in order to move her toward Phil's point of view, and as a first step to move Phil toward Janet's point of view. In other words, the first step of any influence strategy is to identify the person's objectives and determine the needs that underlie those objectives.

Maslow's Hierarchy of Needs

The classic theory that relates motivational needs to human behavior is Maslow's hierarchy of needs. Abraham Maslow was a psychologist who wrote *A Theory of Human Motivation* in 1943. The theory has stood the test of time as it is routinely referenced and described in current textbooks and coursework in the areas of psychology, organizational behavior, and marketing.

Maslow proposed a framework to explain how human needs motivate behavior. The framework rests on the assumption that normal human beings experience five basic needs. These needs exist in a hierarchy extending from the lowest-order need that Maslow described as "physiological" and progressing sequentially up to the highest need respectively as the needs for safety, love, esteem, and self-actualization. Associated with each of these needs, which we will discuss in turn, Maslow also proposed two working principles. First, according to the "deficit principle," only an unsatisfied need can motivate behavior. In other words, a need that has already been satisfied has no power to motivate behavior. Second, according to the "progression principle," the needs exist in a hierarchy of prepotency. In other words, meeting a lower-level need takes precedence over meeting a higher-level need. With these two principles in mind, let's take a look at each of the five basic needs.

Physiological Needs

These needs pertain to what the body needs to survive and to maintain a state of physical balance and equilibrium. Obvious needs exist for food, water, regulation of fluids and temperature, and so on. For a person deprived of food, for example, life is defined in terms of eating. Everything else is deemed irrelevant. Once hunger is satisfied, it no longer dominates the individual's awareness. However, if threatened with the deprivation of food or a food source, all concerns about higher-level needs will leave consciousness and the individual will be compelled to satisfy the physiological need. Modern cultures are organized to virtually eliminate concerns about physiological needs. Most of us simply take them for granted through the availability of food, stylish clothing, furnaces, and air conditioners to keep us protected and comfortable and the practice of modern medicine to preserve and prolong our lives. Only when threatened or victimized by emergencies that deprive us of these conveniences do we begin to recognize the potency of unsatisfied physiological needs. While usually not planning with any conscious awareness of "physiological needs," young couples desire to move from an apartment to their first house, middle-aged couples want to pay off their mortgage to ensure that they'll always have a roof over their heads, and older adults want to ensure that they won't be a burden to their children. These concerns reflect the driving capacity of the physiological needs. As such, a concern for these "future" needs reflects the next level in the hierarchy, which is the safety needs.

Safety Needs

Our need for a predictable and orderly world is an indication of our need for safety. People tend to organize their lives and rely on routine patterns as a way to feel secure. Generally, the need can be recognized among individuals whose behaviors reflect that they are trying to preserve and protect what they already have. For example, insurance policies protect us against financial harm, seat belts prevent bodily harm, burglar alarms provide peace of mind against home intrusion, classes in self-defense protect us against an assault, and so on. Safety needs are powerful motivators of behavior even though most of us live in a society in which we are already relatively safe and secure. Consider for a moment all the products and services that target our need for safety. Beyond the insurance policies and protective devices and services we've already mentioned, we don't have to think far ahead to uncover many more. Parents plan for their children's education to ensure a safe and secure future. Think of all the products and services associated with this need. The vitamin industry markets to our anxieties about heart disease, cancer, and obesity. Programs to reduce substance abuse among teenagers, detect weapons and bombs in airports, and maintain the purity of our environment are all focused on meeting our need for safety.

Belongingness Needs

When not preoccupied with the need for physiological satisfaction or safety, people become aware of their desire for human companionship and interaction. These needs include the desire for intimacy in a loving relationship as well as companionship from friends, social groups, and business relationships. In the absence of any or all of these relationships, the drive to satisfy this need can be perceived as just as powerful as previously unsatisfied needs for food and/or safety. When deprived of human companionship, the need will predominate the person's life. Once again, consider how products and services are designed to target our need for belongingness. We find ample evidence throughout history as well as in modern society of how we value the need for belongingness. The music we listen to, the books we read, and the movies we watch focus on fulfilling our desires for meaningful relationships. Certainly, products and services potently target our need for love and acceptance. Industries such as cosmetics, health clubs, and clothing revolve around our search for satisfying relationships. Closely related to our need for belongingness is the next higher-level need, the need for self-esteem.

Esteem Needs

According to Maslow, all normal people have a need or desire for self-respect that is firmly rooted in a high evaluation of themselves and an appreciation for who they are. In the mentally healthy individual, these needs are entirely normal, and their validity is based in actual achievements as well as evaluations from other people. Maslow goes on to say that the needs can be subclassified into the desire for

1. Strength, for achievement, for adequacy, for confidence in the face of the world, and for independence and freedom
2. Reputation or prestige, respect from others, recognition, attention, and a feeling of importance or appreciation

As these needs are satisfied, the individual is aware of feeling self-confident, worthwhile, strong, capable, adequate, and in general feeling useful and of value to the world. If the needs go unsatisfied, people tend to feel inferior, weak, helpless, and discouraged.

Self-Actualization

The concept of self-actualization relates to a person's desire to become whatever they are capable of becoming. The outcome and the means for getting there will vary from person to person. For one, it will be expressed athletically, for another musically, and for someone else mathematically. Through the course of a lifetime, the person may seek self-actualization through a variety of choices. The types and range of choices are limited only by the person's prior degree of movement through the hierarchy of needs as well as their own desires, interests, ingenuity, and degree of fulfillment.

To review, Maslow's hierarchy of needs includes

Level I	Physiological
Level II	Safety
Level III	Belonging
Level IV	Self-Esteem
Level V	Self-Actualization

The ranking of the five needs (Maslow's hierarchy) illustrates the Deficit Principle. This principle explains that we act to satisfy whatever need we are deprived of. Do the needs associated with one level have to be completely satisfied before the needs of a higher level exert influence on behavior? In a general sense, according to Maslow, probably so. Maslow refers to this state as the Progression Principle. When deprived of food and water, people are not likely preoccupied with making friends. Before being concerned with friendships, they must first satisfy their hunger. In our everyday lives, however, our needs and our awareness for satisfying them are seldom absolute. They overlap among the five levels. Consider an example:

Barbara: John, when you pull the car out of the garage, make sure you close the garage door. I don't mean to nag, but yesterday you left it open all day. I don't want to walk in the house when I get home from work to be greeted by an intruder.

John: You are starting to nag more and more lately and I'm getting tired of it.

What's Barbara's need? What level does it reflect? The answer clearly is level II—safety. Does that mean that she has not progressed beyond level II in any of the rest of her life? Of course not. Her concern for safety is integrated into a broad spectrum of needs across all five levels. However, the progression principle states that if she were preoccupied with safety and it infiltrated most of her mental life, she would not be aware of needs at any of the higher levels.

In John's case, his behavior reflects unsatisfied needs at level IV—self-esteem. His reaction to Barbara's concern about safety surfaced as a sensitivity to criticism. That doesn't mean he isn't concerned about safety or belonging or even self-actualization. It simply indicates that during the conversation, Barbara's behavior triggered his "neediness" in the area of self-esteem.

The hierarchy of needs can be used not only to "diagnose" the unsatisfied need, but also to develop an influence strategy for the purpose of changing the person's behavior. Remember Mr. Metler and the request by Mr. Hastings for his vote and the use of his yard for the political sign? What did the politician use to motivate Mr. Metler? To answer the question, first try to identify Mr. Metler's need. At first, the politician asked for Mr. Metler's vote and the use of his yard without any regard for Mr. Metler's state of need. As a result, he was unsuccessful. Mr. Metler resisted:

Mr. Metler: Move along now. I've got to finish up my chores here.

The breakthrough came only after Mr. Hastings realized Mr. Metler's needs (saving time and effort in order to do what he wanted such as sleep to satisfy his physiological needs, go to the football game with his friends to satisfy his need for belonging, or read to satisfy his need for self-actualization). Once he developed these insights (and they were only educated guesses), Mr. Hastings could then reframe these needs into an influence strategy—*a vote for me will mean spending less time leaf raking and more time doing what you want to do.*

Let's consider the case of the employee (Peter Manchester) whose manager (Sherry Walker) wanted him to broaden his work. Peter resisted as a matter of pride (his self-esteem was threatened). By talking to him only in terms of how he would need to change, Sherry only caused Peter to be more resistant. But by tying his needs (self-esteem and, to some extent, self-actualization) to the necessary direction for change, Sherry smoothly influenced Peter to take control of the change. In other words, while he didn't want to teach more classes (Sherry's objective), he did want to help develop a profit center in the company. Sherry pointed out that to achieve this objective, Peter would need to become more visible with senior managers. This made sense to Peter since the senior managers would need to approve the idea for the profit center. One way to become more visible would be for Peter to become an instructor in classes that senior managers would take. They could then get to know his competence and as a result would be confident in his ability to develop a profit center. Through her understanding of the hierarchy of needs, Sherry was able to link her objectives (establishing a direction) to Peter's needs and motivate Peter to change.

And going back to the situation between Barbara, John, and the garage door, we can observe that their communication broke down because they were talking across two different levels in the hierarchy of needs. As we discussed earlier, Janet was talking from the perspective of safety, whereas Peter was talking from his need for self-esteem. If they could recognize their mutual needs, they could more clearly communicate and stand a much better chance of either preventing or resolving their disagreement (more about communication in Chapter 8).

Influence Strategies that Pressure, Manipulate, and Deceive

As we have now seen, the first step for persuading someone to change is to understand what motivates that person. The hierarchy of needs is a useful tool to "diagnose" why people cling to a particular attitude and why they choose to do what they do. In order to change those attitudes and behaviors, first determine the underlying need. By identifying that need, you'll have discovered the current motivation. At that point, you can begin to consider from a wide array of influence strategies to replace current motivators with "new" motivators to move people closer to what you want them to do.

The knowledge that people can be changed as a result of determining their "needs" can be used for unfair advantage. An influence strategy would be "unethical" if the influencer tried to manipulate a person by withholding information or deceived her into believing she would receive a benefit when in fact she may not. Based on our discussion from Chapter 6, this is not only unethical, but it is risky in terms of consequences that could cause harm. To that extent, it is worthwhile to learn about these tactics in order to be prepared for them and to defend against them.

In his book entitled *Influence—The Psychology of Persuasion*, Robert Cialdini argues that influence strategies become weapons when placed in the wrong hands. According to Cialdini, influence strategies trigger "automatic" patterns of human behavior. In other words, people often respond to an influence strategy almost as though the response were a type of reflex. Just as when a doctor taps your knee with a rubber hammer to produce an involuntary movement, the use of certain influence strategies can trigger an automatic response. Cialdini claims that this stimulus–response pattern is somewhat like a computer program that runs through our human circuits. When the program runs, we respond in a way that we are "supposed to."

The reason for this automatic behavior, says Cialdini, is that it offers us "shortcuts" as alternatives for having to think through the otherwise thousands of decisions we make every day:

> We haven't the time, energy or capacity for it. Instead, we must very often use our stereotypes, our rules of thumb to classify things according to a few key features and then to respond mindlessly when one or another of these trigger features is present.

And as the decisions in our lives become more numerous and complex, we rely more and more on our "shortcuts" to reduce the amount of thinking we have to do.

One example that Cialdini offers is the use of coupons. The automatic response many of us have toward coupons is "discount." Some people go to great lengths to look for, cut out, save, catalog and eventually "cash-in" these little pieces of paper. "Coupon" equals "discount." That's the shortcut. In many cases, it is indeed a valuable shortcut. It saves us time and energy during our otherwise hectic day. The coupon offers a win–win relationship between the user (who now doesn't have to think about which product to buy) and the manufacturer (who makes a sale).

Now let's take a look at Cialdini's seven influence strategies: (1) reciprocity, (2) commitment/consistency, (3) social proof, (4) liking, (5) authority and (6) scarcity.

Reciprocity

The influence strategy of reciprocity relates to repaying other people "in-kind" for what they have given to us. Some examples are inviting people to parties after they have invited us, sending holiday cards in return for those sent to us, and making sure that we give someone a birthday present if they have given one to us. Doing a favor for someone or giving someone an unexpected gift tends to create a sense of obligation.

Here's one situation that will demonstrate reciprocity in action:

Johnny and his mom are at the pet store.

Johnny: Mom, look at this cute puppy. Can I hold him, Mom, please!

Mom: Absolutely not, John. I told you we would only stay a minute. Come on now, it's time to go.

Johnny: But, Mom, please, please!

Salesman: Hi, I couldn't help overhear. I don't mean to intrude, but it's fine for your son to hold a puppy. In fact, we appreciate it because they get to enjoy some companionship. Why don't we pick one out and go into our private petting room.

Mom: I, uh, don't think that would . . .

Salesman: Johnny, which one would you like to hold?

Johnny: That little white one with the cuddly fur and great big eyes.

Salesman: Good choice. Oh, is he going to like you! Now, Johnny, when I give him to you, you hold him nice and tight, okay?

Johnny: Mom, I can't wait. I'm so excited!

Salesman: Look how they are taking to one another. That little pup has a new best friend.

Mom: He's really cute.

Salesman: And very smart. His breed is known for not only being good with kids like Johnny, but they're quite intelligent.

Mom: Not that we're ready for a dog, but how much is he?

Salesman: Oh I'd have to go look up the price. You know what, I just had a thought. Hey, Johnny, it gets kind of cold here in the store when we close over the weekend. Do you have someplace at home that's real warm and real soft where he could stay maybe tomorrow and the next day?

Johnnie: You mean take him home with us? Could we really take him home with us?

Salesman: Well, only if it was okay with your mom and if you could think of someplace he could sleep.

Johnnie: He could sleep on my pillow. Oh, my pillow is so soft and I could keep him real warm, mister. Mom, please. Can we, can we?

Salesman: It would be perfectly okay, Ma'am. We'll pack up some of the pup's favorite food. We don't open again until Monday at noon, so there's no rush bringing him back. In fact, you can keep him even longer if you like.

Mom: Do we need to pay rent or a deposit for taking him?

Salesman: Absolutely not. It's our pleasure.

Mom: Well, I guess it would be okay. It might even be kind of fun. Okay, let's take him home.

Is reciprocity gong on here? Might Mom feel any obligation? Let's find out.

Us: Do you feel like you owe anything to this salesman?

Mom: Well, he was awfully nice. I've been thinking that at some point I should get John a pet. Now that the salesman let us take him home and sort of try him out, I can't very easily give my business to another pet store. Besides, John is already getting attached to the little dog. So I suppose I do feel some obligation.

Reciprocity is used quite often as an influence strategy by salesmen to create a sense of customer loyalty. Salesmen frequently buy dinners, give gifts, and provide entertainment to clients in the hope that they will feel that sense of obligation. Fund-raising organizations use the same method to "hook" prospective donors. Imagine getting a gift of holiday cards in a package from "mothers" who are asking for a small donation in order to get drunk drivers off the road. Will you throw the cards away? Will you send them back? Will you use them without making a donation? If you choose to do any of these things, you might end up feeling guilty and perhaps even ashamed of yourself. Wouldn't it be easier on your conscience if you just sent in a few dollars? If so, you just "complied" with the obligation that was created by the influence strategy of reciprocity.

Commitment

Cialdini describes an experiment in which the investigator of the project went to a crowded public beach and took along a large beach towel and a portable radio. In the first phase of the experiment, the investigator lay on the towel for a few minutes in order to establish a presence in that particular location. Suddenly, he stood up and walked down the beach until out of sight. At that point, a coexperimenter approached the towel, quickly swooped up the radio and started to run away. The objective of the study was to determine how many times over separate trials someone would try to stop the apparent "thief" from stealing the radio. Of the twenty people who clearly witnessed the "crime," only four tried to intervene. In the second phase of the experiment, the conditions remained the same except for one difference. Before the first experimenter walked away from the radio, he asked someone nearby if they would please keep an eye on the radio until he returned (in other words, "would you make a commitment to me?"). Under this condition, nineteen out of twenty people either questioned or physically restrained the thief. Their word was their bond.

According to Cialdini, once we have made a commitment, we behave in ways that are consistent with it. If we try to do otherwise, we will encounter personal and interpersonal pressures to get us back on track. Commitment and consistency are powerful motivators precisely because of these pressures. People whose behavior contradicts what they said they would do are often viewed as two-faced, untrustworthy and indecisive. Going back to the concept of public scrutiny, they are regarded with shame, scorn, and criticism. In contrast, people who are consistent in what they say and what they do are often regarded as strong, logical, rational, honest, trustworthy, and as having a sense of integrity.

How are commitment and consistency used as an influence strategy? Does someone believe in you? If so, they can influence you to do what they want by reminding you of "what you stand for." Do you hold a position in which you are expected to uphold morals and principles? If so, others can "leverage" your need to make sure you conform to their expectations. Let's consider some examples.

The marketing tactic of certain toy manufacturers is to create an intense demand for a toy shortly before the holiday season. Thousands of children see the ads on TV and plead with their parents to buy them the toy for the holidays.

> **Child:** Dad, look, here's that toy I told you about. Look, it's on TV now. See, there it is. Please, can I have it, oh please. Please, promise you'll buy it for me.
>
> **Dad:** I promise, I promise. We'll get it for you.

The only problem is that when Dad gets to the toy shop, they're sold out of the toy. Reassured by the customer service department at the toy store that they will hold the first one that comes in, Dad is directed to the next most popular toy that just happens to be made by the same manufacturer. How could he face his son if he came home empty-handed? After all, he did make a promise. He decides to purchase the alternate toy to ease his son's disappointment and to purchase the original toy (which had been underproduced on purpose) as soon as it arrives so as not to break his promise to his son. The toy manufacturer relies on the influence strategy of commitment and consistency to make a record-breaking profit for not only the months of the holiday season but also for the traditionally low-volume months that usually follow it.

A sophisticated "influencer" understands that the obstacle of fear protects a person from taking too big a leap into unfamiliar territory. There is danger in the unknown. So it is easier to influence a person to say "yes" to a much smaller decision that carries with it virtually no risk of getting hurt. That first yes represents a commitment. To build on that commitment and to expand it, the influencer proceeds to collect a sequence of yesses. At any time that the person resists, the influencer steps back to earlier commitments, neutralizes the resistance by removing the reasons to be afraid, and then once again proceeds until able to gain an unconditional commitment. Here's an example:

> **Ski Instructor:** You know that ski jump that they make in the Olympics? You know, the one where they ski down this steep incline, sail into the air, and then land effortlessly on the mountain to glide gracefully down on the glistening snow?
>
> **Reluctant Customer:** Sure, I've seen that on TV dozens of times.
>
> **Ski Instructor:** If I gave you a free ski rental, would you be willing to do that today?
>
> **Reluctant Customer:** What are you nuts! I've never had a pair of skis on in my life ("no" #1).
>
> **Ski Instructor:** Okay, I understand. But would you agree that even those Olympic skiers were beginners at one time and had to start somewhere?
>
> **Reluctant Customer:** Sure, I would agree with that ("yes" #1).
>
> **Ski Instructor:** Okay, would you at least be willing to try on a pair of skis today and just try to stand up here in the shop?
>
> **Reluctant Customer:** I guess so ("yes" #2).

Ski Instructor: And once you see you're able to stand up, would you allow me to put a one-inch elevation on the carpet here and help you lift your skis up onto that tiny one-inch elevation? Do you think that would be okay?

Reluctant Customer: Sure, I wouldn't see any harm in that ("yes" #3). How much would all that cost?

Ski Instructor: Not even a penny. Let's take it a step at a time and make sure you're comfortable with every little thing we do. What do you say, shall we give it a try?

Reluctant Customer: Let's do it ("yes" #4)!

Written statements also provide a way for the influencer to build a commitment from a person and then ensure that they will act consistently with it. Car salesmen use this approach when they ask the customer to sign a sales agreement that they will buy the car at that price.

Salesman: I stand a much better chance of getting my sales manager to agree to your price if I go in there with your signed sales contract.

The same kind of power to build commitment comes from asking for a deposit. Once again, these tactics tend to make a person feel bound to the agreement. After all, they've made a commitment. Surely they will honor it, right? No one wants to look like a hypocrite or be thought of as "wishy-washy," so we tend to follow through with what we said we would do, even when we no longer want to do it.

In her book *Talking Back to Sexual Pressure—What to Say to Resist Persuasion*, Elizabeth Powell describes a powerful example of this type of influence strategy that can be used to deceive and manipulate an innocent and unsuspecting person. Watch for the telltale signs of commitment and consistency.

Boy: Do you want me to take you home now or would it be okay if we stopped and talked for a while?

Girl: I'd like that.

Boy kisses girl.

Girl: I was hoping you would kiss me tonight.

Boy: I have a confession. Would you like to hear it?

Girl: Yes.

Boy: I wanted to kiss you since we first went out a few weeks ago.

Girl: Why didn't you?

Boy: Because I wanted you to know that I think what we have is special and that it was worth waiting for.

Boy kisses girl again.

Boy touches girl's shoulder and lowers his hand.

Girl pushes hand away.

Boy abruptly withdraws and moves away.

Girl: What's wrong?

Boy says nothing.

Girl: What's wrong? Why did you move away?

Boy: I've just made a complete fool of myself.

Girl: What? What are you talking about?

Boy says nothing.

Girl: I'm confused. I don't understand what you mean. Why do you think you made a fool of yourself?

Girl puts her hand on boy's hand.

Girl: Please tell me.

Boy: I thought we had something special. I thought you really cared about me. I can see now that you think I'm just another guy who only wants one thing and that really hurts. Look, I'm really sorry. Why don't we just go?

Girl: You are special to me. You are special to me. I don't want to go home now. I want to stay here with you.

Girl kisses boy.

Girl positions boy's hand.

What happened here? The girl resisted. The boy said a few words. Then the resistance was neutralized. Was the boy being sincere? Not according to Powell. Unsuspecting women aren't the only ones who need to beware of this tactic. It is a potent use of the power of commitment and consistency. Here's how it works. The implied (unspoken) messages are in italics.

Boy: I thought we had something special.

> *(The girl's silence signals a concession.)*

I thought you really cared about me.

> *(The girl's silence signals another concession.)*

I can see now that you think I'm just another guy who only wants one thing and that really hurts.

> *(Having made two unspoken concessions, the girl is now being set up to feel guilty for doubting the boy's intentions. She is being led to believe that she broke a commitment—so she feels ashamed of herself.)*

Look, I'm really sorry. Why don't we just go?

> *(The boy offers "proof" that he is honorable by getting upset that she could even think he was taking advantage of her. He's behaving consistently; she's behaving inconsistently. To prove that she is not a hypocrite, she must demonstrate that she doesn't believe he was taking advantage of her and so she makes the final concession.)*

What we've just observed is a powerful weapon in the hands of a deceitful tactician. Powell labels it as such and warns prospective victims to be ever the wiser for its use.

Another common example of commitment and consistency is the use of political scare tactics.

Political Candidate: My opponent promises to lower taxes. Just look at his record during the last term. He's raised taxes more than any other president in the history of this country. *(Notice the allegation of inconsistency.)* Now look at my record. When I was governor, I promised to lower taxes and, by God, I lowered taxes. *(The message is that he makes a commitment and his behavior is consistent with that commitment.)*

As with each of the influence strategies, commitment and consistency can be used in ways that are fair and balanced (Chapter 6) or in ways that break promises and cause harm. Influence strategies are nothing more than tools. If you use them with integrity, people will respond by trusting you and wanting to continue their relationships with you. However, if you use them with an intent to deceive, and that intent is discovered, people will judge you as duplistic and as someone to avoid for any future relationships.

Social Proof

The principle of social proof states that one way we can determine what is "correct" or "best" is to find out what other people think is correct or best. The principle is more effective when there are conditions of uncertainty or unfamiliarity and when the other people are those we know and respect. We tend to value the opinions of others who have succeeded in the past, who are already credible in our minds, and who may be recognized as celebrities or experts. This principle often works well to help reduce uncertainty. Generally, we feel that when we do what others are doing and they appear to be doing okay, we'll be okay too.

As an influence strategy, social proof can be easily recognized.

Life Insurance Salesman: I want to help as best I can. Let me tell you about a fellow just like you who thought he had enough life insurance. Despite what I tried to tell him, he took the least expensive policy. He died six months later, leaving his wife with no means to send his kids to college and virtually no money to even make ends meet.

Fund-Raiser: Listen to those phones ringing. Call in and join the hundreds of caring folks in our city.

TV Commercial: I lost fifty pounds in three weeks and developed "washboard" abs with the Roll-O-Plex Ab Toner.

The message is that if it works for us, it can work for you. If you trust us, follow us. Yet, as with any of the influence strategies that Cialdini describes, social proof is based on the notion that it is a shortcut for thinking. In this case, we make the assumption that if a lot of others are doing it, they must know something we don't. They may not. They may just be blindly following the crowd. Second, just because other people are doing it, even hundreds or thousands of people, does not necessarily make it correct or best.

Liking

One of the greatest success stories that illustrates the strategy of liking is that of Joe Girard. Girard sold Chevrolets in record numbers. Among his secrets was to find out the birthdays of his prospective clients and send them birthday cards. He developed a personal relationship with them and created the illusion that he was their friend. It's gratifying to be liked. All else being equal, who would you buy a car from, someone who made you feel liked or someone who made you feel like what you really were, a perfect stranger?

As an influence strategy, there is nothing inherently deceitful about "liking." Treating people with dignity, respect, and courteousness goes a long way toward building cooperative relationships in which productive business can take place. Consider the marked contrast in the following two examples at an airline check-in counter.

Dissatisfied Traveler: Young lady, my wife and I were seated in different rows on this flight and I wonder if you can seat us together.

Attendant: Sir, I'm sorry there's nothing I can do about it. All of the seats are full.

Dissatisfied Traveler: Then upgrade us to first class.

Attendant: I can't do that, sir.

Dissatisfied Traveler: The hell you can't. We both know it's done all the time. I'll just book with another airline next time. I want to talk to your supervisor.

Attendant: My supervisor will just tell you the same thing, sir.

Dissatisfied Traveler: Do I get to talk to your supervisor or not?

Attendant: Certainly, sir.

Supervisor: May I help you?

Dissatisfied Traveler: Your rude attendant told me there was nothing either she or you could do to get my wife and I seated together on this flight. No wonder your airline is going broke. You're all too stupid to take care of your customers. I want you to seat us in first class.

Supervisor: Sir, as Miss Jones explained, it's not our policy to upgrade our coach customers. We can book you on another flight.

Dissatisfied Traveler: That's not acceptable. Who's your boss? I'm going to write him a letter. In fact, I'm going to send a letter to your competitor and give them some ammunition they can use against you.

Supervisor: I'm sorry I couldn't help you, sir. Here is the address of our regional sales executive.

Now compare what just happened with this example:

Dissatisfied Traveler: My wife and I were booked in different rows. Can you help us out?

Attendant: I'm sorry, sir, all seats are filled. I can book you on a different flight.

Dissatisfied Traveler: No, that won't work. We need to get home as soon as possible. Can you upgrade us to first class?

Attendant: I'm afraid not. That's against our policy.

Dissatisfied Traveler: Can I talk to your supervisor?

Attendant: Of course, but he'll just tell you the same thing. I'll get him on my line and explain what we've talked about so far. Then, he'll come on and you can talk to him. Would that be okay?

Dissatisfied Traveler: That would be fine. Thanks for listening and explaining your policy to me.

Supervisor: Hi, I'm Jim Appleby.

Dissatisfied Traveler: Thanks for taking the call. My name is Fred Aptman. My wife and I were booked in different rows. The attendant I just spoke to was very patient and took the time to explain the policy to me. I want you to know I appreciate her courteousness and her patience. It must be very trying to deal with people like us all day.

Supervisor: Actually, it's people like you who make our job so much easier. Most folks under the same circumstances get pretty tense and seldom show us their best sides.

Dissatisfied Traveler: I'll bet. I understand that your normal policy doesn't permit you to upgrade coach passengers to first class.

Supervisor: That's right.

Dissatisfied Traveler: Mr. Appleby, I wonder if you would consider making an exception. We really need to get home on this flight. Since this is the last part of a vacation planned for months, it would just about be ruined if we had to sit apart for a three-hour flight. Do you think you might be able to help us out?

Supervisor: Can you hold the line, Mr. Aptman? Let me see what I can do. (*Returns after about two minutes.*) Mr. Aptman, as the attendant explained, we don't normally upgrade our passengers to first class. I was able to find a special coupon that was part of a promotion. I can fax it to the check-in counter at the airport. Would you be able to pick it up?

Dissatisfied Traveler: Certainly. I really appreciate that you can do this.

Supervisor: The fact is, I didn't think I could. I'm virtually certain I couldn't do it again, but in any case I've enjoyed talking with you and I hope you and your wife have a good flight.

Authority

Findings from numerous research investigations indicate that people will often comply with an order from an authority figure without ever thinking to question it. Doctors' orders have been a prime example. As a result, unnecessary surgeries have been documented, incorrect limbs have been amputated, and even deaths have occurred due to prescriptions given to the wrong patients.

In some cases, grown adults with healthy egos fail to question authority figures. When stopped by a police officer, how many of us simply surrender our driver's license before asking why we were pulled over? When given a grade that's less than what we think we deserve on an exam, how many of us give up our right to question the professor's judgment? "It's rude." "It shows disrespect." "We might make things worse."

Yet, "authority" is an influence strategy. Once again, it is a shortcut for thinking. That doesn't mean that it should not be used to lead someone to a particular outcome. But its use should be bound by the principle of mutual gain and fairness rather than deception and manipulation.

Scarcity

The last influence strategy that Cialdini describes is scarcity. If stores are about to run out of a product, most of us feel the need to stock up whether we need to or not. The trouble is that some advertisers create a sense of urgency when there really is none. The psychological motivator in the scarcity principle is the fear that we will lose our sense of control. Given a normal sense of mental balance, if we are threatened with an impending loss of something that has been readily available, we move to maintain control by trying to prevent that loss. With the prospect of losing what we've had, we may even inflate its value and either pay more than its traditional worth or go to extraordinary efforts to make sure we don't lose it.

If, in fact, scarcity is a reality, its use as an influence strategy is entirely ethical and justified. However, if a sense of urgency is manufactured, it is done with an intent to deceive and is therefore unfair and manipulative.

Gambits—Maneuvers for Advantage

Cialdini's book was written to explain the psychological underpinnings that render people vulnerable to "unethical" influence strategies. Roger Dawson describes similar tactics in his book *You Can Get Anything You Want—But You Have to Do More Than Ask*. However, instead of focusing on psychology, Dawson describes the tactics as methods of negotiation. Dawson's methods are called gambits. According to Dawson, a gambit is "a maneuver for advantage." Just like the strategies described by Cialdini, these gambits can easily deceive and manipulate the unsuspecting person into complying with the desires of the influencer. We'll consider (1) reluctance, (2) the flinch, (3) the vise, (4) the nibble, (5) higher authority, and (6) the split-the-difference split.

Reluctance

The objective of this gambit is to lower the other person's expectations that you will do what he wants. Despite how interested you might really be, you pretend that you're not in order to lower his expectations. The phrase "playing hard to get" captures the essence of reluctance. As an example, when a consultant delivers a proposal that could make huge profits for your company, a "reluctance" gambit might be "Mr. Epworth, thank you for all the time you've put into this proposal. Your quote is certainly fair. As you can imagine, we are considering many others, and we're in no hurry to move on it right away. But just to be fair, if we were to consider your proposal, let's put aside your quote. If we were to make a decision today, and we probably wouldn't, but if we could reach an agreement, what's the lowest figure you could agree to right now?"

The Flinch

The objective of the flinch is also to lower the other person's expectations. You react to her proposal or request with utter astonishment. The intent is to show your shock at the nerve of her to ask for whatever she is asking. An example would be "Ms. Jones, what kind of figure did you have in mind for a salary with our company?" When Ms. Jones replies "$50,000," you flinch (a loud voice with a questioning tone) "FIFTY thousand dollars? Ms. Jones, I don't know where you got the idea that we would ever pay FIFTY thousand dollars." What makes this gambit deceitful is that your budget for the position is well above that amount, and Ms. Jones is worth even more than what you could afford to pay her. But you're using the gambit to lower her expectations in order to come out ahead and force her to take a loss.

The Vise

Like the first two gambits, the vise is also intended to lower expectations. The phrase is simply "you'll have to do better than that." Here's how it works. "Mr. Wilmont, what did you think of the report I submitted on the Fairfax project?" Mr. Wilmont responds with, "Jenkins, you'll have to do better than that." When Jenkins inquires what else he could do (he felt really good about the work he had already done), Mr. Wilmont replies, "Are you saying it couldn't be any better?" The gambit is manipulative in that it preys on Jenkins's need for security and self-esteem without giving him the fair and balanced feedback he certainly deserves.

The Nibble

In this gambit, the influencer first leads the other person to believe that they've reached an agreement. The gambit is particularly effective in manipulating and deceiving the other person if the two parties have invested a great deal of time and energy into their discussion. "Mr. Forsythe, have we reached an understanding that your company will purchase fifty Ztech computers?" Mr. Forsythe replies with, "Let me make sure I understand the terms, Mr. Westchester. The price of each computer is $1,875. We will agree to these terms if you include the surge protectors at $25 each and the delivery charge of $5.75 each." What makes this a gambit is that Westchester purposely complicated the issue of the purchase price and caused Mr. Forsythe to doubt whether or not they would ever reach an agreement. The tactic in part was to wear him down, cause him to be frustrated and worried, and then finally to give him a feeling of relief that the agreement would go through. Then, when Forsythe thought they had reached an agreement, Westchester "nibbled." To preserve the agreement, Forsythe feels pressured to give away hundreds of dollars.

The Higher Authority

The influencer pretends that even though the counterpart's terms are fair and reasonable, approval would have to be given by a higher authority such as a boss, a sales manager, a partner, or maybe a spouse. The "trick" is that the counterpart never gets to meet or talk with this mysterious person who has "absolute power." The influencer says something like, "I think that's a great offer. Let me see what I can do." Then, the influencer returns with the bad news that despite her hardest effort, the "higher authority" will not agree to the proposed terms. After several back-and-forth attempts, the influencer "succeeds" in convincing the higher authority to make a concession, which is inconsequential in comparison to what the counterpart was hoping for. This gambit is similar to the "good guy–bad guy" gambit that is typical in many car dealerships where the salesperson is your "friend" and will "fight" for you with her sales manager. The gambit is of course based in deceit in order to lower your expectations and convince you that your offer was never reasonable. If successful, the gambit puts the influencer and the higher authority at a significant strategic advantage. By manipulating and deceiving the person making the offer, the gambit results in an overpayment by the buyer and unfairly gained profits for the seller.

The Split-the-Difference Split

This gambit begins with the more basic gambit of "splitting the difference." For example, "Mr. Fryman, you offered $1,500 for our painting that we have priced at $2,000. How about if we split the difference and agree on a price of $1,750? By combining this gambit with "higher authority," the process is manipulative and the results are deceiving. Here's how it works. "Mr. Fryman, I think we could split the difference and agree on $1,750. Let me check with my partner first." Later, the seller returns and says, "Mr. Fryman, I'm terribly sorry and, I have to tell you, very upset. My partner will not agree. We priced it at $2,000 and you graciously agreed to come up from your generous offer of $1,500 to $1,750. But my partner says we just can't go down that much. There's one more possibility. Suppose we split the difference again. What I mean by that is that we are now just $250 apart. My partner and I are at $2,000 and you are at $1750.00. Suppose we agree on a price of $1,875. In fact, if you'd be willing to agree on that price, I'll sign the agreement without even consulting my partner. What do you say?" Is this deceitful? Is Mr. Fryman being manipulated? What would you say if you found out there never was a partner? The seller made it all up, strategically positioned Mr. Fryman to believe the partner was a higher authority, and positioned him to fall for a gambit. That gambit caused him to pay $1,875 for an item that the seller would have likely sold for the original offer of $1,500.

To summarize, our needs can sometimes render us very vulnerable to being manipulated and deceived. Leadership, by itself, is not necessarily ethical. As we know, history is filled with accounts of leaders who have violated human rights, caused people to suffer unspeakable horrors, and even resulted in the ruin and destruction of countries and cultures. On the other hand, leadership can be uplifting, glorifying, and cause changes that advance technology and the quality of life itself. Such leadership is usually based on influence strategies that bring benefits not only to the leader but to the followers as well. Such leadership is based on influence strategies that do not deceive or manipulate but instead are fair, balanced, principled, and ethical.

The Power of Fairness

One of the most powerful and at the same time ethical strategies for influencing people is described in *Getting to Yes* by Roger Fisher and William Ury. The now famous book is a description of how to get what you want through what Fisher and Ury call "principled negotiation." Unlike other styles of negotiating which are based on "gambits" or tricks, Fisher and Ury's approach is based on the principle of fairness. Here's how it works.

Let's say that you want to buy a house. You find an ad in the Sunday paper for a house that sounds like it's exactly what you're looking for. You call up the owner who is listing it himself, make an appointment, and take a tour. Since you like what you see, you decide to start talking about the price.

You: I like your house and want to talk about the price.

Owner: What about the price? It's listed at $185,000. The price is firm. That's what I've listed it for and that's what I'll take. Unless, of course, you want to offer me more.

You: $185,000. That's an interesting number. How did you come up with that number?

Owner: I told you. That's what I want for the house. I won't take a penny less.

You: That's not what I asked you. I asked how you determined that $185,000 was your selling price.

Owner: Look, mister, I'm not into these haggling games. Do you want the house or not?

You: Well, I don't know yet. I can tell you that I'm interested in the house. I just want to make sure that the price I pay is really a fair price.

Owner: Are you saying my price isn't fair?

You: That's my point. I don't know if it's fair or not.

Owner: Why wouldn't it be fair?

You: Well, it may be. And if it is, I will gladly pay you what you are asking. I just need to be convinced that it is a fair price.

Owner: Well, it is a fair price.

You: Maybe it is. May I tell you what I've found out so far before I looked at the house?

Owner: I suppose so.

You: Well, I did a little research and found out that there were five houses on the same block as this one that sold within the last eighteen months. Now I know that covers a lot of time. I need to take that into consideration since houses have gone up in value recently. Anyway, these houses all had the same floor plan as this one, and they were built within two years of this one. What's puzzling to me is that these five houses sold anywhere from $128,000 to $142,000. So you see, I'm having trouble convincing myself that this house is worth $185,000. Have you added some rooms or done some structural remodeling?

Owner: No.

You: Is the lot size substantially larger than other homes in the area?

Owner: Not really.

You: I see. Then, maybe I'm missing something. Can you help me convince myself why I should pay nearly $40,000 more for this house than any of the others that sold around here?

Owner: Look, mister. Maybe it is priced a little high. Would you pay $175,000 for it?

You: Hmm, $175,000. Again, please don't interpret my question as disrespectful, but how did you arrive at that number? Do you have an appraisal that says the house is worth that amount? I want to offer you what the house is worth. The reason that's so important to me is that I want to be fair to you and I want to be fair to me. Can you think of a way we can accomplish that?

The fairness principle is an influence strategy that is inherently and visibly straightforward. To make it work, one or both parties search for mutual benefits, objective information, past practices, and whatever else they can identify to ensure that each is getting what they want without jeopardizing the other person.

It can certainly be combined with other influence strategies such as liking, reciprocity, and social proof as long as there is no intent to manipulate, cover up information, or deceive the other person.

The Power of Reason
(Logic and Cause and Effect)

The ability to influence someone ultimately depends on the power to shift the direction of their thinking. One way of doing so is to use force. In other words, either you do it my way "or else." While force can temporarily overpower resistance, once it is removed, the one who was forced usually finds a way to either retaliate or at the very least resume the original behavior. As an influence strategy, force can overpower behavior but has little effect over a person's thinking, which drives behavior.

The influence strategies that we've discussed in this chapter are powerful precisely because they attempt to change the way people think. Once their thinking shifts into the "desired" direction, they themselves will change their own behavior to fit the "new" way they think.

To illustrate this principle (change their thinking to change their behavior), let's return to the pro–con (double-T) chart we developed for Mr. Stipple.

Manufacture/Distribute for Paper Only		Expand/Specialize for Electronics	
Benefits	**Risks**	**Benefits**	**Risks**
Keep current customers happy. Retained employees do what they have always done which avoids stress associated with change. I continue to be the expert and in control of the entire operation. Maintain relationships with current suppliers including cost advantages and preferred delivery schedules. Continue to use existing manufacturing machines and equipment. Overall costs are predictable; new expenses are kept to a minimum.	Risk buyout from larger companies. Competitors may expand and take away our current customers. Market will likely continue to shrink. Operating capital would dry up. Stipple's would need to lay off loyal employees. Production schedules could be delayed. We could lose even more customers. Face even greater losses and spiral into bankruptcy. Market is rapidly drying up which means less and less need for Stipple's as we now are.	Make products that meet customers' needs. Build on our reputation among our current customers. Expand into a company of the future with new technologies and work processes to produce the best "electronics" for office use in the world! Give our loyal employees something to hope for—new and exciting work, the chance for job security. Share the burdens with business associates from the executive staff rather than retain all the burden myself. Keep the company alive & prosperous.	A great deal of capital needs to be invested in a start-up venture—new machines, work processes, training, marketing, equipment. I currently know little about the new products and markets. I need to work with people I don't even know yet. Current production, customers, profits could dry up while we convert to the new system. Stipple's would be competing with companies already established in the industry; they could eat us alive. We would need enough funds to meet our costs for at least two years which could erode our economic base if we don't make a profit by then.
Status quo	**Lose everything**	**Build a future!**	**Lose everything**

Remember when we first discussed Mr. Stipple's case? The reason Mr. Stipple is uncertain about what to do is because he's locked into a paradigm. His paradigm is that "office supplies" equals "paper." To change his paradigm requires that he change (or someone change for him) his thinking. And to change his thinking, he must be given reasons. That's precisely what the double T-chart does. You only have to look at it to discover that it is literally filled with reasons. The most powerful reasons for changing are located right in the center of the chart. Look at the risks column on the left side and the benefits column on the right side. These two columns offer a "cause–effect" logic that builds a strong case for making a change from the old way to the new way. Here's the way it works:

1. Say the first two benefits.
   We could better meet our customers' needs and build on our reputation with our current customers.
2. Say the new idea.
   If we shift our focus from paper products to electronic products . . .
3. Say the old idea.
   But if we limit ourselves to paper products . . .
4. Say the first two losses.
   We risk buyout from larger companies and our competitors might expand and take away our current customers.

Notice the logic. The new idea causes benefits. The old idea causes losses. The new idea could make our sweetest dreams come true. The old idea could cause our worst nightmares to come true. To strengthen the persuasiveness of the argument, continue to give reasons using the same sequence of (1) benefits, (2) new idea, (3) old idea, and (4) losses.

> We could expand into a company of the future with new technologies and produce the best products by shifting our focus to electronics. But by staying with paper, the market will likely continue to shrink, our operating capital would dry up, and Stipple's would need to lay off our loyal employees.
> On the other hand, we could keep our loyal employees, give them new and exciting work to do, and provide them with some real hopes for job security if we concentrate on electronics. Our old paper-based focus might cause us to lose even more customers and might spiral us into bankruptcy, which means we could lose everything.
> So, we stand a greater chance of keeping the company alive and prosperous and building ourselves a wonderful future if we move into electronics.

What about the risks of charging ahead? Clearly, they need to be considered carefully. To do so, we consult the first column on the left side of the chart (the benefits of the old way) and the last column on the right side of the chart (the risks of the new way). Once we conclude that it makes sense to proceed because the risks can be managed, then we can use the persuasive sequence of (1) the new idea results in benefits and (2) the old idea causes losses. This sequence and logic is not only powerful, but also incorporates a fair and balanced approach to decision making and persuasion.

Summary

The information in this chapter has been based on the notion that at the very core of leadership is the ability to influence people. We have considered influence strategies from the perspectives of resistance to change, our vulnerability to influence strategies based on our human needs, the types of influence strategies that manipulate and deceive people into compliance, and the types of influence strategies that persuade people to change based on principles of fairness and mutual gain.

The next chapter will describe methods for communicating clearly in order build effective working relationships. The material will cover both interpersonal communication skills such as listening and problem solving and presentation skills including vocal and visual methods for delivering effective presentations.

Bibliography

Blanchard, Kenneth, *Leadership and the One Minute Manager* (New York: Morrow, 1985).

Bennis, Warren, and Joan Goldsmith, *Learning to Lead* (New York: Addison-Wesley, 1997).

Cialdini, Robert, *Influence—The Psychology of Persuasion* (New York: William Morrow, 1993).

Clark, Kenneth, and Miriam Clark, *Choosing to Lead* (Richmond, VA: Leadership Press, 1994).

Clark, Kenneth, and Miriam Clark, *Measures of Leadership* (West Orange, NJ: Library of America, 1990).

Dawson, Roger, *You Can Get Anything You Want—But You Have to Do More than Ask* (New York: Simon & Schuster, 1985).

Fisher, Roger, and William Ury, *Getting to Yes* (New York: Houghton-Mifflin, 1981).

George, Jennifer, and Gareth Jones, *Understanding and Managing Organizational Behavior* (New York: Addison-Wesley, 1996).

Kotter, John, *Leadership—A Force for Change* (New York: Free Press, 1990).

Powell, Elizabeth, *Talking Back to Sexual Pressure—What to Say to Resist Persuasion* (Minneapolis: CompuCare, 1991).

Mayer, Robert, *Power Plays—How to Negotiate, Persuade, and Finesse Your Way to Success in any Situation* (New York: Random House, 1996).

Rosen, Robert, *Leading People* (New York: Viking-Penguin, 1996).

Tichy, Noel, and Mary Anne Devanna, *The Transformational Leader* (New York: John Wiley & Sons, 1986).

Trout, Jack, and Steve Rivkin, *The New Positioning* (New York: McGraw-Hill, 1996).

CHAPTER 8

Communication Skills

You have now learned how to establish a direction for leadership, anticipate consequences, and use influence strategies for persuading people to follow your lead. The final step is to communicate your thinking in ways that others will quickly understand and find meaningful in their own lives.

The communication skills in this chapter are divided into two primary areas. The first is a set of methods for preventing and resolving interpersonal problems within relationships. Included are skills in the areas of listening, assertive confrontation, and collaboration. The second is a set of methods to help you manage the attention of any sized audience through effective presentation skills. Included are techniques for capturing and maintaining attention by controlling how you look, how you sound, and what you say.

The Relationship Life Cycle

The Relationship Life Cycle is a theoretical model that represents how relationships develop, function, and in some cases disintegrate. The unsuccessful relationship follows a sequence of events marked by accumulating tensions over unresolved conflicts that ends in the termination of the relationship. The successful relationship follows a cycle through which conflicts are confronted and resolved so that the productive functions of the relationship are maintained. The model applies to business as well as social and family relationships.

The model consists of up to eleven phases that will each be described in detail. To facilitate your understanding of the model, we will be looking at a case study, "the Owner versus the Manager," as we proceed through the various steps of a working relationship.

Credibility

The first step in the model is *credibility*. In this stage, the prospective members evaluate their impressions of each other. This process may take place formally or informally. A formal evaluation might include reviewing résumés and professional testimonials. An informal evaluation might include an opinion from a mutual friend. Credibility is established when each of the prospective members believes that the other person can perform the functions expected within the relationship (see Figure 8-1). The members may not have even met each other as yet. (If the mutual scrutiny is favorable to both parties, the relationship proceeds to the next step, which is called Becoming Acquainted.)

FIGURE 8-1   The Relationship Life Cycle: Establishing Credibility

The Owner versus the Manager

Barbara Collins is the owner of a video store. Her husband Nathan, who established the business, recently died from a heart attack. Mrs. Collins knows very little about running a store, or about business practice in general. She placed an ad for a manager in a local trade journal. The person who responded was a man named John Baker. His credentials indicated that he currently managed a video store in a major shopping mall. Letters of reference documented that had it not been for Mr. Baker's expertise, the owners of the store would have been forced to go out of business. Instead, Mr. Baker had increased their profits significantly in less than one year. In his cover letter, John Baker remarked that, although he was happy in his current position, the job description for Mrs. Collins's store fit very closely with his career objectives.

Becoming Acquainted

The second step is becoming acquainted. This process may include interviews, as might occur within a job setting, or informal conversations over coffee in a first-time social meeting. The nature of the interaction helps each person determine the other's qualifications for stepping into the roles of the potential relationship. Each person measures each other against his or her expectations and personal desires. For example, the members of an audience might realize that a speaker's personal warmth is just as sincere as their master of ceremonies had led them to expect. As another example, a couple of college coeds might blissfully discover that they really do have as much in common as their matchmaking friends had promised. In either case, the individuals learn firsthand of the other's characteristics and qualifications. The relationship may terminate at this stage if either party is not satisfied. (See Figure 8-2.)

FIGURE 8-2　The Relationship Life Cycle: Becoming Acquainted

Mrs. Collins was impressed by the documents Mr. Baker had forwarded. She decided that she would invite him for an interview. He arrived promptly, was dressed appropriately, and expressed appreciation for the opportunity to learn more about the position. His conversation revealed that he knew a great deal about the video industry as well as about retail business. He acknowledged to Mrs. Collins that he would eventually like to develop a franchise of video stores that could operate at such volume that the price of movie rentals could be lower than any of the competitions'.

　　From John's point of view, Mrs. Collins badly needed help. She seemed to be a nice person who wanted to make her business succeed. He learned that her husband had died shortly after he opened the store. His death left Mrs. Collins with a considerable financial obligation and virtually without resources to run the business. John sensed that she would give him a considerable amount of autonomy. Through his expertise and her support, he believed they would make the business a great success.

Forming Attachments

In the next stage, the individuals form attachments to each other. Each has so far invested a certain degree of time and energy into the prospect of developing the relationship. As the process of becoming acquainted continues, each person begins to relax defensive guards and develops early forms of trust. Once this early trust begins to emerge, the individuals form an interconnective bond that represents the shell of the newly developing relationship. Each would feel at least some sense of regret and disappointment if the relationship did not develop beyond this point. (See Figure 8-3.)

Mrs. Collins began to get her hopes up that John would accept her offer for the position. She believed that he could run the store well. His self-confidence and authoritative manner gave her a sense of strength that made her feel that the business could succeed. He seemed to know what he was talking about, had great visions for what the store could accomplish, and had the courage

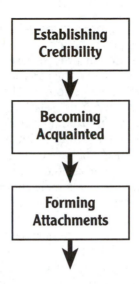

FIGURE 8-3   The Relationship Life Cycle: Forming Attachments

*to make it all work. She worried though that he might not feel challenged
enough in such a small-time operation.*

*John hoped he hadn't come on too strong. This lady seemed anxious any-
way. The last thing she needed was some high pressure type person to shake
up what little self-confidence she had. He really did want the position. By
building it to its economic potential, he could make a great deal of money
and perhaps eventually move into a partnership.*

Clarifying Roles and Defining Expectations

Following the attachment stage, the individuals take an active role in developing the
relationship by formulating the functions of each member. An effective leader will
specify the tasks that she expects the subordinate to perform. The subordinate will
indicate the extent of his willingness and ability to comply with these expectations.
Negotiations may occur; limitations will be defined; and consequences for hard work,
success, and failure will be delineated.

The participants in this phase of the Relationship Life Cycle will define their expectations and clarify relationship roles through two possible channels. One channel
is direct negotiations, and the other is through a process called modeling. Through
the direct route of negotiation, the roles that each participant would like to perform
as well as have the other person perform are put on the table for discussion. Participants air their differences, discuss prospects for compromise, and ultimately resolve
the issues. They might begin discussing roles as defined by the job description. The
subordinate might state reasons for wanting to change certain aspects of the proposed
position, such as working hours, benefits, and compensation. After considering the
subordinate's needs and wishes, the leader might adapt his or her expectations and
modify the proposed roles in ways that might work for both parties.

The process of defining expectations and clarifying roles could also occur through modeling. Modeling determines roles within the relationship through an unconscious process based on role models from the participants' previous relationships. That is, the participants "carve out" their respective roles in ways they may be totally unconscious of. The structure of people's lives is often determined by past influences. Adults' relationships frequently resemble relationships that shaped their lives as children. For example, a male subordinate might expect that a female boss will behave toward him the way his mother related to him as a child. The female boss might behave toward a male subordinate either in a manner similar to the way her mother related to her father or in the way she herself related to her younger brothers. The female subordinate might expect her male boss to treat her the way her father treated her mother, the way her father treated her, or the way her older brothers treated her.

To illustrate how past models really do affect one's current relationships, consider who performs certain roles in your own family today. For example, who washes the clothes and who mows the lawn? Who makes arrangements for the babysitter and who pays the check in a restaurant? Now consider the family you grew up in. Are the roles that you currently perform in your relationships more similar to those that your mother performed or to those that your father performed? If what you are doing now is in any way similar to the things your parents did when you were a child, then the roles that characterize your current relationship have probably been influenced by the process of modeling.

Modeling is no more or less effective a means for determining roles within a relationship than is negotiation, as long as it works. When it does not, you can make your expectations much clearer to the other person by expressing them openly through the process of negotiation. As a result, both of you have a better chance of finding out what you want for yourselves and from the other person. (See Figure 8-4.)

Both Mrs. Collins and John Baker felt optimistic about the prospects for their working relationship. Mrs. Collins stated very clearly that John would have freedom to make decisions regarding matters that concerned the day-to-day operations of the store. She expected him to consult with her prior to altering any of the existing store policies.

John indicated his willingness to work in line with her expectations. However, he did not feel that he could accept the position at the salary that she offered him. With his knowledge of the video industry and his realistic potential for increasing the store's profits, he believed that he should have more money. He clearly stated the dollar figure he needed in order to become the store manager.

Mrs. Collins considered his comments for a long time. However, she said that she could not meet the figure. After a great deal of discussion, they developed a plan through which John could share any profits that would exceed the store's current level of net receipts.

Mrs. Collins felt tremendous relief when John accepted the position. She was certain that the prospects for paying off her business loan were no longer in question. John was someone that she could count on to make the business run the way Nathan had developed it. After all, he had intended it to be a neighborhood store. Their customers were their friends and neighbors. New customers had come in by word of mouth. Nathan loved to cater to them. She sensed that this warmth toward people was just as important to John.

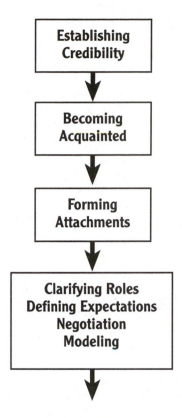

FIGURE 8-4   The Relationship Life Cycle: Clarifying Roles and Defining Expectations

As for John, the position was ideal. He would finally have his own store to run the way he saw fit; no more having to answer to some corporation that ran the operation from across the country. He knew he could bring Mrs. Collins around to the latest trends in the industry. It might take time, but he had a way with people like her.

Integration and Commitment

Once the roles have been clarified and mutually understood, the individuals strengthen their attachment to each other, forming what becomes a sense of integration and commitment. They begin to regard each other as members of a functioning unit. They develop camaraderie and loyalty to each other as well as to the organization itself. People outside of the unit recognize the relationship as a separate and viable entity. (See Figure 8-5.)

Mrs. Collins held a special sale to introduce the community to her new manager. She walked John up to people arm in arm and talked about how Nathan would have been so proud to have him on board.

John praised the Collins family for their service to the community. He greeted the customers on behalf of the store and talked to them about the movies they would like the store to carry.

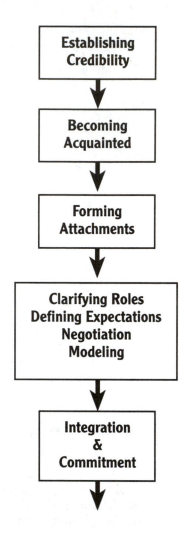

FIGURE 8-5 The Relationship Life Cycle: Integration & Commitment

Stability

As the individuals begin performing the roles, the relationship becomes operational, serving the purpose of fulfilling the collective and individual needs of its members. In a business setting, the relationship accomplishes the company's objectives. In a social setting, the relationship takes care of interpersonal needs. As the needs and objectives are met through the functions carried out by the members, the relationship enters a period of stability. It runs smoothly and does what the individual members expect it to do. Each member performs the functions in accordance with the other's expectations, and neither behaves in a surprising or disturbing manner. (See Figure 8-6.)

Throughout the first quarter after John became store manager, the amount of business began to grow noticeably. With Mrs. Collins's approval, he implemented a system for checking out the videotapes by computer. Customers were thrilled when they could reserve the "hottest" titles at times to suit their

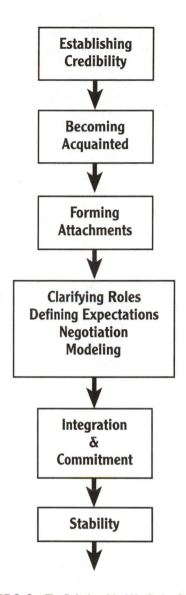

FIGURE 8-6 The Relationship Life Cycle: Stability

schedule. They knew they could count on the movies being there in the store when they came to call for them. Mrs. Collins was available to consult with John on a regular basis. His watchful eye of the industry trends and his sense of responsibility to the business enabled her to have a life of her own again outside of the store. She simply didn't need to be there day and night anymore. Not only was she drawing a nice salary, but she began to prepay on her loan and even started to make long-term investments.

Jolts

At some point, an obstacle will inevitably arise that interferes with the operations of the relationship. One of the members behaves in a manner that disturbs the other.

The behavior is inconsistent with the other's expectations. This disturbance is called a jolt. Jolts can and do occur in the most functional of relationships. By themselves, jolts simply reflect that one person's needs are never completely understood by another, nor do they ever remain constant. As such, changes that emerge in the role performance of one person may cause tension in the other person and disrupt the stability of the relationship. (See Figure 8-7.)

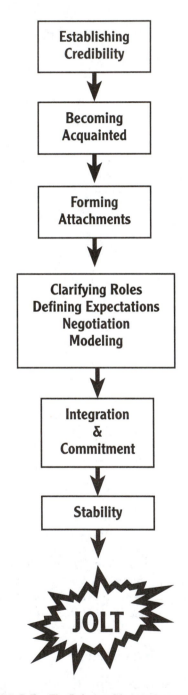

FIGURE 8-7   The Relationship Life Cycle: The Jolt

Tuesday was Mrs. Collins's customary day for checking the mail and paying bills. John was out to lunch when she came in. After greeting the counter attendant, she went into her office and closed the door. She liked to hear the sound of business from the intercom Nathan had installed, so she turned it on and then proceeded to deal with her mail.

A few minutes later, John came back into the store. Mrs. Collins was somewhat surprised when she heard him raise his voice to the employee who had been attending the counter. "Get off your rear end," John said in a condescending voice. "Don't just sit around when there aren't any customers."

"What am I supposed to do?" the employee asked meekly. "It was always okay with Nathan for me to watch a movie when I was waiting for a customer."

"Don't you ever let me hear you call him Nathan again," John said in a scolding tone of voice. "You refer to him as Mr. Collins and to his wife as Mrs. Collins. Get it in your head that I'm your boss now. You are not to be watching movies at any time unless a customer wants to see a portion of one before renting it. As far as what you're supposed to do, restock the movies, sweep the floor, and dust the counters. Don't be sitting around."

Mrs. Collins had never heard John talk to anyone like that before. She couldn't believe it. He left again for an appointment before she had a chance to say anything to him. Besides, she was so taken aback by it all, she wasn't sure what she could say.

Instability

Following a jolt, the relationship becomes unstable and no longer functions smoothly. The interactions between the individuals become strained, and their functions may be performed inefficiently or perhaps even at the expense of the other person.

Unfortunately, it is difficult for many people to talk about their differences, especially when such differences cause problems in the relationship. It is often easier to overlook a problem or perhaps find a "Band-Aid" solution. The intent is to get the relationship back on a stable course again. When the attempted solutions bypass or cover up the jolt, however, seeds are sewn for festering tension. In domestic situations, couples commonly deal with their difficulties by ignoring them, pretending their differences don't exist, or making sarcastic and critical remarks. None of these attempts really do anything about the differences growing between them. In business relationships, people sometimes express their anger and frustration just as they might at home by making sarcastic remarks or by talking behind an associate's back. These maneuvers sometimes help the angered person calm down enough to get back into a facade of stability in the working relationship. Since the jolt itself was never actually resolved, the tension between the two members lies just under the surface waiting to erupt at the first sign of the next conflict. (See Figure 8-8.)

About a week had gone by since Mrs. Collins had heard John scolding the employee. She had been in the store several times since then, but found herself avoiding John. She felt almost as though he had scolded her. She kept meaning to say something to him, but she never found the right moment.

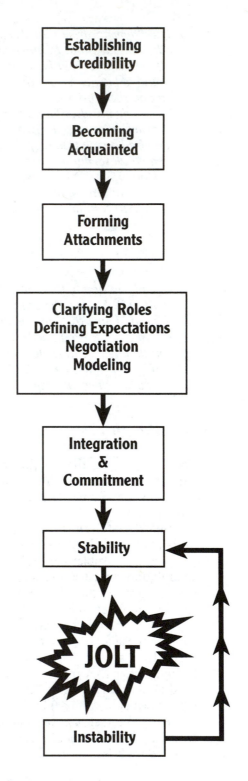

FIGURE 8-8   The Relationship Life Cycle: Instability

One day, while she was sitting at her kitchen table, she got a call from one of the customers, a Mrs. Filmore. The person told her that John had treated her very rudely. He upset her so much that she was considering not coming back.

"What happened?" Mrs. Collins asked with great concern. "Well, I know you have this policy about charging fifty cents if the movies aren't returned by 7 o'clock in the evening. Last night, my basement leaked and I couldn't get over to the store in time. Well, little Freddy, the boy behind the counter, wasn't going to charge me the fifty cents. Then, Mr. Baker found out about it. I told him what happened and that Nathan never would have charged me."

"What did Mr. Baker say?" Mrs. Collins asked.

"He said that Nathan almost ruined this business and that if I wanted to keep my membership in the store's video club, I would pay the money. Then he grabbed the movie out of my hands. He grabbed it! I said to him, 'We'll just see about this, young man.' Then I walked out."

"Mrs. Filmore, I am so sorry that happened. I'm sure that Mr. Baker must not have been feeling well. Please accept my apologies. I would personally like to give you your next ten movie rentals without charging you."

"Oh, that won't be necessary, dear. I feel better just talking about it. I tell you, though, I won't go back in the store when that Mr. Baker is there," the woman said.

Mrs. Collins decided to say something to John this time. She made a trip into the store the next day and told him to come into her office right away.

"John," she started, "Mrs. Filmore called me last night and told me how rudely you treated her. I want to hear what you have to say about it."

"Mrs. Collins, don't come in here all of a sudden and start playing boss with me after five months," John said defensively. "You have no reason to complain. Your profits are up and so is your free time. If I'm going to make this store work for you, you have got to give me a free hand. Maybe I came on a little strong. I'm sorry. But you can't watch over every little thing I do."

Something about the way John talked to her was making her feel more like the employee than the boss. "What am I supposed to do when I get a call from customers who are upset because of the way you treated them?" she asked.

"Mrs. Collins, no store can please all of the people who walk into it. You do your best with most everyone. Our balance sheet from last quarter is proof enough. Let me worry about the customers, okay?" he asked reassuringly. "Don't worry, please."

"He did make me feel better," Mrs. Collins thought. "Besides, Mrs. Filmore was unreasonable herself sometimes." The next time she was in the store to do her office work, she would make a point of calling Mrs. Filmore to give her the free movies.

During the next two weeks, more and more customers called Mrs. Collins with complaints about John. Two of the counter attendants quit, and others were keeping to themselves when they worked.

Eroding Commitment

If the partners in a relationship do not resolve jolts as they occur, tension mounts and intensifies over time. More and more jolts crop up. The commitment and integration that once bound the partners together begins to erode. Their working relationship becomes marred by resentment, mistrust, and emotional distance. One partner starts to believe rumors about the other person and wonders how to defend him- or herself against what the other person might do. Necessity or convenience rather than camaraderie now keeps the physical structure of the relationship intact. (See Figure 8-9.)

> *Mrs. Collins came into the store once again for her Tuesday office work. She started sorting the mail when, about halfway down the pile, she noticed a business envelope from a supplier that she didn't recognize. The return address read "Adult Capers, Inc." She examined the invoice and discovered that John had ordered several thousand dollars worth of pornographic titles. The company promised delivery by the fifteenth of the month. That was tomorrow.*
>
> *She was shocked and felt betrayed. Her skin was flushed and her heart pounded relentlessly. Nathan always insisted that adult titles would never have a place in the store. He condemned other dealers for making such trash available. Now, all of a sudden, this bill appears on her desk. She struggled with all sorts of feelings. Not only was she upset about this filth John ordered, but he had been causing bad will with many of the store's long-time customers. She wondered what happened to the commitment he had given her about clearing new policies with her first. She didn't know what to do. He was bringing more money into the store than she ever thought possible. But he was doing it in a way that she could never support. He went behind her back, he had been alienating the customers, and he had berated the employees. As far as she was concerned, he was hurting the store more than helping it. She decided that she would have to let him go.*

Disintegration

When relationships do not mold to fit the changing needs of their members, additional jolts occur, and eventually the commitment begins to erode. Continued erosion of the commitment spawns additional jolts, and eventually the commitment disintegrates. The relationship often terminates, usually with a great deal of resentment and hostility. (See Figure 8-10.)

Adapting to Change

Conflict between people is completely normal. It is a natural way through which individual differences are expressed. People never stay the same. As such, their needs also change. In order for a working relationship to remain functional, it has to accommodate the changes that its members experience. Conflict arises between the members when they change in ways that threaten each other. One member perceives that the other may be trying to hurt her in some way. This perception

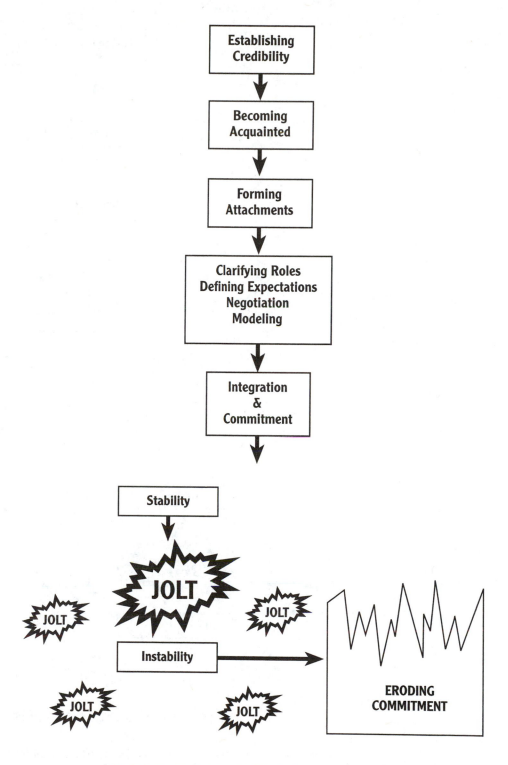

FIGURE 8-9   The Relationship Life Cycle: Eroding Commitment

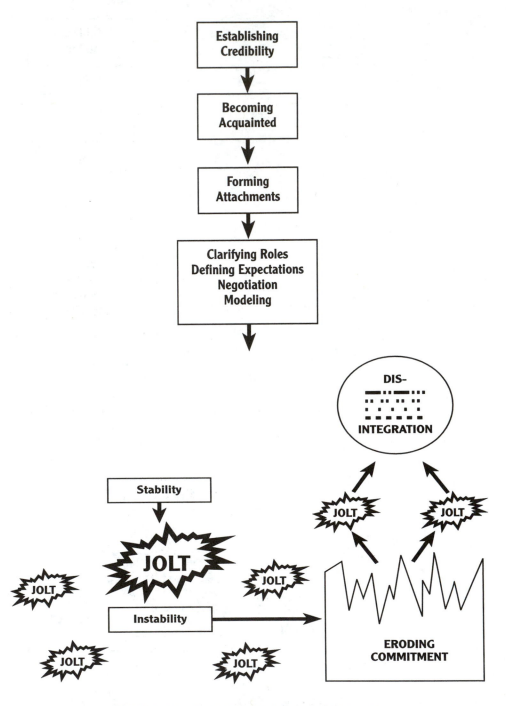

FIGURE 8-10   The Relationship Life Cycle: Disintegration

triggers anxiety. The natural reaction is to try to defend oneself against what feels like an attack. Often the defense takes the form of a counterattack. The stage is then set to intensify the conflict rather than to resolve it.

The most effective way to deal with a jolt is to recycle the conflict back to the phase of role clarification. By recognizing that the strained interaction actually represents some need that the relationship is not meeting, both individuals have an

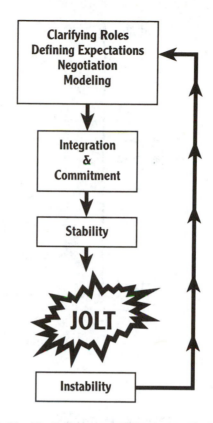

FIGURE 8-11   The Relationship Life Cycle: Adapting to Change

opportunity to renegotiate their roles within the relationship. In other words, as one or both of them change or perhaps their lives outside the relationship change in some unexpected way, they can work together so that the relationship can expand to accommodate the change (see Figure 8-11). This process would involve identifying their differences, discussing their individual needs, and negotiating ways to accommodate each other.

Interpersonal Communication Skills

When a jolt occurs in a relationship, one, both, and potentially all, of the members of the relationship usually become closed minded. Their minds slam shut. When this happens, they can no longer hear what the other person is trying to tell them. Each person defends himself by "attacking" the other. Figure 8-12 illustrates this dynamic by showing how one person's emotional temperature can escalate. The relationship is clearly unstable, and productive work can no longer occur.

The leader's objective is to lower the emotional temperatures within the relationship. Through the use of interpersonal communication skills, the leader can help to rechannel the energy from frustration and anger to cooperation and collaboration. These skills include listening, assertive confrontation, and collaborative problem solving.

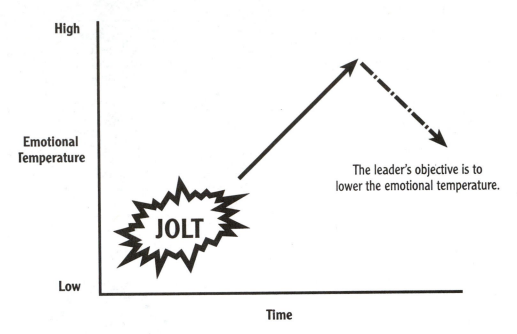

FIGURE 8-12   The Emotional Temperature Chart

Listening Skills

The objectives of listening skills are to

1. convince the speaker that the listener wants to hear what the speaker has to say
2. demonstrate that the listener has accurately understood what the speaker wants to communicate.

The leader can convince the speaker that she wants to hear what the speaker has to say through a tool called *passive listening*. The leader can demonstrate that she has accurately understood what the speaker wanted to communicate through a tool call *active listening*.

Passive Listening. Passive listening is designed to convince the speaker that the listener really wants to hear what the speaker has to say. During a jolt, when emotional temperatures are quickly escalating, each party in the relationship is typically fending for himself. Since the minds of both parties have slammed shut, they close out what the other person is trying to tell them. They are only interested in talking about themselves because they are focused on meeting their own needs. Since both parties perceive that the other is attacking them (their pride, self-esteem, and self-interests), their energies are funneled into protecting themselves. Passive listening works to first defuse this energy and then to rechannel it away from impulsive outbursts and toward clear and rational thinking.

As a part of an overall competency, passive listening includes several tools. These tools consist of eye contact, supportive nonverbal behaviors, acknowledgments, and open-ended questions.

Eye contact is used to communicate that the passive listener is interested in what the speaker has to say. By looking in the general direction of the speaker rather than at "distractions," you demonstrate to the listener that she is your primary concern. Recall that the emotional temperature has been escalating because the other person feels that no one is interested in her, that she has to "attack" in order to gain the attention for her point of view. Eye contact is your first attempt to show her you are tuned in to her.

Appropriate eye contact is evident when the listener looks at whatever the speaker is concerned about. Certainly if he is concerned about himself and his issues, look at him. If he calls your attention to an object such as a report or document, look at it right along with him.

Eye contact certainly does not mean staring. If the speaker feels that you are looking "at" him, rather than tuning in to his concerns, he will once again feel "under attack." His emotional temperature will once again rapidly escalate.

Supportive nonverbal behaviors such as eye contact communicate to the speaker that you are available to hear her concern. You are not off "daydreaming" and not preoccupied with your own concerns. The tone of these behaviors is generally "quiet." Your body position should communicate that you are calm and relaxed. Your hands should be still rather than "fidgety."

Try to see yourself through the eyes of the speaker. If the speaker sees you looking out the window, playing with a paper clip, tapping your fingers on the desk or frequently looking at your watch, he will quickly conclude that your interest in him is a sham. Once he reaches that conclusion, he will close back up and do whatever he needs to do to defend his position. Stay quiet.

Acknowledgments can be both verbal and nonverbal. What the speaker should see as she explains her point of view is you nodding your head as if you were saying "Yes, go on," and "I see." This nonverbal movement is both reassuring that what she is saying is "okay" as well as a confirmation that you want to hear more. The verbal equivalent of this movement is of course to actually say these types of words and phrases in a tone of voice that is supportive and convincing.

Open-ended questions are asked to invite the speaker to continue talking and to say more about her concern. Rather than questions that permit an answer of only "yes" or "no," open-ended questions draw out and extend the answer. This is particularly valuable since the speaker's primary concern is to talk about herself. The open-ended question is effective in allowing her to say more.

One type of open-ended question is structured in such a way that it invites the speaker to say more. Examples include variations on such phrases as "Tell me more" and "Go on."

A second type of open-ended question, the "probe" focuses on specific words, phrases, or issues that the speaker says or brings up. For example, the listener might say:

Mary, a minute ago you mentioned that you're tired of Jack's condescending attitude. Help me understand what you meant by that.

The listener is probing on the words "condescending attitude." For Mary, these words are emotionally charged. She has many feelings packed into them. There is much she wants to say and certainly there is much we as listeners can learn. The probe invites her to talk more not only about the words themselves but about herself. After all, people enjoy talking most about themselves. Passive listening through probing gives them a chance to do so.

To make the best use of the probe, offer some sort of softening phrase that implies you are asking permission to inquire, such as "Help me understand what you meant by..." or "Could you tell me more about..." Then identify the issue you want the speaker to talk about further. The order can be interchanged:

Softening Phrase: Help me understand what you meant by
Issue to be Probed: Jack's condescending attitude.

Issue to be Probed: You mentioned Jack's condescending attitude.
Softening Phrase: Help me understand what you meant by that.

Passive listening is called "passive" because the listener is using behaviors that support rather than add to what the speaker has discussed. Even though the speaker "talks" through acknowledgments and open-ended questions, listening has been passive. It is designed to communicate openness and acceptance. As such, the speaker perceives that since it is "okay" to talk about his concerns, needs, and interests, he no longer has to funnel his energies into defending himself. Consequently, his emotional temperature begins to come down, and he begins to calm down. His mind begins to open back up, and he can start to hear once again.

Active Listening. Like passive listening, active listening is a tool to help bring down the emotional temperature of the speaker. But unlike passive listening whose only purpose is to create a supportive listening atmosphere, active listening is designed to verify to the speaker that you have actually understood what she has been trying to say.

Active listening involves summarizing what you think the speaker was trying to tell you. Listen to several sentences (whatever constitutes a complete thought), and then in your own words feed back to the listener what you believed she was trying to tell you.

After you have completed this brief summary, the speaker will respond by saying the equivalent of "Yes, that's right," or "No, that's not what I mean." If you get a *"yes"* response, you will know that you have in fact understood what the speaker was intending to communicate. On the other hand, if you get a *"no"* response, you will also have achieved a valuable insight. Thanks to your attempt to understand and thanks to the listener's reply, you will have established that you and the speaker are not in sync. The speaker has verified for you that you in fact do not understand what she is trying to tell you. That knowledge (the fact that you do not yet understand) is important information. If you had proceeded in the conversation without that knowledge, subsequent misunderstandings would likely have occurred which could have triggered jolts, and the instability in the relationship would have continued and perhaps worsened. However, with the knowledge gained from your active listening, even though it did not hit its target, you now have an opportunity to try again. Here's an example of active listening on target:

Bill: Every time I ask you to cover for me and you agree, you've let me down.

You: So even if I were to give you my word, you feel like you wouldn't be able to count on me.

Bill: That's right.

Here's an example of when active listening initially misses the mark followed by a second attempt in which the listener tries again with success:

Bill: Every time I ask you to cover for me and you agree, you've let me down.

You: So you think I'm just like everyone else around here, is that it?

Bill: No, that's not it. I'm not talking about everyone else. I'm talking about you. You're the one I can't count on. You're the one who promises you'll cover for me and you're the one who lets me down. Then I end up looking like I'm irresponsible in front of the boss.

You: So, when you've asked me to do something for you and I've given you the idea that I will take care of it, you depend on me to get it done. And when I don't get it done, you have to face the consequences. Is that it?

Bill: That's it exactly.

The example illustrates that active listening doesn't have to be "right" on the first attempt in order to be considered "good" active listening. The process of active listening is successful whenever the listener establishes a useful two-way communication.

How long do you actively listen? Active listening in combination with passive listening continues until the speaker agrees that you understand her side of the issue. Your "final" summary should represent a description of the problem from the speaker's point of view. Once that is accomplished, you are ready to help the speaker become a listener in order to understand your side of the problem.

Assertive Confrontation

As a speaker, you now want to help the listener (the person you've been in conflict with) understand your side of the issue. Your objective is to keep the listener's mind open to "hearing" what you want her to understand. The skill you can use for this purpose is called *assertive confrontation*. "Confronting" simply means presenting the issues openly and directly to the other party as opposed to avoiding the issue or talking about the other person behind his back. Being assertive means that you will present the issue without apology and in a firm and clear manner. By contrast, the word *aggressive* would communicate an intent to get your needs met at the expense of the other person. Aggressive styles of communication tend to be blameful, harsh, critical, threatening, and destructive to the relationship as well as the other person's self-esteem.

Consider the following example of an aggressive confrontation:

Brian: How many times have I told you to contact the vendor by Friday, not Monday. Are you dense? Don't you pay attention when people talk to you?

Notice how these words communicate that something is wrong with the person to whom Brian is talking. How would you feel if you were talked to in this way—angry, resentful, vindictive?

Now compare the next example, which makes use of an assertive rather than an aggressive style.

Brian: Kevin, I'm confused about something I thought we've discussed. Do you have a few minutes now so that we can talk?

Kevin: Okay, what's up?

Brian: A few days ago, I sent you a memo in which I outlined the procedure for when to contact our vendor. I got a confirmation on E-Mail that you received the memo. Maybe it was my mistake to assume that you understood and would follow the procedure. I would like to hear your side of it. The problem is that when you contacted the vendor on Monday instead of Friday, we missed a price break. As a result, we have to pay nearly twice as much for the supplies. Now I've got to explain to my boss why we're overpaying. As I'm sure you've guessed, I'm pretty upset about this.

An assertive confrontation is based on a skill from *Leader Effectiveness Training*, a book and training program by Dr. Thomas Gordon. The skill is called the "Three-part I-message." The "I" portion of the skill refers to the pronoun "I" indicating that the message describes the concern from the perspective of the sender. In other words, "let me tell you about a problem that I am having." The three parts represent both a structure for preparing the message and a vehicle for delivering it to the receiver—the person whose behavior is causing the problem. Here's how it works.

Part I is called *the nonblameful description of behavior*. This phrase objectively focuses on the behavior causing the problem. In the earlier example, the behavior would be calling the vendor on Monday instead of Friday. This behavior is factual. It can be observed by anyone, and it is beyond refute. It happened just as stated. The receiver, in this case Kevin, would have to agree as a matter of fact that he did indeed contact the vendor on Monday rather than on Friday. Note that the nonblameful description sticks to the behavior and is free from judgmental, blameful, or opinion-based words.

Part II is called the *concrete and tangible effects*. In this part, the sender describes the consequences of the behavior. In other words, because of this behavior, there has been a cost. The cost can be measured in terms of something concrete such as money, time, safety, reputation, and so on. The cost to Brian could be expressed in terms of both money and reputation.

Part III is *feelings*. As a result of the behavior and its associated consequences, the sender has certain feelings. Typical feelings include mad, sad, scared, glad, and variations of each.

The three-part I-message can be expressed in any order. The assertive communication can be considered complete when the sender has described the problem from his perspective, and the listener has indicated that she understands the speaker's concern.

Collaborative Problem Solving

Once the two parties (or however many people are involved in the conflict) agree on the substance of the problem and acknowledge each other's perspective, the next step is to use collaborative problem solving to resolve the disagreement. Once again, drawing from Gordon's model, collaborative problem solving includes six steps:

1. *Defining the Problem.* By using both listening skills and assertive confrontations, the problem can be defined so that each of the parties agrees on the issues and acknowledges the other person's point of view. Agreement is less important than acceptance.

2. *Brainstorming Solutions.* Both parties agree to think of and list as many possible solutions as they can without judging or evaluating any of them at this step. The objective here is quantity rather than quality. If judgments are allowed to be expressed and considered, the receiving party might be offended, another jolt could occur, and the cooperative process could break down. Instead, simply encourage

more ideas by saying things like, "that's one idea, let's write it down and then we'll take a look at it later."

3. *Evaluating Solutions*. Once the parties agree that they have enough ideas to work with, they begin the process of evaluating each one. Evaluation is done in terms of whether or not any particular idea satisfies the needs of both parties. The needs should have been identified back in Step 1, *Defining the Problem*. If any given idea satisfies the needs of one party but not the other, it is crossed off. Only those that meet the needs of both parties are allowed to remain. They can be underlined, checked, or otherwise highlighted.

4. *Choosing a Solution*. From among the remaining items, the parties discuss the merits of each idea in terms of its ability to mutually satisfy their needs. Together they collaborate and choose the best solution.

5. *Implementing the Solution*. The parties decide the steps required to implement the solution. They also decide who will do what to carry out the plan.

6. *Feedback*. Before implementing the solution, the parties agree on a time in the relatively near future to review the outcome of the solution. The question to be addressed is how satisfied each party is with the solution and the extent to which it is meeting the needs they defined back in Step 1. They might also discover that their needs may have changed, and the entire process may need to be done again to solve the original problem or a new one.

Once again, consider the Relationship Life Cycle (Figure 8-13). Notice first that conflict is unavoidable and inevitable. It is part of any relationship. People assume

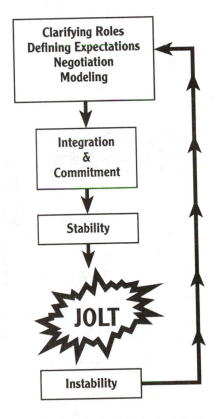

FIGURE 8-13 The Relationship Life Cycle: Adapting to Change

they understand others when in fact they don't. People change over time and don't keep others up to date with evolving roles and new expectations. To be successful, the relationship must adapt.

The line rising from Instability to Clarifying Roles and Defining Expectations illustrates that when jolts occur, the first thing to do is to recognize that people's needs are in conflict. Instead of ignoring the Jolt or using aggressive confrontations that place blame, the leader can use interpersonal communication skills to help the members of the work team (the leader included) adapt to change. Listening skills and assertive confrontations can help define the problem, and collaborative problem solving can help the parties get their individual needs met and work together as an effective team.

Presentation Skills

Every aspect of leadership ultimately depends on the ability to speak effectively to an audience. The audience may be the person sitting across from a leader in an office or it may be millions of people watching and listening to a leader deliver a message on TV.

A listener's attention span can be compared to an open window shade that slowly descends to a closed position. Research indicates that this window shade of attention moves from a fully open to fully closed position in seven seconds, plus or minus two. This means that a speaker must either (1) introduce, deliver, and summarize the message in less than seven seconds or (2) use tools that will refresh the seven-second time frame at various points during the presentation. (See Figure 8-14.)

To ensure that the audience continues to listen throughout the presentation, the speaker needs to periodically refresh the audience's attention before a seven-second time span runs out. The ability to keep an audience alert and interested will determine the speaker's overall effectiveness.

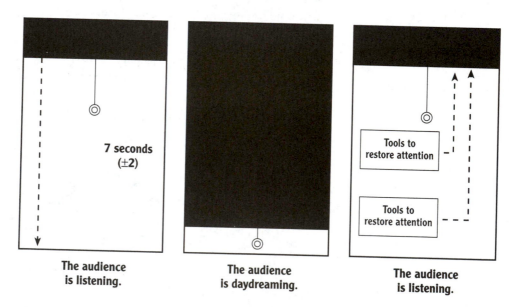

FIGURE 8-14   The Window of Attention

The Speaker Effectiveness Index (SEI) is a model that has been developed to help speakers manage how long their audience pays attention as well as how much they retain and understand. The model provides a framework so that the speaker can achieve two primary objectives. First, by focusing on how they look and sound, speakers can control how long the audience pays attention. Second, by structuring what they say, speakers can help audiences more fully understand their message.

SEI—Audience Management Model		
Attention		**Understanding**
Look	*Sound*	*Say*
Eye contact Gestures Dress Posture	Fluency Vocal energy Timing	Introduction Major points Closing Questions & answers

You can use the Speaker Effectiveness Index for planning and delivering your own presentations as well as for evaluating the presentations of other speakers. To help you achieve each of these objectives, the model will first describe each skill and then provide a checklist to help you determine if the speaker used the skill effectively.

How You Look

Eye Contact.   Select any member of the audience and look at that person until you complete a thought. This period typically lasts from one to five seconds. Then, shift your attention to another person. When people in the audience believe that you are talking directly to them, they pay attention in much the same way they would in a one to one conversation. This simple procedure can instantly put people at ease. By using conversational eye contact at all times during your presentation you can continually keep your audience's attention focused where you want it.

Eye Contact—Effective

_____ You faced and looked at one person at a time.

_____ You talked to one person until you completed a thought.

_____ You made equal eye contact across the audience.

_____ You looked at the visual aid briefly, then looked at the audience.

_____ You looked at notes briefly, then looked at the audience.

Eye Contact—To Improve Next Time

_____ Face and look at one person at a time.

_____ Talk to one person until you complete a thought.

_____ Make equal eye contact across the audience.

_____ Look at the visual aid briefly, then look at the audience.

_____ Look at notes briefly, then look at the audience.

Gestures. There are three basic reasons to use gestures: (1) to relieve your own nervous tension, (2) to energize the audience, and (3) to enhance communication. Distracting movements (tie pulling, hand clasping) relieve the speaker's nervous tension, but divert the audience's attention. Purposeful gestures include both animated and descriptive movements. Animated movements (raising hands in the air, sweeping arms out to the side) positively discharge anxiety, communicate excitement, and energize the audience. Descriptive movements (outlining the dimensions of an object and using movements to convey concepts) better enable the audience to pay attention and gain meaning from the presentation. When you are not purposefully gesturing, stay in a neutral position. In the neutral position, your shoulders and feet face the audience while your hands are relaxed at your sides.

Gestures—Effective

_____ You made frequent use of animated gestures.

_____ You made frequent use of descriptive gestures.

_____ Your gestures appeared natural and spontaneous.

_____ Your gestures were effectively timed.

_____ You used an effective neutral position when not gesturing.

Gestures—To Improve Next Time

_____ Use more animated gestures.

_____ Use more descriptive gestures.

_____ Use gestures as a natural outlet for your energy.

_____ Gesture on meaningful words and on strong vocal inflections.

_____ Keep your hands at your sides when not intentionally gesturing.

Dress. As a rule of thumb, speakers should dress a bit more conservatively than most members of their audiences. The most important aspect of appropriate dress is to present a clean, neat, wrinkle-free, and "finished" appearance. Remove visible objects from shirt pockets, tightly tuck in a shirt or blouse, evenly tie a tie, and make sure that shoes are clean and shined and that hair is well groomed. Overall, check to be certain that the image of you that the audience sees through the way you dress augments rather than detracts from your credibility.

Dress—Effective

_____ Your appearance was free from distracting objects.

_____ You presented and maintained a wrinkle-free appearance.

_____ Your choice of clothing was appropriate for this group.

_____ Your style of dress augmented your credibility.

_____ Your hair was well groomed and caused no distraction.

Dress—To Improve Next Time

_____ Remove distracting objects from view.

_____ Present and maintain a wrinkle-free appearance

_____ Select clothing that conforms to the group's standards.

_____ Choose a style of dress that augments your credibility.

_____ Make sure that your hair remains combed and in place.

Posture. First impressions will influence how the audience will pay attention to you and how much impact your presentation will make. In many cases, your face is the primary cue on which people rely to determine what you are really trying to say. Speakers who smile more are considered more enthusiastic and interesting. Speakers whose facial expressions are consistent with their tone of voice are considered more believable and trustworthy. Head movements, much like gestures, add interest and variety to a speaker's delivery. Moving your head in time with other gestures and in response to your voice adds vitality by animating your presentation.

The way you sit and the way you stand often provide your audience with an immediate first impression of the kind of speaker you will be. When you sit up straight with arms relaxed and legs crossed at the ankle, you communicate that you are relaxed and self-confident. When standing, hold your head erect and square your shoulders and feet to the audience.

Posture—Effective

_____ Your facial expression conveyed interest and enthusiasm.

_____ Your head movements conveyed interest and enthusiasm.

_____ You held your head erect.

_____ When seated, you crossed your legs at the ankles.

_____ When standing, you squarely faced the audience.

Posture—To Improve Next Time

_____ Use facial expressions to convey interest and enthusiasm.

_____ Move your head to convey interest and enthusiasm.

_____ Hold your head erect.

_____ When seated, cross your legs at the ankles.

_____ When standing, square your shoulders and feet to the audience.

How You Sound

Fluency.   Fluency is the continuity with which the speaker's words flow within and between units of thought. Disruptions in fluency give the impression that the speaker is stumbling, unsure, and unprepared to expertly discuss the topic. Fluency problems are noticed through inappropriately placed pauses, word repetitions, fragmented sentences, meaningless words (*uh-uh, you know, I mean, I guess*) and vocal noises (throat clearing, nervous laughter). Continuous fluency can quickly distinguish the effective from the ineffective speaker in any speaking context.

As an important component of fluency, clear pronunciation is achieved when people listen to what you have to say rather than how you actually pronounce your words. Problems in pronunciation become noticeable when the speaker substitutes one sound for another, transposes sounds within words or phrases, uses culturally different productions of sounds, or produces distracting nonverbal sounds such as tongue clicking or lip smacking. Pronunciation need only be changed when it detracts the listener's attention from what the speaker intends to communicate.

Fluency—Effective

_____   You produced word sequences without halting or hesitating.

_____   Your speech was largely free from filler-type words.

_____   Your fluency was largely free from word or phrase repetitions.

_____   You spoke in complete rather than fragmented sentences.

_____   Your pronunciation was clear and easy to understand.

Fluency—To Improve Next Time

_____   Produce word sequences without halting or hesitating.

_____   Eliminate or greatly reduce filler words from your delivery.

_____   Eliminate or greatly reduce word and phrase repetitions.

_____   Replace false starts with complete sentences.

_____   Modify your pronunciations to prevent distractions.

Vocal Energy.   Your voice is a powerful tool for shaping feelings, attitudes, and behavior. Your audience will become interested, enthusiastic, and even excited only when they believe you are interested, enthusiastic, and excited. To convey and subsequently shape these emotions, carefully control the force and range of your vocal energy. Effective vocal energy includes speaking louder than competing noises, with greater emphasis on meaningful words, and strategically dropping or raising your speaking volume.

You can avoid attracting unwanted attention by identifying any abnormalities that might be associated with your voice. These could include volume levels that are too loud or soft, pitch levels that are excessively high or low, or a rate of speech that is so slow that it dulls attention or so fast that words become imprecise.

You can help to establish your image as an authority by speaking with increased vocal energy. You will tone down your authoritative image or convey lower levels of self-confidence by speaking at reduced levels of vocal force.

Vocal Energy—Effective

_____ You spoke loudly enough to convey meaning and enthusiasm.

_____ You emphasized important words by using vocal inflections.

_____ You raised and lowered volume and pitch to create impact.

_____ You spoke with authoritative vocal force when appropriate.

_____ You spoke with less than authoritative vocal force when appropriate.

Vocal Energy—To Improve Next Time

_____ Speak loudly enough to convey meaning and enthusiasm.

_____ Emphasize important words with vocal inflections.

_____ Raise and lower volume and pitch to heighten emotion.

_____ Increase your volume to establish your image of authority.

_____ Decrease your volume to tone down your image of authority.

Timing.   The timing of your delivery consists of your base rate of speaking, the degree that you speed up and slow down within phrases or sentences, and the strategic placement of pauses. Speakers generally hold attention for longer periods of time by using faster than normal base rates of speech. The faster you speak, the better your listener will pay attention. In order to speak faster, you have to use more energy. By using more energy, you will also tend to become more animated. The more animated you are, the more interesting you will be to listen to. So speak faster than usual to capture and hold attention.

Besides increasing your base rate of speaking, you can also create impact by changing your speed within the same phrases and sentences. Start off fast, then slow down, Start off slow, then speed up.

Along with variations in the actual speed, you can also emphasize the importance of your points by strategically placing your pauses. And just as with speed, you can also vary the length of the pause. Put pauses wherever you want to emphasize, hold attention, and build suspense.

Timing—Effective

_____ You spoke at a faster rate to capture attention.

_____ You spoke at a slower rate to capture attention.

_____ You varied your rate within phrases and sentences.

_____ You strategically placed your pauses.

_____ You varied the length of your pauses.

Timing—To Improve Next Time

_____ Speak at a faster than normal base rate.

_____ Slow your base rate to capture and hold attention.

_____ Vary your rate of speaking within phrases and sentences.

_____ Strategically place your pauses.

_____ Vary the length of your pauses.

What You Say

Introduction.   The Introduction establishes the speaker's credibility with the audience. By initially conveying what the audience can gain from your presentation, you can focus and control how your listeners pay attention. You can help them stay focused throughout the entire presentation by using the Introduction to clearly establish a strong sense of purpose.

Use the Introduction to give an overview of your main points. By doing so, you will help your listeners organize their own thinking and enable them to recognize and appreciate the consistency in yours.

Introduction—Effective

_____   You began with an attention getter.

_____   You conveyed how your information related to your audience.

_____   You established a strong sense of purpose.

_____   You established your credibility.

_____   You gave an overview of the major points that you would present.

Introduction—To Improve Next Time

_____   Begin with an attention getter.

_____   Convey how your information relates to your audience.

_____   Establish a strong sense of purpose.

_____   Establish your credibility.

_____   Give an overview of the major points that you will discuss.

Major Points.   An effective presentation is somewhat like a road map. It first presents an overall view and then leads the audience to the destination through a series of landmarks and stop-off points along the way. Like the well-marked road map, the effective presentation moves the audience to consider its purpose by discussing the major points.

Each major point is well marked, thus making it easy to recognize and consider. The major points are also logically organized and, as such, appeal to the listeners' sense of reason.

To create an easy flow, move the listeners' attention from one major point to the next through transitions. Throughout the presentation, the effective speaker enables the audience to stay in tune with the train of thought by speaking in familiar terms, defining technical terms as needed, and avoiding words that could be offensive. While transitions are used to shift from one point to the next, the speaker recaps several points with periodic, brief summaries.

Major Points—Effective

_____   You organized the major points with logical patterns of thought.

_____   You supported the major points with a variety of evidence.

_____   You used familiar terms and defined technical terms as needed.

_____   You used words with good judgment so as to be nonoffensive.

_____   You linked the major points with transitions and summaries.

Major Points—To Improve Next Time

_____ Organize the major points with logical patterns of thought.

_____ Support the major points with a variety of evidence.

_____ Use words that are familiar and define technical terms as needed.

_____ Avoid using words that could be offensive.

_____ Link the major points with transitions and summaries.

Closing. A fundamental concept in learning is that repetition is essential to building comprehension. To make sure that the listener comprehends your message, say a little a whole lot of times rather than a lot only once. The closing is a critical time to create a lasting impression in the listeners' minds. The following five steps will help you create that lasting impression:

1. Acknowledge that the presentation will soon be coming to an end.
2. Refer back to the objectives that you introduced during your Introduction.
3. Summarize the benefits that the listeners will gain from your presentation.
4. Let them know exactly what you would like them to do.
5. Close with a final message that will enable them to remember what you consider to be the most important point from your presentation.

By including these five steps in your closing, you will effectively build comprehension and leave a lasting impression by design rather than by chance.

Closing—Effective

_____ You acknowledged that the presentation would be ending.

_____ You referred back to your objectives.

_____ You summarized the benefits to your audience.

_____ You called for the audience to take certain actions.

_____ You closed the presentation with a final message.

Closing—To Improve Next Time

_____ Acknowledge that the presentation is coming to an end.

_____ Refer back to your objectives.

_____ Summarize the benefits to your audience.

_____ Call for the audience to take certain actions.

_____ Close the presentation with a final message.

Question and Answer Session. To determine your listeners' level of understanding and the extent to which they agree with your point of view, you should provide them with opportunities to ask questions. However, even though the Q&A session is an effective means to do this, it could easily backfire. You could lose control of the interaction and, as a result, lose your credibility. To ensure that you stay in control of the content, direction, and length of the Q&A session, you can use any of the following tools:

1. *The Solicitation*—you ask for questions as a way of demonstrating your willingness and availability to discuss and clarify areas of interest.
2. *The Common Question*—you pose a question as though it had actually been asked by "many people." Then provide the answer.
3. *The Rephrase*—you rephrase the question in your own words to make sure that you've accurately heard and understood it.
4. *The Bridge*—you rephrase the question but do so in a way that allows you to shift the focus of the question from a specific level of inquiry to one that is more general and less risky to answer.
5. *The Tieback*—you relate your answer back to one or more of the objectives that you want the presentation to achieve.

Question and Answer Session—Effective

_____ You actively solicited questions to demonstrate your openness.

_____ You used common questions to create interest in your answers.

_____ You rephrased questions to ensure shared understanding.

_____ You bridged to reduce risk and create common bonds.

_____ You used tiebacks to relate answers back to your objectives.

Question and Answer Session—To Improve Next Time

_____ Actively solicit questions to demonstrate openness.

_____ Use common questions to create interest in your answers.

_____ Rephrase questions to ensure shared understanding.

_____ Bridge sensitive issues to establish common bonds.

_____ Use tiebacks to relate answers back to your objectives.

Tracking Results and Evaluating Progress

You can use the form on the next page to document the results of your presentation or to evaluate the effectiveness of another speaker.

Summary

This chapter has discussed the last of the four competencies in leadership—communication skills. Our discussion of the communication skills included the Relationship Life Cycle, interpersonal communication skills, and presentation skills.

Speaker's Name _____   Date _____

SEI—Skills Summary		
Attention		**Understanding**
Look	**Sound**	**Say**
+ − Eye contact + − Gestures + − Dress + − Posture	+ − Fluency + − Vocal energy + − Timing	+ − Introduction + − Major points + − Closing + − Questions & answers

(+) Currently effective   (−) Needs development

Bibliography

Arredondo, Lani, *How to Present Like a Pro* (New York: McGraw-Hill, 1991).

Bechler, Curt, and Richard Weaver, *Listen to Win* (New York: Master Media Limited, 1994).

Berg, Karen, and Andrew Gilman, *Get to the Point* (New York: Bantam, 1989).

Boettinger, Henry, *Moving Mountains—The Art of Letting Others See Things Your Way* (New York: MacMillan, 1969).

Bowling, Evelyn, *Voice Power* (Harrisburg: Stackpole Press, 1980).

Clark, Elaine, *There's Money Where Your Mouth Is—An Insider's Guide to a Career in Voice-Overs* (New York: Backstage Books, 1995).

Cooper, Morton, *Winning with Your Voice* (Hollywood: Fell, 1990).

Detz, Joan, *How to Write and Give a Speech* (New York: St. Martin's Press, 1992).

Flesch, Rudolph, *The Art of Readable Writing* (New York: Harper Brothers, 1949).

Flesch, Rudolph, *How to Write, Speak and Think More Effectively* (New York: Signet, 1960).

Gilbert, Judy, *Clear Speech—Pronunciation and Listening Comprehension in American English* (Cambridge: Cambridge University Press, 1984).

Gordon, Thomas, *Leader Effectiveness Training* (Solana Beach, CA: Effectiveness Training Press, 1978).

Griffin, Jack, *How to Say It Best—Choice Words, Phrases and Model Speeches for Every Occasion* (Upper Saddle River, NJ: Prentice-Hall, 1994).

Gunning, Robert, and Richard A. Kallan, *How to Take the Fog Out of Business Writing* (Chicago: Dartnell Press, 1994).

Hilton, Jack, and Mary Knoblauch, *On Television—A Survival Guide for Media Interviews* (New York: AMACOM, 1980).

Kinder, Herbert, *Managing Disagreement Constructively—Conflict Management in Organizations* (Menlo Park, CA: Crisp Publications, 1988).

Leeds, Dorothy, *Power Speak—The Complete Guide to Successful Presentations* (New York: Berkley Press, 1991).

Martel, Myles, *Fire Away—Fielding Questions with Finesse* (New York: Irwin Publishing, 1994).

Morgan, Rebecca, *Calming Upset Customers—Staying Effective During Unpleasant Situations* (New York: Crisp Publications, 1989).

Peoples, David, *Presentations Plus* (New York: Wiley Press, 1992).

Portnoy, Robert, *Leadership, What Every Leader Should Know About People* (New York: Prentice-Hall, 1986).

Sarnoff, Dorothy, *Speech Can Change Your Life* (New York: Dell Publishing, 1970).

Sarnoff, Dorothy, *Make the Most of Your Best—A Complete Program for Presenting Yourself and Your Ideas with Confidence and Authority* (New York: Doubleday, 1981).

Schloff, Laurie, and Marcia Yudkin, *Smart Speaking—Sixty Second Strategies for More Than 100 Speaking Problems and Fears* (New York: Penguin Press, 1992).

Wade, John, *Dealing Effectively with the Media* (Los Altos, CA: Crisp Publications, 1992).

Wells, Theodora, *Keeping Your Cool Under Fire—Communicating Non-Defensively* (New York: McGraw-Hill, 1980).

SECTION III

Applications

Chapter 9:   Frequently Asked Questions
about Leadership
Chapter 10: Assessment Guidelines and
Some Final Thoughts

CHAPTER 9

Frequently Asked Questions about Leadership

In this chapter, we'll consider common questions about leadership as well as questions from specific topics and concepts from throughout the book. Where appropriate, references to the book will be offered for further information.

Q: How is leadership different from management?

A: According to John Kotter, professor of business at Harvard, management is concerned with maintaining predictability and order, whereas leadership focuses on change. Managers establish direction, while leaders plan. Managers organize, and leaders align others to their vision. Managers control, whereas leaders motivate and inspire people to do whatever is needed in order to make things change.

Managers are people who are selected to fill a position in an organization. Through their position, the organization gives them the authority to manage the decisions and activities of the organization. Leaders are people who lead whether or not they occupy a position in an organization and even if they lack any kind of formal authority. People listen to them because they believe that the leader has something to offer that will benefit them in some way. Leadership is tied to leading, whereas management is tied to a position.

Q: Why does this book talk about leadership in terms of competencies and why are there four competencies rather than two or six or some other number?

A: Anyone who observes leadership quickly perceives that the leader exercises power over those who follow. Many types of power can be used when one person attempts to influence another. For example, a patient follows "doctor's orders" because she respects the doctor's knowledge and credentials. A subordinate follows a manager's directive because of the manager's position of power in the organization. A citizen obeys a police officer as a matter of recognizing the authority conveyed by the state or local government.

Leadership derives its power internally rather than from any external source such as a university degree, an organization, or a government. People follow a leader once they become convinced that their allegiance will benefit them.

The competencies in this book refer to the behaviors that anyone can use to convince a follower to do what the leader wants him to do. Through directional thinking, the leader paints a picture in the follower's mind of how things could change. Consequential thinking encourages the leader to consider carefully the outcome of changing things in light of the potential cost and risks. The leader uses influence strategies to shape followers' emotions and thinking. By so doing, the follower can be persuaded that he will benefit by doing what the leader wants him to do. Through the use of communication skills, the leader can overcome resistance, solve conflicts, and present her case in a pleasing, convincing, and overall effective way.

Competencies represent the leader's internal power to attract and lead followers. Since the competencies are completely internal, the leader is effective as long as the competencies are effective. Because leadership is tied to competencies as the source of its power, leaders can come from anywhere, can be any age, and can lead for as long as their competencies remain effective.

Q: I'm an executive in an organization. We have about two hundred people whom we've identified as candidates for future positions in leadership. How can we best apply the material in this book as a leadership development program?

A: First, take a careful look at how you identified the candidates. Ask if you used any particular method, theory, or model that sets out clear and consistent selection standards. How do you know that the current group of two hundred are really the people best suited for your future positions? Who selected them? What criteria were used for the selection? How was it determined who was eligible for consideration and who was excluded? What safeguards were in place to prevent favoritism or to prevent excluding someone because of her reputation as a "troublemaker"?

Second, select a development method and apply it consistently to all of the candidates, then measure the results to determine if the program is meeting your expectations. The four competencies model will enable you to meet each of these criteria.

Mentoring is a process many organizations use to identify and develop candidates for leadership. By definition, a mentor is a trusted counselor and advisor. Organizations assign candidates to their current leaders so that an exchange of knowledge and experience can occur through the working relationship that develops.

By incorporating the four competencies model, the organization can structure the mentoring relationship so that the mentors can identify and develop future leaders consistently and effectively.

The first step is for the mentors (any existing leader can be a mentor) to agree on how the candidates should be identified. Self-selection is the most fair and will nearly always enable the organization to prevent allegations of illegal discrimination.

The second step is to assess the candidates. Section I of this book provides a thorough set of assessment materials for the candidates to complete. Any given mentor, a team of mentors, or a team of assessors can analyze the results. The process of analyzing the assessments includes searching the candidates' responses for evidence of the four competencies. Recall that Chapter 4 presents a complete set of instructions. The scoring form displays a matrix that will tell you which of the four competencies the candidates use most and least often. The target result should be the equal use of all four competencies. The differences between the actual result and the target result represents the gaps that the mentor can use to develop the "underdeveloped" competencies.

The third step is for the mentor and the candidate to discuss the results of the assessment and agree on the target result toward which the candidate should aspire. Using that target as an objective, the mentor can assign various projects and activities for the candidate to complete as a way to build the "underdeveloped" competencies. Periodic meetings between the mentor and candidate would consist of discussions regarding these projects and activities. The discussions would consist of the candidate briefing the mentor on what occurred, by the mentor analyzing the results in light of the competencies to be developed, and the mentor and the candidate agreeing to the next actions.

The fourth step would be for the candidate to retake the assessment in order to determine how the developmental experiences impacted his growth in the four competencies of leadership. The mentor would analyze the results, review the findings with the candidate, and repeat the overall process in order to continually improve the candidate's skills.

Q: How do I know if I have what it takes to be a leader?

A: Leadership is not about "being a leader." It is about leading. By approaching a situation, any situation, with the four competencies in mind, you will be taking the appropriate steps to lead. Leadership is observable through the four competencies in action. To determine how effective you are in using the four competencies, take the assessment, measure your results, and do whatever the results indicate to develop whichever of the competencies are less developed than others. Anyone can lead by using the competencies. There is simply no need to complicate the issue by trying to categorize people as leaders and nonleaders.

Q: Can you give me an example of how ordinary people could use leadership in their daily lives?

A: Actually, the book has already illustrated many such examples. One in particular was how the woman convinced the theater manager to honor the tickets of her party after having been denied admission. That example specifically illustrated the competency of directional thinking. It also demonstrated several influence strategies that the woman used to persuade the manager to do what she wanted him to do.

Here's another example. Let's suppose you wanted to lease a new car. Directional thinking enables you to imagine yourself and your family in this beautiful car equipped with all the options. Through the use of Consequential Thinking, you thoroughly research the repair record of this type of car, and you determine the cost factors for the buy versus lease options as well as the market value to trade in your car. You consider the various possibilities through the use of influence strategies, and you decide the various things you'll say to the salesperson and sales manager as you contemplate your communication skills. Here's how it could all come together.

> **Salesperson:** Are there any other models you and the family would like to test-drive, or did you like this one?
>
> **You:** This one is exactly what we've been looking for.
>
> **Salesperson:** Let's sit down and write up the order so you can take it home tonight.
>
> **You:** Sounds exciting. What do we need to do?
>
> **Salesperson:** Let's fill out this form so we can get credit verification, okay?
>
> **You:** Fine. How long will it take?
>
> **Salesperson:** Actually, less than ten minutes. In the meantime, I want to make sure I understand how you'd like the terms to read. You want the car leased for

three years with a term that includes thirty-six thousand miles. You also want the contract that calls for no down payment and no credit life insurance. Do I have it right?

You: Yes.

Salesperson: Ah, here's the credit check, and everything looks fine. The next step is for me to take the terms to the sales manager so we can get a monthly payment. I'll be right back. Would you like some coffee or a soft drink while you're waiting.

You: No thanks, we'll be fine.

(Fifteen minutes later)

Salesperson: You're going to love these numbers. I can't believe he was able to come in with such a low monthly payment. The figure is $397 per month for thirty-six months. The capital reduction cost is $2,500, the security deposit is $250 and the first and last months' payments come to $794. Sign right here and in thirty minutes you'll have the keys and your brand new car.

You: Let me make sure I understand. What I will owe you once I sign is $2,500 for the cap reduction, plus the security deposit of $250, and the first and last payment of $794 for a total of $3,544 that I will need to give you to take the car tonight. Is that right?

Salesperson: That's right.

You: I want to thank you for all the time that you and your staff have given us tonight. We really like the car. We'd like to think it over and we'll get back to you.

Salesperson: I thought you wanted the car tonight. I don't understand.

You: You were thinking that we were ready to buy tonight?

Salesperson: Frankly, I'm confused. With these numbers, I figured there would be no doubt. What would it take for you to sign right now?

You: You mean, you could give us a lower price?

Salesperson: That car is a beauty and it's perfect for you. I would hate to see someone else drive it away. For the last two hours, I've been picturing you and your family in that car. I'll do everything I can to put those keys in your hands tonight. What do you say?

You: It's really been two hours that we've been here? Thank you so much for spending that much time with us. That's the car that we want, or one just like it anyway. We do want to think it over for a bit.

Salesperson: What would be a good time for me to call you tomorrow?

You: Well, the best thing for all of us would be for you to just sit tight until we get back to you.

Salesperson: Would you like to take the car home tonight and keep it until tomorrow? No obligation, of course.

You: That's a generous offer. Thank you, but we'll just be on our way for now.

Salesperson: How about if we knock off a hundred dollars from the cap reduction?

You: Could you do that now?

Salesperson: I'd have to clear it with my sales manager, but if I could, would you take the car tonight?

You: No, that won't be necessary. Thanks again.

Salesperson: Give me a call tomorrow, okay?

You: We'll see. Good night.

Analysis. Let's consider the leadership skills we've observed so far. Because you (the buyer) know what you want, and since you've done your homework, you can remain calm and in control during the sales presentation. Your directional thinking has convinced you that you want the car. Your consequential thinking has allowed you to put your impulses aside (the thrill of driving it home, showing it off, etc.) and to use rational decision making in order to determine the best outcome. Through your use of influence strategies, you concentrated on the principle of fairness to guide you in making your counteroffer (for now you want to think about it). You used communication skills to summarize what you heard the salesperson say to make sure you understood the present terms, and you used an assertive confrontation to firmly and politely express what you intended to do. Let's continue by returning to the showroom the next day after having done some additional research of other car dealerships that carry the same model.

Salesperson: Hi, ready to take that car home?

You: Actually, it's not looking too good.

Salesperson: Whatever the problem is, I'm sure we can take care of it. Want me to try for that hundred-dollar reduction?

You: I wish a hundred dollars was all that is keeping us from doing business.

Salesperson: I don't understand.

You: Let me see if I can help. I really would like to do business here. We live in the neighborhood, and it would be much more convenient to close the deal here rather than having to drive up north to get the terms that I want.

Salesperson: You found a better deal up north? No problem, I'm sure we can match it.

You: Oh, I'm sure you can. That's not what's bothering me.

Salesperson: It's not the money?

You: Indeed it is. But it's also the principle.

Salesperson: You lost me, I'm sorry.

You: Let's start by my telling you the terms that the other dealer quoted. The same car, the same months, and the same mileage as you told me, but with a $2,000 cap reduction—not $2,500. That's a $500 difference. There was no need to put up the last month's payment. And, the monthly payment was $326 instead of $397. That's a difference of $2,556 over the three-year term for a total savings of $3,056 over your deal. That's a lot of money. What's disturbing about all of this is that unless I did my homework, I would have taken your deal. I'm extremely angry about this because I feel you were taking advantage of me.

Salesperson: I'd better get my sales manager.

(Five minutes later)

Sales Manager: Hi, sorry to keep you waiting. I now understand the terms that the other dealer offered, and I want to apologize for any misunderstanding. May I ask you a few questions?

You: Certainly.

Sales Manager: Is the same car available in that dealership today?

You: No. It's at a dealership a couple of hundred miles away. It could be here tomorrow if I wanted it.

Sales Manager: Will you have to pay a delivery charge?

You: No, that's included in the price.

Sales Manager: Do you have a signed sales agreement?

You: Yes, it's binding on the dealership subject to my approval in twenty-four hours.

Sales Manager: Did you check with any other dealers, and if so, how do we compare?

You: I checked with every one of the other dealers. Four of them could beat your deal. One of them could match it. The best deal represents the one I've told you about.

Sales Manager: Could I see the sales agreement?

You: No, I gave my word that I would not use the name of their dealership in any discussions with other dealers. I also did not tell them the name of your dealership. I firmly believe that you will not contest the numbers I've shown you though because you recognize their legitimacy.

Sales Manager: What would you like from us?

You: I want you to beat their deal by $300.

Sales Manager: Why did you choose that number?

You: Because they told me that at the terms they quoted me, they would make a profit of $500. If I were to buy from them, I would pay them according to these terms.

Sales Manager: Why do you want us to take off another $300?

You: Because last night you quoted terms that would have netted you over $3,500 profit at my expense. To ensure that I will be a happy customer, it would be worth your while to recognize how angry I am about all of this. Isn't it worth sacrificing a bit of your profit to restore my good will? You'll still make $200 on the deal, and if your service department treats me well over the life of the lease, I would certainly give your dealership a chance at my next car.

Sales Manager: Thank you for giving me the opportunity. I will meet your terms and I would like to give you an explanation of how we came up with our original numbers. May I?

You: Of course.

Sales Manager: Our pricing structure is guided by the suggested retail price for the car and the suggested retail price for the lease. That's the figure we quoted you the other night. Because of the clientele that we cater to in this area of the country, believe it or not, most people pay the price that we quote them. Since the industry provides the price guidelines and people are willing to pay them, we do not feel we are taking advantage of anyone. Other dealers work with a different client base and often aren't as successful in moving cars as we are. To protect their market share, they lower their prices and sell their cars closer to their cost. We haven't needed to do that and, frankly, we don't expect that we will have to do that in the near future. As far as this deal is concerned, I hope we can earn your business. I appreciate your openness, and I admire your resourcefulness and sound judgment. Are you willing to sign the agreement with us?

You: Let me make sure I understand the terms. The lease will be for thirty-six months with an allowance for 45,000 miles. The cap reduction will be $2,000, the security deposit will be $250, only the first payment is due now, and the monthly payment will be $317.66. Am I correct?

Sales Manager: Entirely. The lower monthly payment reflects our profit of $200. A payment of $326 would have given us a profit of $500.

You: Yes, if that's agreeable, then I'm ready to sign.

Analysis. The primary influence strategies were (1) working from the principle of fairness (why should I pay more than the car/lease is worth?) and (2) lowering the seller's expectations (I'm angry because I feel that I would have been taken advantage of). The communication skills included resolving differences through clarifying roles and defining expectations (the Relationship Life Cycle), assertive communication ("Let me tell you what I expect"), and active listening ("Let me make sure I understand"). This example is based on an actual incident. While circumstances will vary, similar results can be duplicated as long as the four competencies are used carefully and completely.

Q: What should I do first as I try to develop my leadership skills?

A: Complete the assessments in Section I of this book. Then let Chapter 4 guide you as you score your responses. Use the four competencies to develop your understanding of where your current strengths are as well as what you need to do to become more effective. Then, as you increase your skills, take the assessment again to measure your improvement.

You can also begin to measure the effectiveness of leadership among your friends, teachers, supervisors, community officials, and government representatives. Another way to observe how the four competencies are used by leaders is to study the portrayal of leadership in dramatic productions. Some good examples are the characters played by William Hurt in *The Doctor*, Michael Douglas in *Wall Street*, Diane Keaton in *Baby Boom*, Melanie Griffith in *Working Girl*, Patrick Stewart in *Star Trek—The Next Generation*, Al Pacino in *Scent of a Woman*, Charlton Heston in *The Ten Commandments*, Gene Hackman and Denzel Washington in *Crimson Tide*, and Tom Cruise in *Jerry Maguire*. These characters provide the viewer with an excellent opportunity for studying leadership through a dramatic method called "the hero's journey." In each case, you'll be able to determine how effectively each of these leaders used directional thinking, consequential thinking, influence strategies, and communication skills. You can even apply the assessment tools to their portrayals and determine their strengths and developmental needs in each of the competencies.

In the next chapter, we'll discuss some guidelines for successfully completing the assessment. To continually improve your leadership skills, retaking the assessment will provide you with ongoing guidance for identifying both your strengths and developmental needs in each of the four competencies.

CHAPTER 10

Assessment Guidelines and Some Final Thoughts

Now that you have completed your study of the four competencies, it would be an excellent time to retake the assessment to measure your progress. The purpose of this chapter is to help you use the four competencies as you complete your responses.

To review, the four competencies are

1. Directional Thinking—the thought process that a person goes through, whether individually or within an organization, that ultimately produces a vision or establishes a direction.

2. Consequential Thinking—the process of identifying the risks associated with a particular action and then determining whether or not to continue the pursuit of a goal.

3. Influence Strategies—a collection of tools to use for the purpose of persuading people that they should follow a particular course of action because it is in their best interests.

4. Communication Skills—a collection of tools to help prevent and solve conflicts within working relationships (interpersonal problem-solving skills) and to manage the attention of an audience in order to effectively deliver a message (presentation skills).

The target outcome for an assessment is a score sheet that reflects a relatively even "percentage of use" across the four competencies. (See Figure 10-1.)

The scores reflect that the person who completed the assessment responded to the questions by using all four competencies with equal frequency. In other words, given a particular situation, it is likely that this individual began with directional thinking to establish a direction, used consequential thinking to anticipate and manage potential risks and consequences, used influence strategies to persuade others,

DT 25%	CT 25%
IS 25%	CS 25%

FIGURE 10-1   Competency Ratios: An Ideal Distribution

and used communication skills to either prevent and solve interpersonal conflicts and/or effectively manage attention.

This type of result is what you should be striving for as you complete each item in the assessment and of course as you attempt to lead people in your personal and professional life. Remember, use all four competencies to respond to each item in the assessment, and use all four competencies whenever your intent is to lead people.

Now let's apply this guideline to examples from the assessment. Recall that the three chapters in the assessment section were The Behavior Interview, The In-Basket, and Ask the Consultant.

The Behavior Interview Questions

Here are the instructions that were provided regarding the Behavior Interview:

In this section of the assessment, you will answer several questions as though you were writing a type of essay for each one. The questions are designed to help you recall certain events in your recent past that required you to think and act decisively. As you answer each question, write your responses so that they focus on your **ACTIONS** rather than on *good intentions*, what you *wish* you had done or what *you think others might have done.*

For example, consider the following question:
Think back to a time when you had to get a lot of things done in a relatively short time. How did you organize and structure your activities in order to succeed?

A "**Good Intention**" type answer might be:
I always organize. Good organization is so important. Without it, you just can't get anything done. I've always done a good job organizing. All my friends tell me how good I am at it.

An "**ACTION**" type answer might be:
I remember a time when our whole team was facing a deadline that was a week away. Then, without warning our boss told us we had two business days to complete the

project. After we whined and moaned for a few minutes, I suggested that we pull out our master planning chart. On the left side of the chart we listed each step of the project. Across the top we had the completion times and names of responsible parties. With all the people standing in front of the chart, we collectively decided what we could compress, what we could eliminate totally, and what would have to remain intact. I took on the role of recorder by standing up at the chart and leading the discussion. We accomplished a great deal by cutting out what amounted to dozens of "nice to do's" that in the end were nonessentials. By pulling together, we extensively revised our timelines, achieved our objectives, and completed the project nearly four hours before the revised deadline.

There are ten questions in this section. One page is devoted to each question. To make it easier for you to later interpret your responses, be sure to focus your answer on a past event that actually occurred in your life. Then, use your answer to demonstrate what you actually did in order to solve the problem at hand. The more specific you are in describing your actions, the easier it will be for you to later identify your most effective and least effective leadership skills. If instead, your answers describe opinions and intentions, it will be more difficult later to determine how to improve your leadership skills.

Now let's take a look back at one of the questions and answer it by using each of the four competencies.

Describe a situation in which almost everyone else was at a loss as to how to solve a problem and you stepped in, took charge, and solved the problem. Give background information, describe what you did, and indicate the outcome.

Background: My name is Jill Pitman. My husband and I along with our friends Leslie and Ed decided to go out to dinner and a movie. To avoid long lines and to make sure the movie wasn't sold out, we stopped by the theater before going to dinner to buy our tickets for the 7:00 P.M. show. After dinner, we got to the theater by 6:45 and noticed that the show was in fact sold out. When we gave our tickets to the ticket taker, he told us we couldn't get in because the show was sold out.

Directional Thinking: I was determined that we would get into the theater and see our movie. We had made plans to do this, we had bought our tickets several hours before the performance, and we arrived fifteen minutes before the time the movie was supposed to start. I was calm and in control of my emotions and realized that I would need to convince the manager that we should be allowed to see the show that we had bought tickets to.

Consequential Thinking: Because I felt that we were entitled to see this movie at this particular time, I believed that to persist with our efforts to convince the manager was entirely right. It didn't make sense to me that management would oversell the performance. That's not good business since it would only anger theater patrons and hurt the theater in the long run. That meant that the theater sold the same number of tickets for which there were seats. Since we had four tickets, there should have been four empty seats to accommodate us. If there weren't and if the theater hadn't oversold, that meant that at least four people had moved past the ticket taker with tickets to a different movie and then illegitimately walked into our movie. In my mind, these people (whoever they might be) were taking something that belonged to us. Now in the big picture, I'm not concerned about the moral right and wrong of what they did. What I am concerned about is that they interfered with our evening. We bought the tickets in plenty of time because we wanted to see that movie at that time. Since this was all very clear to me, I was prepared to convince the manager to honor our tickets.

Influence Strategies: To convince the manager that he should let us in, I needed to present him with an argument that he couldn't refute. I needed to show him that it would be wrong not to let us in. My case would have to be irresistible, believable, and compelling so that he would have no choice but to agree. I decided to put myself in his shoes and think as though I were a manager. As a manager, I represent the good image of my business. My business stands for something. Certainly it stands for honesty and fairness. I need to protect that image because if customers perceive that our company is dishonest or unfair or fails to honor its commitments, then they will stop patronizing us. Now, with this in mind, I decided to try to convince the manager that if he refused to honor our tickets, he would in effect be breaking a promise. He would be condoning cheating on the part of people who snuck in, and he would be acting in a manner inconsistent with the values that his business stood for.

Communication Skills: I decided to express my argument calmly but firmly. I would look directly at him and remain committed to my convictions. I would be assertive, not aggressive. Here's what happened:

Manager: The problem is that our doors for this movie opened at 6:30. By then, everyone had tickets, and every seat ended up being sold. So you see, we have no more seats. They're all occupied. I'd be happy to try to accommodate you in some other way.

Ed: Jill, Max mentioned free tickets. Since we already have tickets, could they honor them for the 9:30 show?

Manager: I could certainly do that.

Jill: I don't want to go to the 9:30 show. Leslie, do you?

Leslie: Absolutely not.

Max: What if they gave each of us a free pass for a month? Ed, what do you think about that?

Ed: Works for me. Would you do it, Mr. Jenkins?

Manager: Well, uh, I don't know if I, uh . . .

Jill: Wait a minute. I want to see this movie now. I paid for it. I bought my ticket in plenty of time. I've been looking forward to it, and I intend to see it. A later show is not acceptable, and I won't be bought off with free passes. What's right is right.

Manager: Well, Ma'am I'm not sure what I can do. There are no more seats. I can maybe give the four of you one pass to share.

Jill: Forget the pass! Now look, you told us that everyone who got in had a ticket and all the seats are taken, right?

Manager: Yes, Ma'am.

Jill: You know what that says to me?

Manager: Uh . . .

Jill: That tells me that people are sitting in my seat and Max's seat and Leslie's seat and Ed's seat. True, they may have tickets, but they don't have tickets to the 7:00 show in this theater. In fact, I'll bet if you look at every person's ticket, you'll find at least four people who have the wrong tickets. Maybe they have tickets to the 7:15 show in that theater next door. Maybe they have tickets to the

9:30 showing of this feature. But they don't have tickets to this show. We have those tickets; they don't.

Manager: What do you mean?

Jill: Let me spell it out for you, sir. They snuck in.

Manager: That's highly unlikely.

Jill: What's showing right now in that theater? Has the feature presentation started yet?

Manager: No, it's just the previews showing now.

Jill: Stop the projector and turn on the lights.

Manager: What? You have to be kidding. I can't do that.

Jill: I have four tickets here that entitle us admission into that theater. There are at least four people in there who are sitting in our seats. This ticket says I have a right to sit in this theater at this time. Now please do what you need to do to honor this ticket. Tell your projectionist to stop the projector, tell your usher to turn on the lights, and then you make an announcement that will correct this problem.

Max: Where's he going? Jill, this is really embarrassing. He'll never let us in. Let's just come back later.

Jill: You just wait. We are going to get in, I promise you.

Leslie: Look, the manager's going into the theater. I can't believe it, the lights just came on.

Manager: Ladies and Gentlemen. I'm terribly sorry to stop the projector and turn on the lights. We have mistakenly admitted some people into the theater who have tickets to another presentation. Please check your ticket stub. If your stub shows a time or a feature other than this one at this time, kindly leave the theater until your presentation begins. We appreciate your cooperation.

As you look back over the response, you'll notice how Jill answered with behavioral statements. Rather than describe what she would have done, she said exactly what she did. A behavioral response is a powerful way to demonstrate how you handled a situation in the past. As such, it offers evidence of your competence to exercise leadership in the future. And in this case, Jill demonstrated that she used each of the four competencies to resolve the situation.

The In-Basket

In the in-basket exercise, a candidate responds to items that are designed to represent correspondence that might appear on his or her desk. In this exercise, the candidate is placed in the role of the new leader of a subdivision's board of trustees. The candidate's challenge is to respond to each of the in-basket items in a manner that demonstrates effective leadership.

The example that follows is from Jane Reynolds who is the associate trustee of the subdivision.

Peter,

You asked me to submit an expense report to our treasurer, Allen Lavell, for the conference I attended on behalf of Twin Lakes. Of all the gall, he rejected over half of my expenses. Come on, now. I made some decisions on behalf of Twin Lakes that I felt would motivate the county to reconsider some of their restrictions in this subdivision. These decisions included buying a few drinks and paying for the meals of two of the county representatives. If our treasurer would have bothered reading my report, he would have realized they paid for two of my meals to reciprocate. By the way, I'm still working on the county to lift some of its restrictions on us already, thank you very much!

Look, Peter, I made what I thought were reasonable business decisions. I feel our treasurer is being petty and shortsighted. Please reconsider my request.

Jane Reynolds
Associate Trustee
Twin Lakes Development

The response below demonstrates how the four competencies can be used to help Jane resolve the problems between her and Allen.

Directional Thinking: These two people should be able to work together to solve their problems. When they presently talk to each other, they seldom see eye to eye, find fault with each other, and come to me hoping that I will take their side. I want them to sit down, talk objectively about the situation, and reach a solution that they can both live with.

Consequential Thinking: If I intervene, these two people will continue to find fault with one another and depend on me to intervene. If I help them solve their own problem and let them know they will need to work together from this point on, I will be helping them to form an effective work team.

Influence Strategies: I need to elevate their concerns with each other to a concern for the welfare of the subdivision. I need to help them feel a sense of pride and ownership in working together.

Communication Skills: Note to Jane and Allen:

Thanks to each of you for your letter. Let's get together and talk through the problems each of you has brought to my attention. It is clear how much you both have been trying to solve many of the problems we've all been experiencing in Twin Lakes. By working together, we'll be in a much stronger position to put a real dent in these issues and come up with solutions that can make a difference for all of us in the subdivision.

I'll give you a call in the next two days and arrange a time for the three of us to meet. I want to hear your concerns, and I'll make sure you have ample time to present all of the issues that have been important to you. Once we get all the cards out on the table, we'll put our heads together and come up with solutions that will take care of these issues once and for all. By working together, I'm convinced that the two of you can help turn this subdivision into a community that we'll all be proud of. Thanks for your help, and I'll talk to you soon.

Notice how the response included all four competencies. By responding to each of the items in the assessment with the four competencies, you'll be able to demonstrate your capacity for leadership through sound judgment and effective behaviors.

Ask the Consultant

In Chapter 3, you were placed in the role of a consultant that people contacted for help in solving their business problems. Rather than returning to one of the cases in that chapter, we'll consider what might happen if the leader from the Twin Lakes subdivision asked for your help as his consultant. We'll call him Tom Demerist.

Tom and his family recently moved into Twin Lakes. He just received a note informing him of a subdivision meeting. Here's what happened.

I got to the clubhouse at about 7:25. I was greeted by one of my next-door neighbors, Terry Waterman. "Any idea what's going on, Tom?" Terry asked. "I was about to ask you the same thing," I replied. "Susan and I tried to call you and Jeanne, but I guess you just got home a few minutes before the meeting."

Several other people came into the clubhouse at the same time. Jim Henderson, the vice president of the board of trustees, asked everyone to sit down so he could call the meeting to order.

"I want to thank all of you for coming on such short notice," Jim said. "I am sorry for being so mysterious in the announcement, but I think you'll soon see what all this is about. There are many things that have recently happened that you need to know about as property owners in Twin Lakes development. First, Larry Phelps, our board president, called me yesterday to say that he was resigning from the board. He and his family are planning to move out of the subdivision as soon as they can. Their home was vandalized early yesterday morning. The Phelps kept most of their valuables out of the home, but many keepsakes were either taken or defaced. In fact, profanities were plastered on many of the walls and mirrors throughout the house." I raised my hand and was acknowledged by Jim.

"I'm Tom Demerist. My wife Susan and I moved in on Lakeside Terrace two days ago. Many of you here have given us a warm welcome and on behalf of my family, I want to say thank you. Jim, I guess I'm somewhat confused. I'm sure it's always a scary thing to have your house broken into, and it shakes everyone up to hear about it, but surely that's no reason to move out of a neighborhood."

"Let me go on," Jim said. "As president of the board, Larry received many anonymous complaints from people in the subdivision nearly every day. Residents have been upset about a number of problems in the subdivision for quite a while now. When they don't get satisfaction, they need to take it out on someone. Larry was the natural target."

"Why Larry?" I asked. "Just because he was the head of the board?"

"Well, it was a little more than that," Jim proceeded. "Larry sort of threatened people when they didn't pay their subdivision fees."

"Oh come on, Jim," Al Reily interrupted. "It was more than sort of threatened. He called people 'irresponsible' to their face. He embarrassed husbands in front of their families. He threatened to take them to court. He made a lot of us feel like he was the only decent person around here."

"Wait a minute," I said. "This really is beyond me. The homes in this area are in the two hundred thousand dollar bracket. The subdivision fee is $300 a year. What is going on here that people aren't paying it?"

"It's a protest," Sharon Dawson added.

"What do you mean? Why a protest?" I asked.

"First of all, you have to understand more about this subdivision fee," Jim said. "We need this income to get street lights, to pay for repairs in our pavement, to get the snow removal company out here the same day it snows; and those are just the absolute necessities. We still have to decide what we want to do about building the subdivision pool, fencing in the tennis courts, and adding to the number of trees on the streets. The simple fact is that more than 80 percent of the property owners are in arrears and substantially so at that."

"But why?" I pressed.

"Tom, I'm Sharon Dawson. My husband Dave and I were one of the first people to build in Twin Lakes development. That was five years ago. We were followed by the Wilkinsons, the Reardons, and the Jacksons."

"You're the folks up in the cul de sac?" I asked.

"That's right," Sharon told him. "Anyway, shortly after the cut de sac filled, interest rates and the price of housing began to come down a bit. Within six months, all of the lots on our street sold. Within six months after that, the robberies started to happen. There hasn't been one house that hasn't been robbed on our entire street. I take it back, there is one."

"All right, Sharon, hold on," Jim interrupted.

"No, I won't," Sharon insisted. "Tom and his family have every right to know. After all, they live right behind them."

"Behind who?" I asked anxiously.

"Sharon, you have no right to stand in judgment," Jim protested. "You have no proof."

"You mean the police won't accept our proof," Sharon insisted. "We have eyewitnesses who would swear on Bibles that they saw those kids. And those cars that sit out in front of their house at all hours and then drive out of the subdivision without their lights on when its pitch black. Tom, we're almost sure that the Peterson kids are financing a drug ring by stealing from us in the subdivision."

"Why aren't the police involved?" I asked.

"That's just it," Sharon said. "We think they are."

"Sharon, for God's sake," Jim said trying to stop her.

"Donald Peterson is the police commissioner," Sharon blurted out. "We have called the police time and again. They come out within minutes, inspect the scene, file their report, and that's the last we hear of it. They tell us that the best thing we can do is to form a Neighborhood Crime Watch that they could supervise. They would help us with the details like inscribing our identification on our valuables and conducting security searches of our homes."

"Sounds like a good idea to me," I remarked.

"It is," Jim said. "But Larry was supposed to organize it. I'm afraid that no one trusted him enough anymore to give him the support. He just wasn't cut out to head up our board. The pressure just got to him."

"It's getting to all of us," said Bob Marshall. "Sorry to welcome you to the neighborhood this way, Tom. The fact is that Twin Lakes development has recently been listed as suffering from the highest crime rate of all the local subdivisions built in the last five years. Aside from the immediate danger to our families and our properties, we *all* are facing a serious financial loss if this thing causes the value of our homes to go down. We've all got our futures at stake here. Yet we're helpless to do anything about it."

"So we've decided to protest," Sharon's husband Dave told me. "We're trying to drive the Petersons out by taking a stand. "

Once again, Jim interrupted. "But don't you see that you all are cutting off your nose to spite your face? We're just hurting one another."

"But if we can hang on together, sooner or later the Petersons will get the message and leave," said Dave.

"Oh, come on," Jim said angrily, "hell could freeze over first. In the mean time, we are all suffering without streetlights or snow removal. Besides that, our streets are all torn up from the construction equipment." Jim paused for a moment. "Look," he said, "it's getting late. We're all tired and frustrated. I called you here to tell you about Larry. As of tomorrow, he's gone. We have no president. We have no leadership. I surely don't want it. We need to elect someone right now."

There was a long silence. Everyone riveted their eyes to the floor dreading that Jim would look at them with expectations. After about two minutes, Sharon raised her hand.

"Sharon, are you volunteering?" Jim asked.

She laughed. "Me, of course not. I could never do it. No, I think we need new blood on this board. I would like to nominate Tom. He's got a stake in this subdivision. He's been asking some intelligent questions all night. Besides that, I happen to know that he and his wife have built one heck of a business up over the last several years. That takes smarts and it takes guts." The people in the room began to applaud. There was almost a sense of desperation for Tom to accept.

I looked over at Sharon for a moment. Then I glanced at his next-door neighbor, Terry. Jim diverted his attention up to the front of the room.

"Tom, what do you say?" Jim asked, almost pleading. "Will you do it?"

"Jim, I don't know what you all expect me to do," I replied in frustration.

"That's the irony of it all," Jim said helplessly. "Neither do we. Just take charge somehow and get us out of this mess."

Now imagine that Tom just told you all of that information and is asking for your advice on what he should do. What would you tell him? How would you go about developing your response? Your approach should be identical to the structure that has been used earlier. In other words, start out with directional thinking. What would Tom ultimately hope to accomplish? That outcome would be his target. Next, consider consequential thinking. What are the consequences that Tom should consider? What are the risks? What are the potential costs? In order to achieve his objectives, Tom will need to consider how to influence the members of the board regarding what he wants them to do. As such, what influence strategies would likely be effective? What do the people in this subdivision want? How can Tom help them get that for themselves and for the subdivision as a whole? Finally, what communication skills should Tom use? Are there relationship issues that need to be addressed and resolved? What interpersonal communication skills might he use to handle the tensions within the group? Would passive listening help? What about active listening? Should he use assertive confrontations? How about collaborative problem solving? How should he deliver his message to the group? How should he sound, how should he present himself, and how should he organize what he is going to say?

Based on your advice, here's how Tom handled the next meeting:

Tom scheduled the next subdivision meeting for a week later. He mailed notices to all of the residents in the subdivision; there were 80 of them. Each night during the week before the meeting he made calls to as many of the residents as he could reach between 6:30 and 9:30. During each call, he introduced himself, mentioned the names of his family members, and indicated that he had been asked to serve as president of the subdivision's board of trustees. Finally, after briefly getting to know the people he spoke with, he reminded them about the meeting and strongly urged them to attend.

Tom arrived at the clubhouse about 45 minutes before the meeting was scheduled to begin. He arranged the tables in a horseshoe with enough seating for nearly 50 people. He figured that if more came, they could bring extra chairs from the storage room. He made coffee and arranged the cups, spoons, cream, and sugar. "I'm going to have to learn to delegate," he said to himself. "Oh well, at least this time, I want to make sure everything is set up just the way I want it."

He called the meeting to order exactly at 7:30. He guessed that nearly 40 people were there. The turnout disappointed him somewhat. Nonetheless, these were the people he would work with to get things under control.

He introduced himself and spoke briefly about his family and home. Next, he had everyone pair up with someone from the subdivision that they didn't know. After everyone got situated in their new seats, he instructed the participants to take a couple of minutes to get to know each other. When he called time, he had each person introduce his or her partner to everyone else by name, names of their family members, and where they lived in the subdivision. Tom was pleased. Everyone seemed to enjoy getting to know their "new" neighbors. The activity succeeded in building some cohesiveness.

Tom then called for the group's attention. "It's now 7:45," he said. "We will work together tonight until 9:00. First, I want to tell you exactly what I want us to accomplish this evening. Then, I'll let you know what the ground rules are so that we can stay focused on solving the problems that we are all so concerned about.

"I want us to consider this an organizational meeting. We'll start out by bringing everybody up to date on what's been taking place here in this subdivision that has us all so concerned. Let's make sure we agree on all of that first before we try to settle anything. Once I'm sure that we have identified our problems, then we'll put our heads together to plan how to work on each one of them. We will end the evening by forming working groups that will each have a specific set of tasks to accomplish. Each group will appoint a recorder and spokesperson to present its results to us at our next meeting. By the way, make a note that we will have standing meetings on the first Wednesday night of the month at 7:30 here at the clubhouse until further notice.

"Now, let me tell you about the ground rules for tonight. Everyone who wants to will get a chance to have their say. Considering that feelings are running high about some of the issues we will be discussing, there will be times when you will disagree with what someone else is saying. That's fine. Raise your hand and I'll give you a chance to have your say. If you feel like you need to interrupt somebody, I am going to have to stop you from proceeding until the other person finishes. I hope you won't be offended by that. If you are, I'm sorry. At the same time, I hope you can understand the importance of keeping our discussion focused at all times. Okay, any questions before we begin?" Tom asked. There were none. Tom then continued.

"There were several concerns that were expressed during our meeting last week. They were all new to me since it was my first meeting. Many of you were there. Some of you were not. I'll review them now. Let me know after I have finished if I've overlooked anything." Tom paused to look around the room. These were the people his family would be getting to know very well over the years. It was important for all of them to believe they could work together.

"Last week Jim Henderson told us that Larry Phelps was resigning as president of our board of trustees. Larry's house had been vandalized. Well, at least I learned that our subdivision suffered from an extremely high rate of burglaries. Suspicions were that a group of teenagers based within the subdivision were committing the robberies as a way to finance their drug racket. I also came to understand that the local police suggested that the subdivision support a Neighborhood Crime Watch project. The police would help by providing equipment for inscribing owners' names on valuables and by conducting security inspections to help us determine ways to increase our home security. Any comments so far?" Tom asked.

There were none. Tom continued. "Up until now, the Neighborhood Crime Watch has not been organized. As I understand it, everyone was depending on Larry to get people together, but it never happened. Besides the vandalism, we also have concerns about the unrepaired pavements, the delays in snow plowing, the pool that is still on the drawing board, and our tennis courts that need fencing. In order for this work to be done, we need revenue from our subdivision fees. Nearly 80 percent of the property owners in the subdivision have not paid the $300 fee as a protest. The reason for the protest is that the local police commissioner, who happens to live in the subdivision, is also the father of some of the teenage kids who are suspected of the home burglaries. The feeling is that the protest will be an effective way to get our message across to the police commissioner. Have I left anything out?" Tom asked.

Paul Jackson raised his hand and said, "Just for the record, Tom, the revenues from the subdivision fees are also supposed to cover adding to the number of trees in the subdivision."

"Thanks, Paul," Tom acknowledged. "Anything else? No? Okay, let's go on. What I want to point out is that the protest is one idea we have been using to try to solve our problems. Some of you may think it's a good idea, others may not. Nonetheless, it is one idea. Instead of debating it right now, I want us to start coming up with even more ideas. Once we have made a list of them, we can talk about the ones we can all live with and would be willing to work together on. There will be plenty of time for discussion before we make our decisions. All right, here's what we are going to do. So far, we have been trying to stop the robberies by a protest. The protest has dwindled our subdivision reserves to the point where we cannot pay for some expenses that many of us feel are important. What I want you to consider now is what other ideas to stop the robberies we can come up with that wouldn't restrict our ability to take care of the subdivision's other needs."

Sharon Davis called out, "Tom, you're not giving it time. The protest will work if we wait long enough."

"As you see it, Sharon, the protest can work," Tom reflected. "It's a matter of biting the bullet in a sense. If we can hang in there just a bit longer, the commissioner will get the message."

"Right," Sharon agreed. "He's not a bad person. It's just been real awkward to talk to him. You know, it would sort of be like accusing the man to his face. This way, he'll get the idea. When he does, he'll do something with those kids. The robberies will stop, and then we'll start paying the fee."

"Okay, we've got one idea," Tom said. "Let's get some more. I want you to think of as many other ways to stop the robberies as you can. It's now 8:05. I will give you five minutes to write your ideas on the paper in front of you. Abbreviate so you don't waste time writing. This time is for thinking. Don't inhibit yourself by worrying what other people might think. Write down whatever comes to your mind. Ready, begin."

Tom stopped them after exactly five minutes. He made a master list on the newsprint board as each person read the ideas. In all, they came up with ten possibilities:

1. Complete the procedures for Neighborhood Crime Watch.

2. Invite the commissioner to a meeting with Tom.

3. Hire a security service to patrol the neighborhood.

4. Invite the boys suspected of the robberies to a meeting with Tom.

5. Report the commissioner to the county supervisor.

6. Establish for sure that the suspected boys are the actual culprits.

7. Phone the license numbers of suspicious cars seen in the subdivision to the local police.

8. Invite the local police to the next subdivision meeting for assistance.

9. Call other subdivision boards to see what they have done when they have had to deal with high crime rates in their areas.

10. Continue the protest by not paying subdivision fees.

By 8:30, Tom had completed the master list. He then informed everyone that this was the time to give their opinions on the various ideas. He structured the task by focusing on each idea one at a time. Whenever one person interrupted, he immediately intervened and refocused the discussion on the main topic. By 9:00 he was ready to pull everything together.

"Seems like we've reached a decision," Tom said. "The consensus is that we first have to establish if the boys down the street are involved in any or all of the robberies. We've appointed three people here to search the public record files in the local newspaper to see if any of the boys' names appear under records of arrest. They will get that information to us next week. If the boys are involved, I will personally meet with our neighbor, the commissioner, and ask for his help. If he is willing to help, we will be well on the way to solving our problems. If not, we will decide what actions we can take from that point on. The secondary issue is the subdivision fee. We have decided that until we can get some closure on whether the boys are actually involved, we will start a campaign to get our property owners to pay their fees. We have a committee of five who will report to us next week on the steps they will take to get that campaign started. Now, suppose we do not establish that the neighborhood boys are involved; then it will be extra important to get this Neighborhood Crime Watch under way. One of us has agreed to arrange to have a police representative here next week to get the project started."

Tom closed the meeting by expressing his appreciation for the willingness that almost everyone expressed for working together. He felt optimistic and was greatly relieved that these people were committed to solving their mutual concerns. He left the clubhouse that night very happy that his family had chosen to live in Twin Lakes development.

Summary

Leadership is a process through which a person develops a direction for change, anticipates and manages the consequences that the change might produce, selects strategies to influence others that such change would serve their interests, and communicates what they should do in order to create that change.

This book offers a practical guide for assessing your leadership skills in these four competencies. Section I included a three-part assessment to first measure your skills and then develop a plan for further developing them. Section II described and illustrated directional thinking, consequential thinking, influence strategies, and communication skills.

With these tools in hand, you can apply them to many situations both personally and professionally. The many examples throughout the book provide illustrations of each.

From a personal perspective, you can use these tools to help you make choices about major purchases such as cars, houses, and investments; anticipate and manage potential consequences of your decisions; and then negotiate the terms using effective influence strategies and communication skills. The competencies could also help you make choices about your personal relationships both in terms of choosing friends and partners and building relationships that work to satisfy the needs and interests of everyone involved.

From a professional perspective, the competencies could help you make career choices, assess the advantages and disadvantages, and prepare you to be persuasive in your interviews. Throughout your professional life, directional thinking, consequential thinking, influence strategies, and communication skills will help you gain visibility as a leader and enable you to demonstrate your ability to make sound judgments and compelling arguments tactfully and diplomatically.

To ensure that you recognize your strengths and developmental needs throughout your personal and professional life, periodically retake the assessment in Chapters 1 through 3 and score your responses using the forms in Chapter 4. As you become more confident in your leadership skills, you might choose to help develop these competencies in other people. Once again, the assessment and scoring tools will be helpful.

In conclusion, remember that leadership is about behavior—what people do, rather than who people are. Anyone can lead. That means you. So set your direction, anticipate and manage the potential consequences, figure out what people want, link your direction to their needs, and give them a reason to listen to you.

DT 25%	CT 25%
IS 25%	CS 25%

FIGURE 10-2　**Four Competencies for Leadership: The Ideal Assessment**

INDEX